THE WEB OF INDIAN LIFE

THE WEB OF INDIAN LIFE

THE SISTER NIVEDITA

GYAN

Published by

Gyan Publishing House
5, Ansari Road
Daryaganj, New Delhi-110002
Phone: 011-47034999, 9811692060
E-mail: books@gyanbooks.com

Distribution Network
gyanbooks.com
India, USA, Canada, UK, Australia, France

ISBN : 978-81-212-9148-4 (PB)
First Published, 1906

2nd Impression 2023

Printed at: Gyan Press, Delhi.

THE WEB OF INDIAN LIFE
Author: THE SISTER NIVEDITA

THE WEB OF INDIAN LIFE

BY

THE SISTER NIVEDITA
(MARGARET E. NOBLE)
OF RAMAKRISHNA-VIVEKANANDA

LONDON
WILLIAM HEINEMANN
1906

IN sending this book out into the world, I desire to record my thanks to Mr. Romesh Chunder Dutt for his constant interest and encouragement, and also to Prof. Patrick Geddes, who, by teaching me to understand a little of Europe, indirectly gave me a method by which to read my Indian experiences.

NIVEDITA,
Of Ramakrishna-Vivekananda.

WAH GURU KI FATE!
VICTORY TO THE GURU

FOR THE FIRM ESTABLISHMENT
OF NATIONAL RIGHTEOUSNESS

CONTENTS

CHAPTER I

THE SETTING OF THE WARP

A HOUSE of my own, in which to eat, sleep, and conduct a girls' school, and full welcome accorded at any hour of day or night that I might choose to invade the privacy of a group of women friends hard by: these were the conditions under which I made my entrance into Hindu life in the city of Calcutta. I came when the great autumn feast of the Mother was past; I was there at the ending of the winter when plague broke out in our midst, and the streets at night were thronged with seething multitudes, who sang strange litanies and went half mad with religious excitement; I remained through the terrific heat, when activity became a burden, and only one's Hindu friends understood how to live; I left my home for a time when the tropical rains had begun, and in the adjoining roads the cab-horses were up to their girths in water hour after hour.

What a beautiful old world it was in which I spent those months! It moved slowly, to a different rhythm from anything that one had known. It was a world in which a great thought or intense emotion was held as the true achievement, distinguishing the day as no deed could. It was a world in which men in loin-cloths, seated on door-sills in dusty lanes, said things about Shakespeare and Shelley that some of us would go far to hear. It was full of gravity, simplicity, and the solid and enduring reality of great character and will.

From all round the neighbourhood at sunset would come the sound of gongs and bells in the family-chapel of each house, announcing Evensong. At that same hour might the carpenter be seen censing his tools, or the schoolboy, perhaps, his inkstand and pen, as if thanking these humble creatures of the day's service; and women on their way to worship would stop wherever a glimpse of the Ganges was possible, or before a bo-tree or tulsi-plant, to salute it, joining their hands and bowing the head. More and more, as the spirit of Hindu culture became the music of life, did this hour and that of sunrise grow to be the events of my day. One learns in India to believe in what Maeterlinck calls "the great active silence," and in such moments consciousness, descending like a plummet into the deeps of personality, and leaving even thought behind, seems to come upon the unmeasured and immeasurable. The centre of gravity is shifted. The seen reveals itself as what India declares it, merely the wreckage of the Unseen, cast up on the shores of Time and Space. Nothing that happens within the activity of daylight can offer a counter-attraction to this experience. But then, as we must not forget, the Indian day is pitched in its key. Tasks are few, and are to be performed with dignity and earnestness. Everything has its aureole of associations. Eating and bathing—with us chiefly selfish operations—are here great sacramental acts, guarded at all points by social honour and the passion of purity. From sunrise to sunset the life of the nation moves on, and the hum of labour and the clink of tools rise up, as in some vast monastery, accompanied by the chanting of prayers and the atmosphere of recollectedness. The change itself from daylight to darkness is incredibly swift.

A few fleecy clouds gather on the horizon and pass from white, maybe, to orange and even crimson. Then the sun descends, and at once we are alone with the deep purple and the tremulous stars of the Indian night. Far away in the North, hour after hour, outlines go on cutting themselves clearer against the green and opal sky, and long low cliffs grow slowly dim with shadows on the sea. The North has Evening: the South, Night.

Tropical thunderstorms are common through April and May at the day's end, and the terrible convulsion of Nature that then rages for an hour or two gives a simple parallel to many instances of violent contrast and the logical extreme in Indian art and history. This is a land where men will naturally spend the utmost that is in them. And yet, side by side with the scarlet and gold of the loom, how inimitably delicate is the blending of tints in the tapestry! It is so with Indian life. The most delicate *nuance* and remorseless heroism exist side by side, and are equally recognised and welcomed, as in the case of a child I knew—a child whose great grandmother had perhaps committed suttee—who ran to his mother with the cry, "Mother! Mother! save me from Auntie! She is beating me with her eyes!"

The foundation-stone of our knowledge of a people must be an understanding of their region. For social structure depends primarily on labour, and labour is necessarily determined by place. Thus we reach the secret of thought and ideals. As an example of this we have only to see how the Northman, with his eyes upon the sun, carries into Christianity the great cycle of fixed feasts that belongs to Midsummer's Day and Yule, approximately steady in the solar year; while the child of the South, to whom the lunar sequence is everything, contributes Easter and Whitsuntide. The same distinction holds in the history of Science, where savants are agreed that in early astronomy the sun elements were first worked out in Chaldea and the moon in India. To this day the boys and girls at school in Calcutta know vastly more about the moon and her phases than their English teachers, whose energies in this kind have been chiefly spent in noting the changes in shadow-length about an upright stick during the course of day. Evidently Education —that process which is not merely the activity of the reading and writing mill, but all the preparedness that life brings us for all the functions that life demands of us—Education is vitally determined by circumstances of place.

The woman pausing in the dying light to salute the river brings us to another such instance. There is nothing occult in the passion of Hindus for the Ganges. Sheer delight in physical coolness, the joy of the eyes, and the gratitude of the husbandman made independent of rain, are sufficient basis. But when we add to this the power of personification common to naives peoples, and the peculiarly Hindu genius of idealism, the whole gamut of associations is accounted for. Indeed, it would be difficult to live long beside the Ganges and not fall under the spell of her personality. Yellow, leonine, imperious, there is in her something of the caprice, of the almost treachery, of beautiful women who have swayed the wills of the world. Semiramis, Cleopatra, Mary Stuart, are far from being the Hindu ideal, but the power of them all is in that great mother whom India worships. For to the simple, the Ganges is completely mother. Does she not give life and food? To the pious she is the bestower of purity, and as each bather steps into her flood, he stoops tenderly to place a little of the water on his head, craving pardon with words of salutation for the touch of his foot. To the philosopher she is the current of his single life, sweeping irresistibly onward to the universal. To the travelled she tells of Benares and the mountain snows, and legends of Siva the Great God, and Uma Himavutee, mother of all womanhood. Or she brings memories of the Indian Christ and His youth among the shepherds in the forests of Brindaban on her tributary Jumna. And to the student of history she is the continuity of Aryan thought and civilisation through the ages, giving unity and meaning to the lives of races and centuries as she passes through them, carrying the message of the past ever into the future, a word of immense promise, an assurance of unassailable certainty. But with all this and beyond it all, the Ganges, to her lovers, is a person. To us, who have fallen so far away from the Greek mode of seeing, this is difficult perhaps to understand. But living in a Calcutta lane the powers of the imagination revive; the moon-setting becomes again Selene riding on the horse with the veiled feet; Phœbus Apollo rising out of one angle of a pediment is a convincing picture of the morning sky; and the day comes when one surprises oneself in the act of talking with earth and water as conscious living beings. One is ready now to understand the Hindu expression of love for river and home. It is a love with which the day's life throbs. "Without praying, no eating! Without bathing, no praying!" is the short strict rule to which every woman at least conforms; hence the morning bath in the river is the first great event of the day. It is still dark when little companies of women of rank begin to leave their houses on foot for the bathing-stairs. These are the proud and high-bred on whom "the sun has never looked." Too sensitive to tolerate the glance of passers by, and too faithful to forego the sanctifying immersion, they cut the knot of both difficulties at once in this way. Every moment of the ablution has its own invocation, and the return journey is made, carrying a brass vessel full of the sacred water which will be used all day to sprinkle the place in which any eats or prays.

Their arrival at home finds already waiting those baskets of fruit and flowers which are to be used in worship; for one of the chief acts of Hindu devotion consists in burying the feet of the adored in flowers. The feet, from their contact with all the dusty and painful ways of the world, have come to be lowliest and most despised of all parts of the body, while the head is so sacred that only a superior may touch it. To take the dust of the feet of the saints or of an image, therefore, and put it upon one's head, is emblematic of all reverence and sense of unworthiness, and eager love will often address itself to the "lotus-feet" of the beloved. Amongst my own friends, health forbade the bathing before dawn, and poverty did not allow of the visit to the river in closed palkee every day. But half-past nine or ten always found the younger women busy bringing incense and flowers and Ganges water for the mother's "puja," as it is called; and then, while she performed the daily ceremonies, they proceeded to make ready the fruits and sweets which were afterwards to be blessed and distributed.

It is interesting to see the difference between a temple and a church. The former may seem absurdly small, for theoretically it is simply a covered shrine which contains one or other of certain images or symbols, before which appropriate offerings are made and prescribed rituals performed by duly appointed priests. The table is only properly called an altar in temples of the Mother; in other cases it would be more correct perhaps to speak of the throne, since fruit and flowers are the only sacrifices permitted. So it is clear that the Eastern temple corresponds to that part of the Christian church which is known technically as the sanctuary. The worshipper is merely incidental here; he sits or kneels on the steps, and pays the priest to perform for him some special office; or he reads and contemplates the image in a spirit of devotion. The church, on the other hand, includes shrine and congregation, and has more affinity to the Mohammedan mosque, which is simply a church with the nave unroofed.

Temples are not very popular in Bengal, every house being supposed to have its chapel or oratory, for which the ladies care, unless the family be rich enough to maintain a chaplain. Even the services of a Brahmin in the house or neighbourhood, however, will not dispense them from the offering of elaborate personal puja before the morning meal can be thought of. I can never forget a reproach levelled at myself on this point.

It was my first morning in a Hindu home. I had arrived at dawn, tired and dusty after days of railway travel, and had lain down on a mat spread on the floor, to sleep. Towards eight o'clock, the thought of my tea-basket brightened my despair, and I turned eagerly to open and secure its refreshment. Suddenly a little boy stood before me like a young avenging angel. His great brown eyes were full of pain and surprise, such as only a child's face ever adequately shows. He did not know much English and spoke deliberately, laying terrible emphasis on each word, "Have—you—said—your—prayers?" he said.

It is a little strange, during the rains, to have to take an umbrella to go upstairs, but without my two courtyards in the middle of the house the hot weather would have been insupportable in Calcutta.

These make the Eastern home, by day, a cave of all winds that blow, and at night a tent roofed in by the starry universe itself. No one who has not experienced it can know quite what it means to return in the evening and open the door upon the sky and stars that one is leaving without. The Indian night is in itself something never to be forgotten. Vast and deep and black it seems, lighted by large soft stars that throb and gleam with an unknown brilliance, while the stillness is broken only by some night-beggar who chants the name of God in the distant streets, or by the long-drawn howl of the jackals crying the quarters of the night across the open plain. Even the moonlight itself, with the palm-trees whispering and throwing ink-black shadows, is not more beautiful than these solemn "dark nights," when the blindness and hush of things brood over the soul with their mighty motherhood.

Just as the housewives of some European university town in the Middle Ages would feel responsible for the welfare of the "poor scholar," so to the whole of Hindu society, which has assimilated in its own way the functions of the university, the religious student is a common burden. Where he is, there is the university, and he must be supported by the nearest householders. For this reason, I, being regarded as a student of their religion, my good neighbours were unfailing of kindness in the matter of household supplies. Perhaps the most striking instance of this lay in the fact that when I was to have a guest I had only to say so, and friends in the vicinity would send in a meal ready-cooked, or the necessary bedding, without my even knowing the names of those to whom I owed the bounty. And with all this, there was no question as to the course of my study or the conclusions I was reaching—no criticism, either, of its form. They simply accorded to a European woman the care they were accustomed to bestow on the ashen-clad ascetic, because they understood that some kind of disinterested research was her object also, and they knew so well that the management of affairs was no part of the function of the scholar. What do we not read of the depth of a culture that is translated and re-applied with such ease as this? And what do we not learn of the intellectual freedom and development of the people?

Few things, even in Indian life, are so interesting as this matter of the social significance of the beggar. That distaste for property which we see in such lives as Kant's and Spinoza's resolves itself readily in the Indian climate into actual destitution. Shelter and clothing are hardly necessities there: a handful of rice and a few herbs such as can be obtained at any door are alone indispensable. But everything conspires to throw upon such as beg the duty of high thinking and the exchange of ideas with their supporters. Hence the beggar makes himself known by standing in the courtyard and singing some hymn or prayer. He comes always, that is to say, in the Name of God. There is a whole literature of these beggars' songs, quaint and simple, full of what we in Europe call the Celtic spirit. In his lowest aspect, therefore, the Indian beggar is the conserver of the folk-poetry of his country. Where his individuality is strong, however, he is much more. To the woman who serves him he is then the religious teacher, talking with her of subjects on which she can rarely converse, and in this way carrying the highest culture far and wide.

It is said that the deep familiarity of Punjabi women with Hindu philosophy is the result of the strong recrudescence of the characteristic national charity under Runjeet Singh. When we think of the memories that would linger behind such a visitor—the man whose whole face spoke knowledge, standing at the door one noon and asking alms—we come upon a trace of the feeling that paints the Great God as a beggar.

It is droll to find that the whole city is parcelled out into wards, each of which is visited regularly on a given day. My days were Wednesday and Sunday, and going out one of these mornings about nine, I was fortunate enough to catch the whole procession coming up the lane. Men and women they were, elderly for the most part, but hale and well, with their long staffs in the right hand, and metal or wooden bowls in the left—amongst the most cheerful human beings I ever saw. The fact of this regular division of the city puts the affair at once on the basis of a poor-rate (of which we have none in India), and shows that in ways appropriate to themselves the Hindu people are as able organisers as any. It may be that in Western cities the workhouse is a necessary solution, but certainly this Indian distribution of want over the wealthier community, with its joining of the act of giving to the natural sentiment, seems a good deal less mechanical and more humane than ours. It is very amusing sometimes to see how tenacious people are of their own superstitions. I have seen an English woman made really unhappy because an Indian beggar would not accept a loaf she bought and handed to him, while he would have been very thankful for the money that it cost. The donor and her friends were in despair at what they regarded as utterly impracticable. Yet to the onlooker it seemed that the obstinacy was on their own side. In England we are warned that alcohol is a constant temptation to the poor and ill-fed; it is better, therefore, to give food than money. In India, on the other hand, there is no risk whatever on this score; for not one man in a hundred ever tasted liquor, and at the same time a Hindu beggar at least may not eat bread made with yeast, or baked by any but Hindus of his own or better caste. Now the offering made in this case was of yeast-made bread, baked by a Mohammedan, and handled by a Christian! To the poor man it was evident that the lady was willing to give; why should she load her gift with impossible conditions? And for my own part I could but echo, why?

Among the quaintest customs are those of the night-beggars. These are Mohammedans, but all fields are their pasture. They carry a bowl and a lamp as their insignia of office. It is common amongst these gentlemen to fix on a sum at sunset that they deem sufficient for their modest wants, and to vow that they shall know no rest till this is gathered. As the hours go on, therefore, they call aloud the balance that remains; and persons coming late home or watching by the sick are often glad to pay the trifle and gain quiet. Yet there is something weird and solemn in waking from sleep to hear the name of Allah cried beneath the stars in a kind of Perpetual Adoration.

Like a strong tide beating through the months, rise and fall the twelve or thirteen great religious festivals, or Pujas. Chief of them all, in Bengal, is the autumn Durga-Puja, or Festival of the Cosmic Energy. A later month is devoted to the thought of all that is gentle and tender in the Motherhood of Nature. Again it is the Indian Minerva, Saraswati, who claims undivided attention. Those who have lived in Lancashire will remember how the aspect of streets and cottages is changed towards Simnel Sunday. Every window is decorated with cakes, and every cake bears a spirited picture in comfits of some coaching or other local scene. And everywhere, with us at Christmas-time, the shops are gay with holly and mistletoe, so that there is no mistaking the time of year. Similarly, in Calcutta, as each puja comes round, characteristic articles appear in the bazaars. At one time it is hand-screens made of beetles' wings and peacocks' feathers, and every shop and every pedlar seems to carry these beautiful fans. Through September and October, as the Durga-Puja approaches, the streets resound with carols to the Mother. But the most charming of all is the Farewell Procession with the Image.

For no image may be kept more than the prescribed number of days, usually three. Up to the evening before the feast it is not sacred at all, and any one may touch it. Then, however, a Brahmin, who has fasted all day, meditates before the figure, and, as it is said, "magnetises" it. The texts he chants are claimed to be aids to the concentration of his own mind, and to have no other function. When the image has been consecrated it becomes a sacred object, but even then it is not actually worshipped. Its position is that of a stained-glass window, or an altar-piece, in an Anglican church. It is a suggestion offered to devout thought and feeling. On the step before it stands a brass pitcher full of water, and the mental effort of the worshipper is directed upon this water; for even so, it is said, does the formless Divine fill the Universe. It would seem that the Hindu mind is very conscious of the possibility that the image may thwart its own intention and become an idol; for not only is this precaution taken in the act of adoration, but it is directed that at the end of the puja it shall be conveyed away and thrown bodily into the river! On the third evening, therefore, towards sunset, the procession forms itself, little contingents joining it from every house in the village as it passes the door, each headed by one or two men bearing the figure of the god or goddess, and followed by the children of the family and others. It is a long and winding march to the Ganges' side. Arrived there, the crown is carefully removed, to be kept a year for good luck ; and then, stepping down into the stream, the bearers heave up their load and throw it as far as they can. We watch the black hair bobbing up and down in the current for awhile, and then, often amid the tears of the children, turn back to the house from which a radiant guest has departed. There is quietness now where for three days have been worship and feasting. But the tired women are glad to rest from the constant cooking, and even the babies are quickly cheered, for it will be but a month or two till some new festival shall bring to them fresh stores of memory.

The great decorum of Oriental life is evident when one has to come or go through a Hindu city in the evening. Doorways and windows are flanked with broad stone benches, and here, after the evening meal, sit numbers of men in earnest conversation. But any woman is safe in such a street. Not even the freedom of a word or look will be offered. As Lakshman, in the great Epic, recognised among the jewels of Sita only her anklets, so honour demands of every man that he look no higher than the feet of the passing woman ; and the behest is so faithfully observed that on the rare occasions when an Indian woman may need to undergo the ordeal I have known her own brother to let her go unrecognised. For one need not say that women do now and then slip out on foot at nightfall, accompanied by a maid bearing a lamp, to enjoy an hour's gossip in some neighbour's house. We are all familiar with the powers of criticism of quiet women who never strayed into the great world, or saw more than the view from their own thresholds would reveal. What is true in this respect of the Western cottage is true also of the Eastern zenana. Woman's penetration is everywhere the same. Her good breeding makes everywhere the same demands. On one occasion I had the misfortune to introduce into my Indian home a European whose behaviour caused me the deepest mortification. But the ladies sat on the case when she had gone, and gravely discussed it in all its bearings. Finally it was gently dismissed with the remark, "she was not well-born." On another occasion I came in one evening at the moment of some distinguished friend's arrival. Such was the *empressement* of her reception, the warmth of the inquiries after her health and so on, that I felt myself to be certainly an intrusion. But a quiet hand detained me when I would have slipped away. "Wait," said the Mother, "till I have finished, for I haven't the least idea who she is!"

There were, however, certain practical difficulties in the life. It had taken some time, in the first place, to discover a house that could be let to an Englishwoman; and when this was done it was still a few weeks before a Hindu caste-woman could be found who would be my servant. She turned up at last, however, in the person of an old, old woman, who called me "Mother," and whom I, at half her age, had to address as "Daughter" or "Jhee." This aged servitor was capable enough of the wholesale floodings of the rooms which constituted house-cleaning, as well of producing boiling water at stated times for the table and the bath. For some reason or other she had determined in my case to perform these acts on condition that I never entered her kitchen or touched her fire or water-supply. Yet hot water was not immediately procurable. And the reason? We possessed no cooking-stove. I asked the price of this necessary article, and was told six farthings. Armed with which sum, sure enough, my trusty retainer brought home a tile, a lump of clay, and a few thin iron bars, and constructed from these, with the greatest skill, the stove we needed.

It took some days to set and harden, but at last the work was complete. Afternoon tea, prepared under my own roof, was set triumphantly before me, and my ancient "daughter" squatted on the verandah facing me, with the hot kettle on the stone floor beside her, to see what strange thing might come to pass. I poured out a cup of tea and held out the pot to Jhee for more hot water. To my amazement she only gave a sort of grunt and disappeared into the inner courtyard. When she came back, a second later, she was dripping with cold water from head to foot. Before touching what I was about to drink she had considered a complete immersion necessary!

How happy were those days in the little lane! how unlike the terrible pictures of the Hindu routine which, together with that of the Pharisees in the New Testament, had embittered my English childhood! Constant ablutions, endless prostrations, unmeaning caste-restrictions, what a torture the dreary tale had been! And the reality was so different! My little study, with its modern pictures and few books, looked out on the cheeriest of neighbours. Here, a brown baby, with black lines under his eyes, and a gold chain round his waist, carried in triumph by his mother or nurse; there, some dignified woman, full of sweetness, as a glance would show, on her way to the bathing-ghat; again, a quiet man, with intellectual face and Oriental leisure; and, above it all, the tall palm-trees, with little brown villages and fresh-water tanks nestling at their feet, while all kinds of birds flew about fearlessly just outside my window, and threw their shadows across my paper as I wrote. The golden glow of one's first sensation suffuses it still. It was all like a birth into a new world.

One evening, as I prepared for supper, a sound of wailing broke the after-darkness quiet of the lane, and making my way in the direction of the cry, I entered the court-yard of some servants' huts, just opposite. On the floor of the yard a girl lay dying, and as we sat and watched her, she breathed her last. Hours went by, and while the men were away at the burning-ghat, making arrangements for the funeral-fire that would be over before dawn, I sat with the weeping women, longing to comfort them, yet knowing not what to say. At last the violence of their grief had exhausted them, and even the mother of the dead girl lay back in my arms in a kind of stupor, dazed into forgetfulness for awhile. Then, as is the way of sorrow, it all swept over her again, in a flood of despair. "Oh!" she cried, turning to me, "what shall I do? Where is my child now?"

I have always regarded that as the moment in which I found the key. Filled with a sudden pity, not so much for the bereaved woman as for those to whom the use of some particular language of the Infinite is a question of morality, I leaned forward. "Hush, mother!" I said, "your child is with the Great Mother. She is with Kali!" And then, for a moment, with memory stilled, we were enfolded together, Eastern and Western, in the unfathomed depths of consolation of the World-Heart.

CHAPTER II

THE EASTERN MOTHER

THESE eighteen centuries has Europe been dreaming of the idyll of the Oriental woman. For Asia is one, and the wondrous Maiden of all Christian art, from the Byzantines down to yesterday—who is she, of what is she aware, save that she is a simple Eastern mother? Of what fasts and vigils are we told in her case, that she should have known herself, or been known, as Queen of Saints? A rapt humility, as of one whose robe was always, indeed, her veil; a touch of deep silence, and that gracious richness of maternity which we can infer from the full and rounded sweetness of the Child who grew within her shadow—what more do we know of the Blessed Virgin than these things?

What more we may desire to know we can learn in the East itself—in India as well as anywhere. For in the period before Islam had defined itself, overflowing Chaldea, with the impulse, perhaps, of the pastoral life, become aggressive, to re-make the desert—in the days when Palestine and Lebanon were cultivated lands, inhabited by peasants of the early type, not as yet made a burnt-offering on the altar of crusading fury, in the closing centuries of the pre-Christian era—the common life of Syria had a still wider identity with that of Hindus than it has to-day. The ceremonial washings of Pharisees and Sadducees, the constant purifying of the cup and

B

platter, the habitual repetition of a single name or prayer, which some later phase of the Christianising consciousness has stigmatised as "vain"—these things were not *like*, they *were*, what we know to-day as Hinduism, being merely those threads of the one great web of Asiatic life that happened to touch the Mediterranean coast.

And in matters so fundamental as the relation of mother and child, religious teachers come only to enforce the message of the race. Is it not said by the Prophet himself that the man who kisses the feet of his mother finds himself in Paradise?

Yet how frail and slight and young is often the mother so tenderly adored! No Madonna of the Sistine Chapel can give that lofty purity of brow or delicate untouched virginity of look of any one of these Hindu mother-maidens, whose veil half covers, half reveals, as he rests on her left arm, her son!

The picture is too central to Indian life to have demanded literary idealising. Poetic and mythological presentments of the perfect wife there are in plenty: of motherhood, none. Only God is worshipped as such by men and children and by mothers themselves as the Holy Child! Here the half pathos of Western maternity, with its perpetual suggestion of the brood-hen whose fledglings are about to escape her, is gone, and an overwhelming sense of tenderness and union takes its place. To one's mother one always remains a baby. It would be unmanly to disguise the fact. And yet for her sake most of all it is needful to play the man, that she may have a support on which to lean in the hour of darkness and need. Even a wife has no power to bring division between a mother and her son, for the wife belongs almost more to her husband's mother than to himself. There can, therefore, be no jealousy at the entry of another woman into his life. Instead of this, it is she who urges the marriage; every offering is sent out in her name; and the procession that wends from the bridegroom's house to the bride's some few days before the wedding, bearing unguents and fragrant oils for the ceremonial bath, carries her loving invitation and goodwill to the new and longed-for daughter.

Even in Indian home life, then, full as this is of intensity of sweetness, there is no other tie to be compared in depth to that which binds together the mother and her child. With the coming of her first-born, be it boy or girl, the young wife has been advanced, as it were, out of the novitiate. She has become a member of the authoritative circle. It is as if the whole world recognises that henceforth there will be one soul at least to whom her every act is holy, before whom she is entirely without fault, and enters into the conspiracy of maintaining her child's reverence.

For there are no circumstances sufficient in Eastern eyes to justify criticism of a mother by her child. Their horror of the fault of Gertrude is almost exaggerated, yet Hamlet's spell is invariably broken when he speaks of the fact. To him, her sin should be sacred, beyond reproach; he ought not to be able to think of it as other than his own.

The freedom and pleasantries of filial sentiment in the West are thus largely wanting in that of the East. A determined stampede of babies of from three to six may, indeed, take place day after day through the room where their mother is at prayer. There may even be an attempt at such an hour to take the city by assault, the children leaping vociferously on the back of that good mother, whose quiet of conscience depends, as they well know, on her perfect silence, so that she can punish them only by turning towards them the sweetest of smiles. "Why, mother," said her family priest to one who appealed to him regarding devotions interrupted thus, "the Lord knows that you are a mother, and He makes allowance for these things!" But though, in the Oriental home, the wickedness of five years old may find such vent as this, the off-hand *camaraderie* that learns later to dub its parents "mater" and "governor" suggests a state little short of savagery, and the daughter who permits herself to precede her father is held guilty of sacrilege. The tenderness of parents corresponds to this veneration of children, and we only learn the secret of feelings so deep-rooted when we find that every child is a nurseling for its first two years of life. Consciousness and even thought are thus awakened long before the closest intimacy is broken, and a dependence that to us of the West is but a vague imagination, to the Eastern man or woman is a living memory.

How completely this may become an ingrained motive we see in the case of that Mogul Emperor who is remembered simply as "the Great." For Akbar had a foster-brother in the Rajput household whither his father Humayum had fled before his birth and where his first six years of life were passed. Akbar's mother dying, the Rajput Queen took the babe to nurse with her own son, and brought up the boys in this respect as brothers, though the guest was a Mussulman of Tamerlane's descent, and her own the proudest Hindu blood on earth. Events swept the children apart in boyhood, and, destiny fulfilling itself, he who came of a race of conquerors ascended the throne of Delhi, after many years, as Emperor of India. Then he found his Rajput subjects difficult indeed to subjugate. In them, the national idea renewed itself again and again, and insurrection followed insurrection. There was one name, moreover, in every list of rebels, and men wondered at the indulgence with which the august ruler passed it by so often. At last some one ventured to point it out, protesting that justice must surely be done now. "Justice, my friend!" said the lofty Akbar, turning on his counsellor, "there is an ocean of milk between him and me and that justice cannot cross!"

This long babyhood creates a tie that nothing can break. The thoughts and feelings of womanhood never become ridiculous in the eyes of the Indian man. It is no shame to him that his mother could not bear a separation; it is right and natural that he should be guided by this wish of hers. None but the hopelessly degraded ever reacts against woman's weakness in active cruelty. If one asks some hard worker in his old age to what he owes his habit of industry or his determined perseverance over detail, it is more than likely that his reply will take us back to his infancy, and the wishes that a young mother, long dead, may have expressed for him. Or the man, in perplexity as to the course he should pursue, will go as naturally as a child, to test his question in the light of her feminine intuition. In all probability, she is utterly unlearned, but he knows well the directness of her mind, and judges rightly that wisdom lies in love and experience, having but little to do with letters.

Surely one of the sweetest happenings was that of a little boy of six who became in later life extremely distinguished. His mother, too shy to express the wish for instruction to her learned husband, confided in her son, and day after day he would toddle home from the village school, slate and pencil in hand, to go once more through his morning's lesson with her, and so, with mutual secrecy, she was taught to read by her own child! With almost all great men in India the love of their mothers has been a passion. It is told of a famous Bengali judge who died some twenty-five years ago —one whose judicial decisions were recorded and quoted, even by the Englishmen who heard them, as precedents in English law, it is told of this man, when on his deathbed, that his mother stumbled and hurt her foot on the threshold of his room one morning, as she came after bathing to visit him. Another moment, and, weak as he was, he had crept across the floor, and lay before her, kissing the wounded foot again and again, and bathing it in hot tears of self-reproach for the pain it suffered. Such stories are remembered and repeated in Indian society, not because they occasion surprise, but because they make the man's own name holy. The death scene with Aase would redeem Peer Gynt himself. None who is sound in this basic relationship of life can be altogether corrupt in the rest, nor can his decisions, however adverse, be completely repugnant to us. How curious are the disputes that agitate Christendom as to the sentiment one may fittingly indulge towards the mother of a beloved Son! Is her supreme position in His life not self-evident? What, then, could be more convincing of union with Him than sweetness of feeling and words of endearment addressed to her? And so, with its wonderful simplicity, the great heart of the East sweeps aside our flimsy arguments and holds up to us the fact itself.

But it is not the great alone who worship motherhood in India. Never can I forget the long hours of one hot March day, when I sat by the bedside of a boy who was dying of plague. His home was of the humblest, a mud hut with a thatched roof. His family were Sudras, or working-folk. Even his father, it appeared, could not read or write. The boy was eleven or twelve years of age, an only child, and he was doomed. The visitor's sole real usefulness lay in taking precautions against the spread of the disease.

Amongst the veiled and silent women who came

and went at the other side of the little court where the boy lay, was one who slipped noiselessly to his bedside whenever she could, and exposed herself to the infection with a recklessness born of ignorance. At last I attempted to reason with her, urging her, as gently as I could, to remain at some distance from the lad, and thus avoid the danger for herself and others.

She turned to obey without a word, but as she went the tears poured down her poor thin cheeks, and lifting the corner of her sari to wipe them away, she tried to stifle the sobs she could not altogether repress. At that moment the words reached me from the doorway. "She is his mother." What I did can be imagined. Suddenly I discovered that the boy must be fanned, and that there was a place behind his pillow out of the line of the air current. Here, with his head almost resting on her feet, his mother sat henceforth, crouched up, attending to her child through happy hours.

Often he would grow delirious, and forget her presence. Then he would toss his head from side to side, and his fever-lighted eyes stared blankly at me, while he uttered his one cry, "Ma! Ma Mataji! —Mother! Mother! *honoured* Mother!" To my Western ears it seemed a strange cry for a child of the slums! Sometimes, as memory returned, he would smile at me, mistaking me for her, and once he snatched at my hand and then carried his own to his lips. Sweet, unknown mother, forgive me these thefts of love, that rent the veil from a graciousness so perfect, an adoration so deep!

That day, alas, was their last together. All through the hours, the child had struggled to repeat the name of God. Late in the afternoon he stumbled on a hymn that was much sung at the time about the streets; but he could not say it, and it was my part to take up the words and stand repeating them beside him. A smile of relief passed over his face; he lay quiet for a moment. Then his breath came shorter and shorter, and as the sun set, with his mother's eyes upon his face, he died.

Of such stuff as this are the teeming millions of the Hindu people made. In moments of mortal agony, when Western lips would frame a prayer, perhaps half an oath, the groan that they utter is ever the cry of the child in its deepest need, "Oh, Mother!"

But it is easy to multiply instances. What we want is that epic of motherhood, of which each separate mother and her child are but a single line or stanza, that all-compelling imagination of the race, which must for ever be working itself out through the individual.

We talk glibly of Dante's "Vision of Hell." How many of us have looked into hell, or even seen it from afar off, that we should appreciate what it means to descend there? When the gloom of insanity falls upon the soul so that it turns to rend and destroy its dearest and best, when the blight of some dread imagination covers us with its shadow, is it lover, or child, or servant, who will still find in our maimed and maleficent presence his chiefest good? There is One indeed whom we cannot imagine as forsaking us. One whose will for us has been the law of righteousness, and yet for whose help we shall cry out instinctively in the moment of the commission of a crime. And like the love of God in this respect is, to Hindu thinking, that of a mother. Transcending the wife's, which may fluctuate with the sweetness bestowed upon it, the mother's affection, by its very nature, grows deeper with deep need, and follows the beloved even into hell. A yearning love that can never refuse us; a benediction that for ever abides with us; a presence from which we cannot grow away; a heart in which we are always safe; sweetness unfathomed, bond unbreakable, holiness without a shadow—all these indeed, and more, is motherhood. Small wonder that the innermost longing of every Hindu is to find himself at home in the Universe, with all that comes thereby of joy or sorrow, even as a baby lying against its mother's heart! This is the dream that is called Nirvana, Freedom. It is the ceasing from those preferences that withhold us that is called Renunciation.

The very word "mother" is held to be sacred, and good men offer it to good women for their protection. There is no timely service that may not be rendered to one, however young or beautiful, by the passing stranger, if only he first address her thus. Even a father, looking at some small daughter, and struggling to express the mystery of futurity that he beholds in her, may address her as "little mother." And the mother of the nation, Uma Himavutee, is portrayed always as a child, thought of always as a daughter of the house. In motherhood alone does marriage become holy; without it, the mere indulgence of affection has no right to be. This is the true secret of the longing for children. And to reach that height of worship in which the husband feels his wife to be his mother, is at once to crown and end all lower ties.

Who that has ever watched it can forget a Hindu woman's worship of the Holy Child? A small brass image of the Baby Krishna lies, or kneels at play, in a tiny cot, and through the hours of morning, after her bath and before her cooking, the woman, who may or may not herself be wife and mother, sits offering to this image flowers and the water of the bath, fruits, sweets, and other things—her oblations interspersed with constant acts of meditation and silent prayer. She is striving to worship God as the Child Saviour, struggling to think of herself as the Mother of God. She is ready enough to give her reason, if we ask her. "Does my feeling for my children change according to what they do for me?" she questions in return: "Even so should one love God. Mothers love most those who need most. Even so should one love God." The simple answer is worth a world of theology. Nor is it forgotten presently that the other children, made of flesh and blood, and answering to her call, are likewise His images. In every moment of feeding, or training, or play, of serving or using or enjoying, she may make her dealing with these an act of devotion. It was her object, during the hours of worship, to come face to face with the Universal Self. Has she done this, or has she brooded over the ideal sentiment till she has made of herself the perfect mother?

By her child, again, her intention can never be doubted. She may turn on him now a smile and then a face of sorrow, now a word of praise and again an indignant reproach. But always, equally, she remains the mother. The heart of hearts of her deed is unfailing love. She knows well, too, that nothing her babies do can mean anything else. The sunny and the petulant, the obedient and the wilful, are only seeking so many different ways to express a self-same dependence. To each she accords the welcome of his own nature. In such a reconciliation of opposites, in such a discovery of unity in variety, lies the whole effort and trend of Eastern religion.

For what thought is it that speaks supremely to India in the great word "Mother"? Is it not the vision of a love that never seeks to possess, that is, content simply to *be*—a giving that could not wish return: a radiance that we do not even dream of grasping, but in which we are content to bask, letting the eternal sunshine play around and through us?

And yet, and yet, was there ever an ideal of such strength as this, that was not firm-based on some form of discipline? What, then, is the price that is paid by Hindu women for a worship so precious? The price is the absolute inviolability of marriage. The worship is, at bottom, the worship of steadfastness and purity. If it were conceivable to the Hindu son that his mother could cease for one moment to be faithful to his father—whatever the provocation, the coldness, or even cruelty, to which she might be subjected—at that moment his idealism of her would become a living pain. A widow remarried is no better in Hindu eyes than a woman of no character, and this is the case even where the marriage was only betrothal, and the young *fiancée* has become what we know as a child-widow.

This inviolability of the marriage tie has nothing whatever to do with attraction and mutual love. Once a wife, always a wife, even though the bond be shared with others, or remain always only a name. That other men should be only as shadows to her, that her feet should be ready at all times to go forth on any path, even that of death, as the companion of her husband, these things constitute the purity of the wife in India. It is told of some wives with bated breath, how, on hearing of the approaching death of the beloved, they have turned, smiling, and gone to sleep, saying, "I must precede, not follow!" and from that sleep they never woke again.

But if we probe deep enough, what, after all, is purity? Where and when can we say it is, and how are we to determine that here and now it is not? What is there sacred in one man's monopoly? or if it be of the mind alone, how can any physical test be rightly imposed?

Purity in every one of its forms is the central pursuit of Indian life. But even the passion of this search grows pale beside the remorseless truthfulness of Hindu logic. There is ultimately, admits India, no single thing called purity: there is the great life of the impersonal, surging through the individual, and each virtue in its turn is but another name for this.

And so the idea of the sanctity of motherhood, based on the inviolability of marriage, finds due and logical completion in the still greater doctrine of the sacredness of religious celibacy. It is the towering ideal of the supersocial life—" As Mount Meru to a fire-fly " compared to that of the householder—which gives sanction and relation to all social bonds. In proportion as the fact of manhood becomes priesthood, does it attain its full glory; and the mother, entering into the prison of a sweet dedication, that she may bestow upon her own child the mystery of breath, makes possible in his eyes, by the perfect stainlessness of her devotion, the thought of that other life whose head touches the stars.

CHAPTER III

OF THE HINDU WOMAN AS WIFE

Of the ideal woman of the religious orders the West to-day has very little notion. Teresa and Catherine are now but high-sounding names in history; Beatrice, a true daughter of the Church, is beloved only of the poets; and Joan of Arc, better understood, is rightly felt to be by birth the nun, but by genius the knight. Yet without some deeper sense of kindred with these it will be hard to understand a Hindu marriage, for the Indian bride comes to her husband much as the Western woman might enter a church. Their love is a devotion, to be offered in secret. They know well that they are the strongest influence, each in the other's life, but before the family there can be no assertion of the fact. Their first duty is to see that the claims of others are duly met, for the ideal is that a wife shall, if that be possible, love her husband's people as she never loved her own; that the new parents shall be more to her than the old; that she can bring no gift into their home so fair as a full and abundant daughterhood and a confirmation of their supreme place in their son's love. Both husband and wife must set their faces towards the welfare of the family. This, and not that they should love each the other before all created beings, is the primal intention of marriage. Yet for the woman supreme love also is a duty. Only to the man his mother must stand always first. In some sense, therefore, the relation is not mutual. And this is in full accordance with the national sentiment, which stigmatises affection that asks for equal return as "shopkeeping." When her husband is present or before honoured guests the young wife may not obtrude herself on the attention of her elders. She sits silent, with veil down, plying a fan or doing some little service for the new mother. But through the work of the day she is a trusted helpmeet, and the relation is often very sweet. Nothing is so easy to distinguish as the educational impress of the good mother-in-law. Dignity, with gaiety and freedom, is its great feature. The good breeding of the Hindu woman is so perfect that it is not noticed till one comes across the exception—some spoilt child, perhaps, who, as heiress or beauty has been too much indulged; and her self-assertiveness and want of restraint, though the same behaviour might seem decorous enough in an English girl of her age, will serve as some measure for the real value of the common standard.

It is not merely in her quietness and modesty, however, that the daughter-in-law betrays good training. She has what remains with her throughout life—a *savoir faire* that nothing can disturb. I have never known this broken; and I saw an extraordinary instance of it when a friend, the shyest of orthodox women, consented to have her photograph taken for one who begged it with urgency. She stipulated, naturally, that it should be done by a woman. But this was found to be impossible. "Then let it be an Englishman," she said with a sigh, evidently shrinking painfully from the idea of a man, yet feeling that the greater the race-distance the less would be the impropriety. The morning came, and the Englishman arrived, but in the Indian gentlewoman who faced him there was no trace of self-consciousness or fear. A superb indifference carried her through the ordeal, and would have been a sufficient protection in some real difficulty.

All the sons of a Hindu household bring their wives home to their mother's care, and she, having married her own daughters into other women's families, takes these in their place. There is thus a constant bubbling of young life about the elderly woman, and her own position becomes a mixture of the mother-*suzeraine* and lady abbess. She is well aware of the gossip and laughter of the girls amongst themselves, though they become so demure at her entrance. Whispering goes on in corners and merriment waxes high even in her presence, but she ignores it discreetly, and devotes her attention to persons of her own age. In the early summer mornings she smiles indulgently to find that one and another slipped away last night from her proper sleeping-place and betook herself to the roof, half for the coolness and half for the mysterious joys of girls' midnight gossip.

The relationship, however, is as far from familiarity as that of any kind and trusted prioress with her novices. The element of banter and freedom has another outlet, in the grandmother or whatever aged woman may take that place in the community house. Just as at home the little one had coaxed and appealed against the decisions of father or mother to the ever-ready granddam, so, now that she is a bride, she finds some old woman in her husband's home who has given up her cares into younger hands and is ready to forego all responsibility in the sweetness of becoming a *confidante*. One can imagine the rest. There must be many a difficulty, many a perplexity, in the new surroundings, but to them all old age can find some parallel. Looking back into her own memories, the grandmother tells of the questions that troubled her when she also was a bride, of the mistakes that she made, and the solutions that offered. Young and old take counsel together, and there is even the possibility that when a mother-in-law is unsympathetic, her own mother-in-law may intervene on behalf of a grandson's wife. Before the grandmother, therefore, there is none of that weight of reverence which can never be lightened in the mother's presence. Even the veil need not be dropped. The familiar "thou" takes the place of the stately "you," and there is no respect shown by frigid reserve.

Long ago, when a child's solemn betrothal often took place at seven or eight years of age, it was to gratify the old people's desire to have more children about them that the tiny maidens were brought into the house. It was on the grandmother's lap that the little ones were made acquainted ; it was she and her husband who watched anxiously to see that they took to each other; and it was they again who petted and comforted the minute grand-daughter-in-law in her hours of home sickness. Marriage has grown later nowadays, in answer amongst other things to the pressure of an increasing poverty, and it does not happen so often that an old man is seen in the bazaar buying consoling gifts for the baby brides at home. But the same instinct still obtains, of making the new home a place of choice, when between her twelfth and fourteenth year—the girl's age at her first and second marriages—the young couple visit alternately in each other's families.

The Hindu theory is that a long vista of common memory adds sweetness even to the marriage tie, and whether we think this true or not, we have all known happy marriages on such a basis. But about the mutual sentiment of old and young there can be no theory, because there is no possibility of doubt. In all countries in the world it is recognised as amongst the happiest things in life. The reminiscence of Arjuna, one of the heroes of the great War-Epic, gives us the Indian explanation of this fact. "I climbed on his knee," he says, speaking of the aged knight Bhishma, head of his house, "all hot and dusty from my play, and flinging my arms about his neck, I called him 'Father.'" "Nay, my child," he replied, as he held me to his breast, "not thy *father* but *thy father's father!*" With each generation, that is to say, the tie has deepened and intensified.

In all cases where one or two hundred persons live under the same roof, a complex etiquette grows up, by which gradations of rank and deference are rigidly defined. Under the Hindu system this fund of observation has so accumulated that it amounts now to an accomplished culture—a completed criticism of life—rich in quaint and delightful suggestions for humanity everywhere. We may not know why a mother's relatives are apt to be dearer than a father's, but the statement will be approved as soon as made. It has not occurred to us that our relations to an elder sister and a younger are not the same: in India there is a different word for each, for whole worlds of sweetness lie a world apart in one name and the other to the Hindu mind. Yet a cousin is constantly called brother or sister, the one relation being merged entirely in the other. The mere use of a language with this degree of definiteness implies an emotional training of extraordinary kind. It is, of course, best suited to natures of great richness of feeling. In these, sentiment is developed in proportion to expression, and the same attitude that makes every one in the village "Aunt" or "Uncle" to the children, produces an ultimate sense of kinship to the world. This is perhaps the commonest characteristic of Hindu men and women; shy at first, and passive to slight stimulus, as are all great forces, when once a relationship is established, they believe in it absolutely, blindly; are ready to go to the uttermost in its name; and forget entirely all distance of birth or difference of association. The weak point in the system appears when it has to deal with the harder, more arid class of natures. In these there is less inner response to the outer claim; expressions of difference, therefore, become less sincere and more abject. This is but a poor preparation for the open air of the modern world, where seniority, sanctity, and rank have all to be more or less ignored, and man stands face to face with man, free and equal so far as the innate manhood of each can carry. But such persons—though, naturally enough, they cluster round the powerful foreigner as moths about a lamp—are the failures of Hinduism, not its types, and they are very few. In a perfected education, Western ideals of equality and struggle would present themselves to these for their choosing, while far away in Europe, maybe, hearts born too sensitive for their more rudimentary emotional surroundings would be thankful in turn to find life made richer by Indian conceptions of human relationship.

In a community like that of the Hindu home—as in all clan-systems—the characteristic virtue of every member must be a loyal recognition of common duties and dangers. And this is so. The wife who refused to share her husband's obligation to a widowed sister and her children was never known in India. Times of stress draw all parts of the vast group together; none of the blood can cry in vain for protection and support: even a "village-connection" (*i.e.*, one who is kin by association only) finds refuge in his hour of need. This great nexus of responsibility takes the place of workhouse, hospital, orphanage, and the rest. Here the lucky and the unlucky are brought up side by side. For to the ripe and mellow genius of the East it has been always clear that the defenceless and unfortunate require a *home*, not a barrack.

Into this complex destiny the bride enters finally, about her fourteenth year. Till now she has been a happy child, running about in freedom, feet shod and head bare, eating and drinking what she would. Till now, life has been full of indulgences—for her own parents, with the shadow of this early separation hanging over them, have seen no reason for a severity that must bring in its train an undying regret. From the moment of her betrothal, however, the girl's experience gradually changes. Just as the young nun, if she runs to find her thimble, will be sent back to bring it "more religiously," so about the newly married girl there grows a subtle atmosphere of recollectedness. The hair is parted, no longer childishly brushed back; and at the parting—showing just beyond the border of the veil with which her head now is always covered—appears a touch of vermilion, put there this morning as she dressed in token that she wished long life to her husband; much as one might, in taking up a fan, blow a kiss from its edge to some absent beloved one. The young wife's feet are unshod, and the gold wedding bracelet on the left wrist, and a few ornaments appropriate to her new dignity, supply the only hint of girlish vanity. But she has more jewels. These that she wears daily are of plain gold, more or less richly worked, but on her wedding night she wore the *siti*, or three-lined coronal, set with gems, and arms and neck were gay with flashing stones. All these were her dower, given by her father to be her personal property, and not even her husband can touch them without her consent, though he will add to them occasionally at festive moments. She will wear them all now and again, on great occasions, but meanwhile the silver anklets and the golden necklet and a few bangles are enough for daily use. The girl knows her right to her own ornaments quite well, and the world will never hear how often the wife or the mother has hastened to give up the whole of this little resource in order that son or husband might weather a storm or receive an education. The one thing from which she will never part, however, unless widowhood lays its icy hand upon her life, is that ring of iron covered with gold and worn on the left wrist, which is the sign of the indissoluble bond of her marriage —her wedding-ring in fact.

With all the shyness of the religious novice comes the girl to her new home. Its very form, with its pillared courtyards, is that of a cloister. The constant dropping of the veil in the presence of a man, or before a senior, is the token of a real retirement, the sacrament of an actual seclusion, within which all the voices of the world lose distinctness and individuality, becoming but faint echoes of that which alone can call the soul and compel the eager feet. For India has no fear of too much worship. To her, all that exists is but a mighty curtain of appearances, tremulous now and again with breaths from the unseen that it conceals. At any point, a pinprick may pierce the great illusion, and the seeker become aware of the Infinite Reality beyond. And who so fitted to be the window of the Eternal Presence as that husband, who is at once most adored and loved of all created beings?

For there is a deep and general understanding of the fact that only in its own illumination, or its own feeling, can the soul find its highest individuation. To learn how she can offer most becomes thus the aim of the young wife's striving. All her dreams are of the saints—women mighty in renunciation: Sita, whose love found its richest expression in the lifelong farewell that made her husband the ideal king; Sati, who died rather than hear a word against Siva, even from her own father; and Uma, realising that her love was given in vain, yet pursuing the more eagerly the chosen path. "Be like Savitri," was her father's blessing, as he bade her the bridal farewell, and Savitri—the Alcestris of Indian story—was that maiden who followed even Death till she won back her husband's life. Thus wifehood is thought great in proportion to its giving, not to its receiving. It would never occur to any one, in writing fiction, or delineating actual character, to praise a woman's charms, as we praise Sarah Jennings', on the score that she retained her husband's affection during her whole life. A good man, says the Hindu, does not fail his wife, but, apart from this, coquetry and vanity, however pleasing in their form, could never dignify marriage. Lifelong intimacy, to be beautiful, must boast deeper foundations—the wife's love, daring all and asking for no return; the mother's gentleness, that never changes; the friend's unswerving generosity. To the grave Oriental there is something indecorous in the discussion of the subject on any but this highest basis. And yet Persia, the France of Asia, must have been a perpetual influence towards romanticism in Hindu life. There is said to be no love poetry in the world so impassioned as the Persian. The famous verse:

> Four eyes met. There were changes in two souls.
> And now I cannot remember whether he is a man and I a woman,
> Or he a woman and I a man. All I know is,
> There were two: Love came, and there is one. . . .

we must believe completely representative of its spirit.* The Persian language, however, has only

* This verse is actually old Bengali, of the sixteenth century.

touched India through the Court of Delhi and through letters. It has been the possession of the Indo-Mohammedan, and of any man here and there who took the time and trouble to master its literature; but the world of Hindu womanhood has remained probably as remote from it as though it belonged to another planet.

This is not true to the same extent of the romantic aspect of Christianity. The letters taught in English schools result very much in novel-reading, and an indigenous school of fiction has grown up, in the form of books and magazines, which is likely to modify popular ideas on this subject profoundly. Meanwhile, and for long to come, it remains true that according to Hindu notions, the eyes of bride and bridegroom are to be directed towards the welfare of the family and not of themselves, as the basis of society: it is the great springs of helpfulness and service, rather than those of mutual love and romantic happiness that marriage is expected to unloose. Selfish wives and jealous husbands there must be, as among all peoples. But it is a fact, nevertheless, that here the absolute stainlessness of the wife is considered but preliminary to the further virtue demanded of her, the sustaining of the honour of her husband's house.

With this clue it becomes easy to understand even what the West considers to be the anomalies of Hindu custom—the laws regarding rare cases of polygamy and adoption. For it is legally provided that if a woman remain childless her husband may after seven years, *and with her permission*, take a second wife, in the hope of gaining a son to succeed to his place. On the European basis of individualism, the permission would probably be impossible to obtain; but with the Eastern sense of family obligation, this has not always been so, and I have myself met the son of such a marriage whose story was of peculiar interest. The elder wife had insisted that the time was come for the alternative to be tried, and had herself chosen the speaker's mother as the most beautiful girl she could find, for the husband. The marriage once over, she made every effort to make it a success, and welcomed the new wife as a younger sister. Not only this, but when the son was born, such was her tenderness that he was twelve years old before he knew that she was not his mother. After her death, however, the younger wife became head of the house. Amongst the children to be fed, there were degrees of kindred, certain adopted orphans, two or three cousins, and himself. He was the eldest of all, and protested loudly that he came in last, and his cousins only second, for his mother's attentions. "Nay, my child," she answered, with a Hindu woman's sweetness and good sense, "if I desired to neglect thee, I could not do it. Is it not right, then, first to serve those who have no protection against me?"

The family life which such a story discloses is singularly noble, and it is not necessary to suppose that polygamy entailed such generosities oftener than we find monogamy do amongst ourselves. In any case, the same tide that brings in individualism has swept away this custom; and whereas it never was common it is now practically obsolete, except for princes and great nobles, and even amongst these classes there are signs of a radical change of custom.

"Where women are honoured, there the gods are pleased: where they are dishonoured, religious acts become of no avail." "In whatever family the husband is contented with his wife, and the wife with her husband, in that house will good fortune assuredly abide." Few books offer such delights to their readers as that known as the "Laws of Manu."

It is in no sense a collection of Acts of Parliament, for the one attitude throughout is that of the witness, and the hastiest perusal shows that it represents the growth of custom during ages, and is in no sense the work of a single hand. This is indeed its first and most striking beauty. As must be, of course, it often happens that the superstition of a habit is stated as gravely as its original intent, but rarely so as to obscure that first significance, or leave it difficult of restoration, and from cover to cover the book throbs with the passion for justice, and the appreciation of fine shades of courtesy and taste, clothed in calm and judicial form. Especially of this type are those dicta on the rights of women, which are household words in Indian homes. We all know the reaction of the written word on life. Fact once formulated as scripture acquires new emphasis, a certain occult significance seems to attach to it, and the words, "it is written" become terrible enough to affright the devil himself. In this way the fear of a feminine curse has become a superstition in India, and I have seen even a low-class mob fall back at the command of a single woman who opposed them. For is it not written in the book of the law that "the house which is cursed by a woman perishes utterly, *as if destroyed by a sacrifice for the death of an enemy*"?—strange and graphic old phrase, pregnant of woe!

It is evident then that the laws of Manu are rather the unconscious expression of the spirit of the people than a declaration of the ideals towards which they strive. And for this reason they would afford the most reliable foundation for a healthy criticism of Indian custom. The conception of domestic happiness which they reveal is very complete, and no one who has seen the light on an Indian woman's face when it turns to her husband—as I have seen it in all parts of the country—can doubt that that conception is often realised in life. For if the characteristic emotion of the wife may be described as passionate reverence, that of the Hindu husband is certainly a measureless protection. If we may presume to analyse things so sacred as the great mutual trusts of life, it would seem that tenderness is the ruling note of the man's relation. Turning as he does to the memory of his own mother for the ideal perfection, there is again something of motherhood in what he brings to his wife. As a child might do, she cooks for him, and serves him, sitting before him as he eats to fan away the flies. As a disciple might, she prostrates herself before him, touching his feet with her head before receiving his blessing. It is not equality. No. But who talks of a vulgar equality, asks the Hindu wife, when she may have instead the unspeakable blessedness of offering worship?

And on the man's side, how is this received? Entirely without personal vanity. The idea that adoration is the soul's opportunity has sunk deep into the life of the people. And the husband can recognise his wife's right to realise her highest through him without ever forgetting that it is her power to love, not his worthiness of love, that is being displayed. Indeed, is not life everywhere of one tint in this regard? Does anything stir our reverence like an affection that we feel beyond our merit?

It is often glibly said that this habit of being served spoils the Indian man and renders him careless of the comfort of others. I have never found this to be so. It is true that Indian men do not rise when a woman enters, and remain standing till she is seated. Nor do they hasten to open the door through which she is about to pass. But then it is not according to the etiquette of their country to do these things. With regard to the last point, indeed, their idea is that man should precede woman, maintaining the tradition of the path-breaker in the jungle; and one of the most touching incidents in the national epic of heroic love is Sita's request to go first along the forest paths, in order to sweep the thorns from her husband's path with the end of her veil. Needless to say, such a paradox is not permitted.

Thus, honour for the weaker is expressed in one way in England and quite otherwise in Hindostan, but the heart of conduct is the same in both countries. The courtesy of husbands to their wives is quite unfailing amongst Hindus. "Thou shalt not strike a woman, even with a flower," is the proverb. His wife's desire for companionship on a journey is the first claim on a man. And it is very touching to notice how, as years go on, he leans more and more to the habit of addressing her as "O thou, mother of our son!" and presenting her to new comers as "my children's mother," thus reflecting upon her his worship of motherhood. In early manhood he trusts to her advice to moderate the folly of his own rasher inclinations; in old age he becomes, as everywhere in the world, more entirely the eldest of her bairns, and she more and more the real head and centre of the home. But always she remains as she was at the beginning, Lakshmi, her husband's Goddess of Fortune. In those first days he ate from no hand but his mother's or hers; and one of her devotions was the fast, not broken till he had eaten and their talk was over, though her evening meal might in this way be delayed till long past midnight. Now, with the responsibilities of her household upon her, she feeds a whole multitude before she takes her own turn, and still the mutual pact of soul and soul has not been broken by the strife of "rights." These two have all these years been each other's refuge against the world. And not once have they felt so separated as to offer thanks, or speak, either of the other, by name, as if head and hand could be different individuals!

On that first bridal evening, the little bride was borne before her young husband, and they were told that the moment was auspicious for their first shy look. Then the old Vedic fire was called to witness their rites of union; the girl flung the garland of flowers about the neck of her bridegroom, in exquisite symbolism of the bond that was to hold them; and finally they took seven steps together, hand in hand, while the priest chanted appropriate texts for each stage of life. Such was their wedding. Since then, the rights of one have been the rights of the other; joys, griefs, and duties have been held in common. Till now, if the bride of that distant night be entirely fortunate, that prayer of her childhood is fulfilled to her in the end of her days, that prayer that said:

> From the arms of husband and sons,
> When the Ganges is full of water,
> May I pass to the feet of the Lord.

It has seemed to me in watching Hindu couples that they were singular in the frequent attainment of a perfect intimacy. To what is this due? Is it the early association, or the fact that courtship comes after marriage, not before? Or is it the intense discipline of absolute reserve in the presence of others? The people themselves, where their attention is called to it, attribute the fact to child-marriage. I remember asking a friend of my own, a man of wealth and cultivation, orthodox and childless, "If you could put away personal considerations, and speak only from the outside, which do you think better in the abstract, our marriage-system or yours?"

He paused, and answered slowly, "I *think*—ours; for I cannot conceive that two people could grow into each other, as my wife and I have done, under any other."

Amongst the luxuries of the West I have sometimes thought that the deepening of the human tie was proportionate to simplicity of surroundings. A people to whom all complexity of externals is impossible must live by thought and feeling, or perish in the wilderness.

But whatever be the truth on this point, I have seen clearly and constantly that the master-note by which the Hindu woman's life can be understood in the West is that of the religious life. This is so, even with the wife. Cloistered and veiled, she devotes herself to one name, one thought, yet is never known to betray the fact, even as the nun steals away in secret to kneel before the Blessed Sacrament. The ideal that she, like the nun, pursues, is that of a vision which merges the finite in the infinite, making strong to mock at separation, or even at change. And the point to be reached in practice is that where the whole world is made beautiful by the presence in it of the beloved, where the hungry are fed, and the needy relieved, out of a joyful recognition that they wear a common humanity with his; and where, above all, the sense of unrest and dissatisfaction is gone for ever, in the overflowing fulness of a love that asks no return except the power of more abundant loving.

CHAPTER IV

LOVE STRONG AS DEATH

As to the skies their centre is the Polar Star, so to the Eastern home the immovable honour of its womanhood. Here is the secret of that worship of the mother in which all union of the family and all loyalty to its chief are rooted. Woman in the West may thirst for the glory of love or the power of wealth: in Asia, her characteristic dreams are of perfectness and purity and faith. Woman in the West is a queen, exposed to the fierce light that beats upon a throne, putting to good or evil use the opportunities of sovereigns. Even queens in the East are too sacred to be looked upon by common eyes. They grow, like the tall white lilies of annunciation, set in the dimness beside some altar, screened from the very glances of the faithful at their prayers. The long silken tent through which such ladies move from palace-door to carriage-step is no vulgar prison, but a shrine. Bereft of its concealment, they would feel dishonoured, unprotected, as does the widowed gentlewoman, compelled to fight for bread, amongst the struggling crowd.

The very possibility of this blaze of publicity shed on delicate high-bred womanhood is repugnant to the Oriental mind. Remoteness and shadow, silence and obscurity, seem to it the true environment of holiness. And woman is held to be so much a sacred mystery that no man may even mention the name of another's wife to him. "Are they at home all well?" is the guarded form which the necessary inquiry for her health has to take. The outer courts of the house, where the men pass the day, the verandah and the stoop, where neighbours meet and chat, these are but public places. Here the intellectual life may be lived, and civic affairs transacted. But it is by the cool grey threshold of the inner, the women's rooms, that the world of *home* is entered. And what an ocean of passionate loving surges through the quiet walls! Here the wife listens for the feet of the returning husband. Here the widow sobs for him who will return no more. Here scamper home the babies to find mother or aunt, grave elder sister, or twin-souled younger comrade. Here youth lays its plans and brings its perplexities, while old age looks on, with the quiet eyes of experience and of faith. Here passes, in short, all that mingling of smiles and tears, of laughter and prayer, of charm and weariness, that goes to make up the bitter-sweet sacrament of daily life. Only the art of mediæval Holland speaks a passion for home as ardent as this of the Orient, which as yet has found no voice!

Standing without in the noonday hush and looking into the semi-darkness of the women's apartments it is as if one caught a glimpse of some convent garden, full of rare and beautiful flowers. This is the women's hour. Their natural guardians are all absent, sleeping, or at business. Only in the outer court a drowsy servant guards the entrance. An air of innocent raillery, of delicate gaiety, pervades all. Friendly confidences and gentle fun are being exchanged. It is now that the long melancholy cry of the pedlar is heard, with his "Bracelets and bangles—who wants?" or "Good, good cloth!" or what not. And the wandering merchant may be called in, to add amusement to the moment by his baiting and bargaining.

Noonday passes, and slender widows in their long white veils fall to telling their beads, unnoticed and absorbed. Here and there a mother glides away to prepare for the children's coming home from school. The sound of laughter and talk dies gradually down, and afternoon wears on to evening, and the hour of prayer. So passes the day's drama, with all its blending of subdued tints, from dainty rose to ashen grey. Yet almost all the windows of the home look inwards, and four blank walls enclose the whole. True indeed is it that silence and shadow are the ideals of this, the life of Eastern womanhood.

But the ideal itself, that it may be fixed and perpetuated, requires its culminating types and centres, its own duly consecrated priesthood, whose main task in life shall be to light its lamp and wait upon its altar. And such persons, in the world of Indian women, are the widows. Literature consists largely of man's praise of woman in relation to himself; yet it remains eternally true that this heroine of man—Helen, Desdemona, Beatrice—is but one modification or other of her who goes unseen, unhymned, unnamed, the woman of solitude, the woman who stands alone.

Neither Europe nor the modern spirit can claim the glory of having created the idea of woman as an individual. Queen Hatasu had it, in ancient Egypt. In still older Chaldea, Semiramis had it. In the sagas of the North, it is true, no woman goes unwed. But no sooner does Christianity—the Mission of the Asiatic Life—appear amongst us, than mediæval history blossoms into its Hildas, and Teresas, and Joans, its Saxon Margarets and its Spanish Katherines. It is the *self-protecting* woman only, who is born perhaps of the nineteenth century. Of old it was held by Frank and Saxon, by Latin and

Teuton, that she who did not marry needed the protection of the Church. And in Asia to this day it is believed that she requires the sanction of the religious life itself, though that life be lived for the most part within the community-house. For the only unmarried woman in India is the widow, and especially the child-widow—that is, one whose betrothed has died before actual marriage.

A kind of faithfulness is implied in this, which is quite different from the faithfulness of the West. There, it is counted for great fidelity if amidst the growing complexities of life there run the stream of a strong and constant memory; if the bereaved wife be true to the idea for which the husband stood; if she carry his name as a banner, whose new adherents are won by the power of her own consecration. In India, no growth of complexity can be permitted. Where the life stood when its companion was smitten down, there it must remain, till a second death completes the releasing of that one being who only seemed to others to be two.

How wonderful is death! So cold, so still! The mind is withdrawn from the senses, and steadied, that enters its presence but for a moment. They who dwell there find release into a great calm. The Hindu widow lives out her life with her soul ever present at the burning-ghat. Her white sari, unbordered, her short hair, her bareness of jewels, her scant food and long prayers, her refusal to meet guests and join in festivities,—all these things are but the symbols of its abiding lights and shadows. She has found her vocation, so to speak, and as a nun must henceforth direct her life. If she be a child-widow, this is only the more true. Then, the church in which she lingers is more apt to be the thought of the Divine itself. But if in her widowhood she can remember what it was to be a wife, her altar will be the name of the dead husband, and her austerities will carry with them the unspeakable gladness of the memory that half of all their merit goes to him. This belief in a mystic union of souls was the motive of suttee,—a sacrifice that was supposed to lift the husband's soul at once into bright places, and bring his wife to enjoy them beside him for thousands of years. Who, with such an idea deep-ingrained, could not laugh at fire?

It is clear that this scheme of the widow's life is inherent in a great simplicity. A marriage which had but one duty could alone have led to this bereavement which has but one thought. And yet we must understand that it is in this terrible blight of love that the strong woman finds her widest individual scope.

It is told of Bhashkaracharya, the mathematician, that he had but one child, the maiden Lilavati. Casting her horoscope carefully, he discovered that there was only a single moment in her life when she could be married without fear of widowhood. Preparations were made for the wedding accordingly, and the father himself constructed an instrument by which to regulate the time of the ceremonies. Water would be admitted drop by drop through a certain hole, from one pot to another, and its reaching a given height was the signal for the sacramental act.

The marriage-rites began, but the child Lilavati grew tired, and went wandering from room to room in search of amusement. In some obscure corner she came upon an unaccustomed-looking pot, and leaned over its edge to watch how the inner section was gradually sinking in the water which it contained. As she did so a tiny pearl fell all unnoticed from her wedding-crown, and stopped the hole through which the water passed! Time went on, but the vessel sank no further. "Ah!" exclaimed Bhashkaracharya sorrowfully, when, the hour already past, he found the jewel that had frustrated all his caution, "it is useless for a man to fight against his destiny!"

Within some few weeks or months the little bride was left a widow. But now her great father resolved to make of her a woman so learned that she should never sigh for earthly happiness—a resolve in which he succeeded to such an extent that to this day it is not known whether the abstruse treatise named "Lilavati" was merely dedicated to her, or whether she asked the questions to which it contains the answers.

This story is historic. But simple instances abound in every village. The kind widowed aunt who lived in the opposite house to ours, did she not count every soul in the Calcutta lane, together with her brother's children, as her own? "Do not leave this country," she would say to some member of our household every now and then, "for you know I count you all my bairns!" When the man in the next house died of cholera, it was not we, the European neighbours, but this Pishi-ma of ours, who was first on the scene with disinfectants. When the immediate necessity of cleansing the whole house was explained, it was still another and older widow lady who listened, and carried out the work with her own hands. Indeed, wherever one is called in time of need, one finds a group of widow-women already present. There is no act of nursing that these are not ready, and even eager, to perform; no disease so loathsome or dangerous that they will not gladly take a sick child into their arms; no injury so bitter that it will prevent their weeping sorrowful tears of sympathy with the injured in his hour of pain and loss.

It is quite natural that widows should be more free for the civic life than other women. Wives have their husbands' comforts to attend to, and mothers their thousand and one maternal cares. But the widow, and above all the childless widow, in her agony of solitude, can hear the sobs of children not her own, can stretch hands across the desert of her own mourning to those who are ill, or in poverty, and desolation. In the last generation lonely women had still more scope than they have now. I have heard of one who never sat down to the midday meal till a servant brought her word that every soul in the village had already eaten. Almost every family can remember some aged dame of its own who was famed for her skill in all sorts of remedies for man and beasts. The very cow-goddesses, who are worshipped in Himalayan villages in time of cattle pestilence, may have been actual Hindu women of this type, raised to the rank of deities. But the last half-century in India has been rapidly accomplishing the decay of the middle classes; and with this decay, brought about by the shrinking of wealth in its old channels, the fall of woman, in social and material power, proceeds apace. Yet still the widows represent the intellectual centres amongst women. The more modern they are, the less likely is it that they can reel off Sanskrit verses, but the more probable that they read books in the vernaculars. In any case, they produce the saints; and the position of a woman-saint in India is such that no man in her neighbourhood will venture on a journey without first presenting himself before her veiled form, taking the dust of her feet, and receiving her whispered blessing.

Widows have constantly distinguished themselves, especially in Bengal, as administrators of land and wealth. Of this pattern was the great Mahratta Queen of Indore, Ahalya Bai. Her husband died while waging war with Scindia and another, and her first act was to disband her armies, and send word to the sovereigns that she was at their mercy, a defenceless woman. The expected result followed in the complete abandonment of all hostilities. After which, Ahalya Bai Rani lived and reigned for many a long year eating the Hindu widow's handful of rice of her own cooking, and spending her great revenues in public works on the largest scale.

For the wife becomes regent when a man dies during the minority of his son; and even if the latter be already of age, his ownership of an estate is by no means free and complete during the lifetime of his mother. The whole world would cry shame if he acted without her occasional advice, and, indeed, the Indian woman's reputation for business capacity is so like the French that it is commonly said of encumbered property that it needs a widow's nursing.

In such a case there is, however, for the wealthy woman one temptation. Throughout her married life her relation with her father's house has remained close and intimate. At least once a year, if not oftener, she has returned to it on visits. Her eldest child was born there under her own mother's care. Her girlhood's friends have perpetually renewed her youthful memories by hastening to see her on her arrival, and talk over old times. It was many a year before the revival of familiar associations ceased to make her wholly a child again, so that she would run bare-headed down the lane to a neighbour's house, rejoicing in the unaccustomed freedom of the fact that the only men she was likely to meet were practically her own brothers, for she had played with them in babyhood.

But if the relation to her early home and to her past be thus deep and exquisite, what are we to say of the bond that knits together the Hindu sister and her brother? Here is the tie that offers to the woman of responsibilities her great temptation; for it is considered hard, and yet essential, for one who administers a dead husband's wealth not to bestow it in these channels, not to submit to management and direction, not to transfer possession gradually from the one house to the other. And the very insistence upon the dishonour of such a course is in itself testimony to the affection that tempts. The perfect wife is she who loves her husband with a love that forgets even father and brothers if need be. But how arduous is such perfection to attain! One day in the Hindu sacred year is known as "The Feast of Brothers," because on it sisters are visited and give their benisons. And so, even about the detached life of the married woman, made independent of her father's care, early associations continue to twine and grow stronger. They never cease to be an organic part of her life; and if the stress of her existence throws her back upon them, she knows that on which she leans, that it will not fail her at her need, or prove a false staff, breaking in her hand.

And yet her natural longing, in the first days of her widowhood, is to remain, unless forbidden by his poverty, in the household of her father-in-law, for herein lies all her loyalty to the dead. Nay, it will often happen that even a child-widow is anxiously retained by her husband's parents, as a token, in some sort, left by him who is gone. All the glory of womanhood lies in such things as these. Even in her own home, too, a widow has the right to be exacting on a thousand little points regarding her dead husband. Do her father and brothers not remember the great days of obligation of the household into which she married? Do they require reminder, instead of hastening to be beforehand with her, in suggesting the gifts and offerings she would do well to send? Ah, then, it is only herself for whom they cease to weary themselves, or do they forget *his* dignity who should be as dear as their own blood. And for her own part she watches with solicitude all that passes in the family whose name she bears. Is a new bride received among them ? From her own diminishing store of jewels will be sent some trifle—may be only a couple of tiny gold jasmine flowers for the ears —by the bereaved to the newly-wedded daughter-in-law. Or she hears of sickness and arrives to nurse. She comes to wait on the aged, or will assume charge of the young while grave elders go on pilgrimage. All this implies a network of social ideals that tends to make it difficult to divert the income arising from alliance.

Over and above her alleged common sense, on the other hand an estate that passes into the hands of a woman ruler enjoys the economic advantage of her freedom from personal extravagance; for the energy with which a widow pursues after abstinence is extraordinary. To this day she lives in an ancient India, created by her own habits. In Calcutta she drinks only Ganges water, holding that the municipal supply is contaminated by European use. She will eat only rock-salt in order to avoid the pollution of manufacturing processes. When ill she accepts treatment only from the old Indian doctors, the *vaidya* or the *kaviraj*, and pays fantastic sums for their medicines if they come from Benares or some other seat of classic learning. If well, she eats one meal of cooked food prepared with her own hands at or after mid-day, and only a slight refection of milk, fruit, and unleavened bread at nightfall. Her hair is cut short (or in some parts of India the head is shaved), perhaps originally to remove the temptation of beauty, but, as far as custom knows and questions, only that she may bathe the more frequently and easily—every bath conveying to her the notion of a baptism.

Such is her ordinary routine. Her occasional dissipations consist in a pilgrimage, an extra visit to a temple at dawn or after sunset, or attendance at some ceremony of epic recitation.

Is it not well said that she knows no extravagance?

It is because her life is holier than that of others that no hand must touch her food, though she may prepare and serve the meals of any in the house. For the same reason, if questions of precedence arise, she stands higher than married women. Did she not rise before dawn to tell her beads, or to sit for an hour in meditation? Then, when her room was cleaned and ordered, did she not go to the river for the morning bath? Returning with the wet sari that she had washed, according to daily custom, with her own hands, did she not don the silken garment and pass to that ceremonial worship, with flowers and offerings, that lasts for at least an hour or more, and only when that worship was ended could she begin to think of cooking her meal. With the waning of the afternoon she falls again to telling her beads, right hand and rosary both concealed in a little bag. At the moment of "candlelight," she passes once more into actual meditation. Then an hour's chat, the frugal evening meal, and so to bed, to begin at dawn on the morrow again the daily round.

An incomparable moment in the history of a Hindu family is that of the return to it of a young daughter freshly widowed. Unspeakable tenderness and delicacy are lavished on her. A score of reasons for the mitigation of her rule are thought out and urged. In spite of her reluctance, the parents or parents-in-law will insist. Sometimes the whole family will adopt her austere method of living for a few months, and keep pace with her self-denials step by step, till she herself discovers and breaks the spell. "Well, well!" exclaimed an old father brooding over the ruin of his child's happiness at such a crisis, "it was high time for me to retire from the world; can we not renounce together, little mother?" And while she is supported by her father's strong arm, the mother's wings are open wide, to fold closer than ever before the bird that has flown home with the arrow in its heart. Indeed, this union of theirs has become proverbial, so that if some small son be uncommonly helpful and chivalrous to his mother, friendly neighbours will say, in banter: "But this is no boy! This is surely your widowed daughter, mother!" So pass the years, till, it may be, the mother, herself widowed, becomes as a child, falling back upon the garnered strength of her own daughter. Life ebbs: but discipline gathers its perfect fruit, in lives stately and grave and dignified, for all their simplicity and bareness; in characters that are the hidden strength alike of village and of nation; in an ideal of sainthood justified; an opportunity of power created.

In the long years of her mature life we picture the Madonna standing always beneath the Cross. And we are right. But patience! not for ever shall she stand thus. It shall yet come to pass that in high heaven a day shall dawn, on which, wearing the self-same meekness, clothed in self-same humility, the Mother of Sorrows shall be crowned—and that by her own Son!

CHAPTER V

THE PLACE OF WOMAN IN THE NATIONAL LIFE

As the light of dawn breaks on the long curving street of the Indian village the chance passer-by will see at every door some kneeling woman, busied with the ceremony of the Salutation of the Threshold. A pattern, drawn on the pavement, in lines of powdered rice, with flowers arranged at regular points within it, remains for a few hours, to mark the fact that cleansing and worship have been performed. The joy of home finds silent expression in the artistic zest of the design. Wealth or poverty betrays itself, according as the flowers are a bright network of neuter gourd-blossoms, a stiff little row of two or three white daisies, or some other offering, more or less humble, as the case may be.

But everywhere we read a habit of thought, to which all things are symbolic: the air upon the door-step full of dim boding and suggestiveness as to the incomings and outgoings which the day shall witness; and the morning opening and setting wide the door an act held to be no way safe unless done by one who will brood in doing it upon the divine security and benediction of her beloved.

Such thought was the fashion of a very ancient world—the world in which myths were born, out of which religions issued, and wherein our vague and mysterious ideas of "luck" originated. The custom bears its age upon its brow. For thousands of years must Indian women have risen with the light to perform the Salutation of the Threshold. Thousands of years of simplicity and patience, like that of the peasant, like that of the grass, speak in the beautiful rite. It is this patience of woman that makes civilisations. It is this patience of the Indian woman, with this her mingling of large power of reverie, that has made and makes the Indian nationality.

On its ideal side, the life of an Indian woman is a poem of the Indian soil. For all that coherence and social unity which the West has lost within the last few centuries remain still in the Orient intact. Eastern life is an organic whole, not only as regards the connectedness of its parts amongst themselves, but also in the larger matter of their common relation to place. Even in a city, the routine of a Hindu home is an unbroken reminiscence of the ancestral village; orthodox life is simply rural life maintained unmodified under adverse conditions.

Perhaps this is nowhere more strikingly illustrated than in all that concerns the place of the cow in domestic life. Journeying over the country, the eye learns to look to the grazing-lands in order to gauge the prosperity of districts. For in climates which horses support with difficulty the patient bullock is the friend of agriculture, and without his aid the fields could not be kept under the plough.* Thus the Aryan and the cow between them have made India what she is; and never does the peasant forget the fact. Five thousand years of love and gratitude have been sufficient, on the other hand, to humanise the quadruped; and the soft eyes of the gentle beast, as we see it in this Eastern land, look out on

* It is a fundamental law of Indian economics, but one little known to present administrators, that for every acre of land kept in cultivation, the village should have the grant of one acre of grazing land free. The reason and the necessity are alike obvious.

us, with a satisfied conviction of kinship and mutual trust, for which the Western barbarian is but little prepared. Its breeds and sizes are almost innumerable. Benares, and the rich mercantile quarters of Northern cities, maintain the lordly Siva's bulls, who come and go about the streets eating from what shop-front or stall they choose, entirely unmolested. The south, again, possesses a kind of bullock little larger than a Newfoundland dog, which is nevertheless strong enough to draw a cart containing a couple of men; and perhaps there are no beasts of draught in the world finer than the Mysore bullocks. But almost all Indian cattle are smaller than their Western compeers and all are characterised by a prominent hump, in front of which the yoke is placed.

It is no wonder that the life of the cow has so large a place in that scheme of the national well-being which we call Hinduism. Who has realised the ages that it must have taken to stock the country with the necessary numbers—ages in which the destruction of one life so precious under the weight of hunger would be an irredeemable crime against society? It is only natural that the poetry of the people should find in these animals one of its central motives; for all that domestic affection which we spend on the dog and cat, making of such dumb creatures actual comrades and hearthside friends, is here lavished on them. Even in the towns, where the stones of the courtyard are the sole pasture, they are kept, and in the huts of the poor the room occupied by the milk-giver is to the full as good as that of any of the family.

We find it difficult in the North to distinguish the natural festivals of fruit gathering and harvest home from purely religious rites. There is an exaltation of feeling and imagination, and a closeness to the powers of nature, in the one case as in the other, which forms a link between them. The occasion of receiving a new cow into a Hindu family is tinged with a like sentiment. The whole household turns out to welcome the incoming member, who is decorated with flowers and fed daintily as soon as she enters the gates of the dwelling, while endearments are lavished on her in the effort to make her accept the strange abode as home. The psychology of this is not purely self-interested, as when we butter the cat's paws that she may never be happy at a distance from our hearth. There is a habitual, almost an instinctive, recognition in India of the fact that mind is the controlling element in life, and it has become a second nature with them to appeal directly to it. Even in the case of what we are pleased to term the lower animals, it requires no argument to show a Hindu that the cow will maintain her health and perform all her functions better if her feeling goes with, instead of against, her new environment. The fact is self-evident to him. And in the ceremony of welcome, the intrusion of any violent thought or emotion upon the family circle would be earnestly deprecated, and every effort put forth to hold the mental atmosphere in gentleness and calm.

This way of looking at things finds striking illustration in the education of girls. For throughout a woman's life the cow is to be her constant companion. It is important, therefore, that she be duly equipped with the knowledge of its management and treatment. This necessity is expressed in folk-form by the statement that few families are blessed with good fortune in the three matters of children, of money, and of milk. Even if the home be full of the laughter of little voices, and if there be money enough to feed them, is not the milk apt to turn sour or the cow to run dry? It is essential, then, to choose brides for our sons who have "a lucky hand with the cow"; and to attain the "lucky hand" little girls are made to rise at five o'clock in the mornings, and to sit for an hour or more before her, hanging garlands on her neck, offering flowers at her feet, giving her delectable things to eat, and repeating texts and verses full of the expression of reverence and gratitude.*

And, indeed, there is no end to the household debt. "Milk is the only food," said a Hindu, "that is the product of love." Probably for this reason—in a country where so much thought is given to the mental effects of what is eaten—it is the favourite, being held, with fruit and honey, to be fit nourishment for the saints. But fuel and medicine also are provided by the bovine mother. Cowdung is held to have antiseptic and purifying properties, and to spread it with her own hands, making the mud floor damp proof, and giving it the breath ever fragrant to the peasant, would be thought no more disgraceful to the princess fallen upon evil days of poverty than to the humbler daughter of any poor but well-descended house.

From the Punjab to Cape Comorin, evenfall—the *who is it?* moment of Japan, and the *yellow dust hour* of China—is known as the *time of cowdust*, recalling in a word the picture of the village, and the herds driven home along the lanes for the night.

It is one of the great glories of countries of the Asiatic type, ranking beside their universal recognition of the sacredness of letters, that in them the simple life of the commonwealth as a whole, and not the artificial and luxurious routine of courts, has always been regarded as the social type. Hence in India, labour, rising into government, stands side by side with prayer and motherhood as the main opportunity of woman, and as her integral contribu-

* I was informed by so authoritative a body as the professors in the Minnesota College of Agriculture, U.S.A., that this procedure of the Hindu woman is strictly scientific. "The cow is only able to yield her full possibility of milk to a milker whom she regards as her own child.

tion to the national righteousness. The domestic necessities of pastoral, may bear less heavily upon her than those of peasant communities, leaving her more time for the use of the needle; but in Arabia, as in India, the ideal must needs be fulfilled, and "Our Lady of the Moslems"* is loved for the fact that, though the daughter of the Prophet, she turned the millstone with her own delicate hands, and toiled in frugal household ways for the good of those dependent on her care, almost as much as for the sweet intercession by which she named "the salvation of all Mussulmans" as the dowry she would claim of God on the Day of Judgment.

In India, the cowhouse, the dairy, the kitchen, the granary, the chapel, with numerous other offices, divide the day-long attentions of the ladies of the family. In rich old houses there will be a large cooking-room and verandah for the cooks, and in addition, not one but a series of kitchens for the use of mother, daughters, and daughters-in-law. And the herb gardens and orchards are accessible only from the zenana. In all these things nothing is more noticeable than the readiness and spontaneity with which work is subdivided, and the peaceable way in which it is carried out. This is most striking with regard to the preparation of food, a service into which the Indian has been taught from childhood to pour a concentrated sweetness of love and hospitality. Perhaps there is no single institution amongst ourselves by which we can convey an idea of the joy it gives the master of a household to see many mouths fed at his cost, or the mistress to feel that she serves them all. Every woman being a cook, and often of great skill, it was in years gone by considered as the highest compliment to receive an invitation from a

* Our Lady of the Moslems.—Fatima, daughter of the Prophet and Khadijah. The Prophet loved her more than any other created being.

neighbouring family on the occasion of some important festivity, to come and help *faire la cuisine.* Even Hindu society, however, is affected by the ideals of Western organisation, and emergency-work nowadays tends more and more to be laid on the shoulders of Brahmins imported for the occasion, but not regarded socially as servants, in spite of the fact that they accept a daily wage.

There is thus a point of view from which the lives of Indian women may be considered as a vast co-operation of the race to perform necessary labour, dignifying it meanwhile by every association of refinement, tenderness, and self-respect. And it might also be claimed that the orthodox Hindu household is the only one in the world which combines a high degree of civilisation with the complete elimination of any form of domestic slavery. Certainly slavery in Asia, under the *régimes* of great religious systems, has never meant what Europe and America have made of it. There are still living persons who were bought in their childhood as *Ghulams* by Rajput and Bengali families. These were orphans, brought up and educated along with the children of the household, but made useful in minor ways. It never occurred to any one that when the days of wage-earning arrived, the quondam master and mistress had any claim whatever upon the emoluments of their dependents, yet they could not be held to have done their duty until they had married and settled them in life appropriately. It is a curious consequence of this humanity of custom that the word "slave" cannot be made to sting the Asiatic consciousness, as it does the European.

As one travels through regions not yet exhausted by famine, the signs of Indian peasant happiness become familiar to the eye. The mud homestead, built on its high plinth with deep verandahs, decently thatched or tiled, and almost hidden in clusters of cocoanut palms, bamboos, and plantains, the stretch of green with its grazing cows, or rice-fields and mango orchards, the unbroken dome of blue, edged off, on the horizon, by the tremulous line of foliage where new bamboos veil some fresh village or farmhouse, such is the picture beloved by the Indian heart. Even in the distant cities, every festival-day brings back its memory; for the jars of water, with cocoanuts for lids, and the green shoots of plantain, standing against the pillars, with the garlands of mango-leaves above the doorway, are the "auspicious," and therefore universal decoration.

It is her longing for this natural setting of grove, river, and meadow, that makes the housewife so contented with the severe architectural form of her home, bidding her seek for no irrelevant decorative detail. The Indian does not live in whom the passion for nature is not conscious and profound. And the marble palaces of Rajputana and the North, in which buildings are made beautiful, instead of having beautiful things put into them, are directly related, through this ideal, to the peasant cottages and farmhouses of Bengal.

Indeed, if we would draw the life of an Indian woman truly, it is in a long series of peasant pictures that it must be outlined. Every plant, flower, fruit, in its own season, calls up some historic or poetic association. Under the kodhumba tree, whose blossoms occur in stiff balls, like those of our plane, stood Krishna, playing on the flute. In the magnificent shade and coolness of the bo—the tree whose leaves are so delicately poised that they quiver like those of our aspen, even in the stillest noon—Buddha, in the heart of the night, attained Nirvana. The soft sirisha flower that "can bear the weight of bees, but not of humming-birds," reminds one of all exquisite and tender things—the lips of a woman, the heart of a child, and so on.

The amloki fruit is not only wholesome and delicious for household use, making the work of preserving it an act of merit, but its very name is famous throughout Buddhist Asia, carrying one back to the great age when it was a constant architectural ornament. The fragrance of the mango-blossom is one of the five arrows of Cupid's bow. The custard-apple was the favourite fruit of Sita.

Such are a few only of the complex associations that have in the course of ages accumulated about the common Indian life. No home is so bare that it is not beautified by this wealth of dreams, for it has long ago sunk into the very structure of the language. No caste is so high, nor is any outcast so low, as to be beyond its reach. It is an immense national possession, creating mutual sentiment and common memory, offering abundance of material also for the development of individual taste and imagination, and above all acting as an organic and indestructible bond, to attach the Indian mind eternally to its own soil, and in every sense involving permanence of relation, silently and rigorously to exclude the foreigner.

Men are of course initiated into their share of this inheritance in infancy. Afterwards, from their study of letters, they may return and refresh the domestic folklore with a greater accuracy. But the women live always in its atmosphere. This is the actuality against whose background their simple pious lives are set. And through them it maintains unabated its volume and continuity.

We see thus that the Indian organisation of life and society is coherent and necessary, and that its methods and ideals, having sprung directly from the soil, have a stability due to correspondence with their environment which is inconceivable to persons who are themselves content to be favoured members of most favoured nations.

The social unity, as of an individual organism, was expressed in quaint form in the old-time myth that Brahmins sprang from the lips of the Creator, warriors from His arms, the people from His thighs, and the working classes from His feet. But the way in which physical conditions imposed themselves upon the Creator Himself in this process could not be recognised by early observers, who had seen nothing outside their own country.

The modern student, however, educated by a wide range of geographical impressions, cannot fail to be struck with another feature of the Indian synthesis—its completely organic character in a territorial sense. Every province within the vast boundaries fulfils some necessary part in the completing of a nationality. No one place repeats the specialised function of another. And what is true of the districts holds equally good of the people as a whole, and the women in particular. In a national character we always find a summary of the national history. Of no country is this more true than of India.

The Bengali wife worships her husband, and serves her children and her household with all the rapt idealism of the saints. The women of Maharashtra are as strong and as actual as any in the West. The Rajputni queen prides herself on the unflinching courage of her race, that would follow her husband even into the funeral fire, yet will not permit a king to name his wife as amongst his subjects. The woman of Madras struggles with agony to reach the spiritual pole-star, building up again and again, like some careful beaver, any fragment of her wall of custom that the resistless tides of the modern world may attempt to break away. And the daughters of Guzerat are, like the women of merchant-peoples everywhere, soft and silken and flower-like, dainty and clinging as a dream.

Or we may penetrate into the Moslem zenana, to

find the same graceful Indian womanhood, sometimes clad in the sari, sometimes in the short Turkish jacket, but always the self-same gentle and beautiful wifehood and motherhood, measuring itself in all its doings as much against the standards of religious obligation, and as little against those of fashion, as any of its Hindu compatriots might do.

Nor, amongst these strong outstanding types, is there any failure of individual achievement. Brynhild herself was not more heroic than thousands of whom the Rajput chronicles tell. Nay, in the supreme act of her life, the mystic death on the throne of flame beside the dead Sigurd, many a quiet little Bengali woman has been her peer. Joan of Arc was not more a patriot than Chand Bibi,* or the wonderful Queen of Jhansi, who, in the year 1857, fought in person with the British troops. The children of men who saw it talk to this day of the form of this woman's father swinging on the gibbet, high above the city walls, hanged there by her order for the crime of making a treaty with the English, to deliver the keys into their hands. They talk, too, of her swift rush at the head of her troops across the drowsy midday camp, her lance poised to pierce, her bay mare Lakshmi straining every muscle, the whizz of the charge so unexpected that only here and there a dazed white soldier could gather presence of mind to fire a shot at the cavalcade already passed. And old men still sing her glory with tears choking the voice.

But the Rani of Jhansi, though a queen, was no purdah woman. She was a Mahratta, with a passion for her country, and practised from girlhood in the chase. She had been the real heart of the kingdom ever since her marriage, for her husband was only a

* Chand Bibi.—The heroic princess, who defended Ahmednagar against the armies of Akbar. Killed by mutineers, 1599.

handsome figure-head, who spent in making feeble poetry the time he might have given to rule or to his wife. Her life had been, in fact, as solitary as that of a mediæval saint. And her ostensible reason for fighting was the right to adopt an heir. There has always indeed been a great development of the political faculty amongst Mahratta women, a development which is by no means lost at the present day. It is well known that, long before the time of the Queen of Jhansi, Sivaji owed the inspiration that led to the national reawakening to his mother rather than to his father.

If again we desire to hear of the woman of romance, is it not sufficient to cite the name of that Empress to whom the Taj Mahal was built? To Hindus as to Mohammedans this palace of the dead is holy, for to the one as to the other it speaks with silent eloquence of the perfect wife. We may dream as inadequately as we please of the Queen Arjmand Banu, Crown of the Palace, but two things we cannot forget. One is the tender thought of the woman who could detach herself from the very pains of death to assure her husband that she desired a tomb worthy of his love; and the other is the image of the passing of Shah Jehan, in the sunset-lighted balcony, with his eyes fixed on the snow-white pile at the bend in the river, and his heart full of the consolation of having wrought for her he loved, through the space of twenty years, a work that she had surely accepted at the last. The words, "Even I, even I, am Beatrice," are not more full of the triumphant close of love than this picture of the death of the Mogul Emperor.

Yet we have to admit that to the Asiatic woman in general society does not offer the kingdom of beauty and charm as her sphere. The foster-mother of Moses the mother of Jesus, the wife of the Prophet, Khadijah, and his daughter Fatima, are the true exemplars of the Moslem woman. And the ideal achievements of Hindu womanhood are likewise of wisdom and service and renunciation, rather than of power and love. Hindu lyrics of romance are always put into the mouth of Radha the shepherdess, singing to Krishna; and it is interesting to note how the motive of each lover is placed always in the feeling of the other, and how quickly any departure from this canon would disgust Indian taste. Even Persian poetry, the classic of the Mohammedan, is said by those who know it to have avoided in a wonderful way the use of "he and she." "Be I the string, the note be thou! Be thou the body, I the life! Let none hereafter say of us that one was I, another thou." Is this spoken between two lovers, or is it entirely of the soul?

There is doubtless some truth in the idea that society in a military state tends always to seclude its women. The fact that in the aristocratic strictness of retreat the Mussulmannin ranks first, the Rajputni second, and the Bengali woman only third, in India, goes far to support this conclusion. But the case of the Rani of Jhansi is sufficient indication that the custom is by no means so universal as is often stated. The lower classes move freely in all countries, for household work and the earning of their livelihood compel; and the screen is always more easily lifted for the Hindu than for the Mohammedan. A thousand considerations intervene to mitigate its severity in the case of the former, while in the South and West, where Moslem rule was brief, and Moslem fashions had little force, it is actually non-existent.

By this it is not to be understood that any Hindu women meet men outside their kindred with the freedom and frankness of their Western sisters. Very old adaptations of the Ramayana show us the brother-in-law who has never looked higher than the heroine's feet, and the wife who blushes rather than mention her husband's name. But the power of the individual to isolate himself in the midst of apparently unrestrained social intercourse is necessary in all communities, and has its correspondence in Western society itself. Freedom is granted only to the self-disciplined. It might be added that a good wife has as little occasion to realise the possible jealousy of her husband in the East as in the West, and that an unreasonable fit of suspicion would be considered the same weakness and insult by the one society as by the other.

The liberty of Madras and Bombay is, however, a reality for all its limitations. And in certain parts of the province of Malabar woman is actually in the ascendency. This curious country, of women learned in Sanskrit, and kings who rule as the regents of their sisters, will have many disclosures to make to the world when India shall have produced a sufficient number of competent sociologists of her own blood. It is commonly said to be characteristically polyandrous; but it is not so, in the same sense as Tibet and some of the Himalayan tribes, for no woman regards herself as the wife of two men at once. The term *matriarchal* is more accurate, inasmuch as the husband visits the wife in her own home, and the right of inheritance is through the mother. Thus, far from India's being the land of the uniform oppression of woman by a uniform method, it represents the whole cycle of feminist institutions. There is literally no theory of feminine rights and position that does not find illustration somewhere within her boundaries.

With regard to the seclusion of women by Hindus, the statement that it arose as a protection against the violence of a ruling race is thoughtless and untrue. The custom in its present rigour dates undoubtedly from the period of Moslem rule.

Where that rule was firm and long established, it has sunk deep into Hindu habit, and in Bombay and Madras, under opposite conditions, has been almost passed by. In the plays of Kalidas, and in old Sanskrit literature generally, there is abundant evidence that it was not practised in its modern form in the Vedic, Buddhistic, or Puranic periods.

But although it dates from the era of Ghazni or Ghor — except where the Rajput made an independent introduction of the purdah—there is nothing to show that the cloistering of women was spread in Hindostan by other means than by the force of fashion and imperial prestige. Indeed, sooner or later we have to face the question : What induced the Mohammedan to screen his women ? Islam derives the religious sanction of its social institutions from Arabia, and the Arab woman is said to enjoy considerable freedom and power. Hence it is sometimes claimed that the Mussulman himself adopted the practice from Persia, from China, or from Greece. Such explanations are little more than recrimination. What are we to regard as the root of a convention which in certain parts of the Orient appears to be almost instinctive ? Climate, inducing scantiness of clothing, cannot be the whole secret, for in that case Madras would be more deeply permeated by the custom than Bengal, whereas the very opposite is the fact.

Might we not as well reverse the inquiry, and try to assign some reason for the Western assumption of *equality* between man and woman ? The first point that strikes us is the very uneven distribution of the theory in Europe itself. It is by no means so strong in Latin as in Teutonic countries, nor so clearly formulated amongst the Germanic peoples as in the Norse Sagas. This fact lends colour to the theory of modern sociologists that fisher-life is the source of all equality between the sexes. For the man, pursuing the conquest of the sea, must leave his wife regnant over the affairs of field and farm. It is supposed by some that the very use of the wedding-ring originated in the investiture of woman at marriage, by means of the signet-ring, with a fulness of authority similar to the husband's outside, over all that lay within the house. Surely it is clear that land and sea are not the only possible antitheses, but that wherever a race is employed in a sustained and arduous conquest of Nature there it will tend towards fulness of co-operation, similarity of manners, and equality of rights as between men and women; and that, other things being equal, under long-settled conditions, from which anxiety is largely eliminated, there is a progressive inclination towards divergence of their lines of activity, accompanied by the more complete surrender of woman to the protection of man, and the seeking of her individuality in the sphere of morals and emotion.

The tendency to divergence of function would be accelerated in Asia by the nature of the climate, which makes stillness and passivity the highest luxury. This fact would combine again with military prepossessions, to make the custom of seclusion especially characteristic of royal households, and having once achieved such social prestige it would speedily extend over wide areas. Thus it becomes characteristic of conquering races, and among Hindus is imitated with marked energy by Bengal, which is not only the most idealistic of all the Indian provinces, but also—owing to the existence of the zemindar class—the most persistently feudal, after Rajputana.

If this theory be correct, the freedom of the Indian woman of the first Aryan period is to be explained as an outcome of the struggle with earth and forest. The early immigrations of agricultural races across the Himalayas from Central Asia must have meant a combat with Nature of the severest kind. It was a combat in which the wife was the helpmeet of the husband. If he cleared the jungle and hunted the game, she had to give aid in field and garden. The Aryan population was scanty, and she would often be required to take his place. Vicissitudes were many. At a moment's notice she must be prepared to meet an emergency, brave, cheerful, and self-helpful. In such a life woman must move as easily as man.

It began to be otherwise, however, when the country was cleared, agriculture established on the Aryan scale, and the energy of the race concentrated on the higher problem of conserving and extending its culture of mind and spirit. It is doubtful whether Indian philosophy could ever have been completed on other terms than on those of some measure of seclusion for woman. "This world is all a dream: God alone is real," such an ultimatum could hardly have been reached in a society like that of Judaism, where love and beauty were held as the seal of divine approval on a successful life. Not that India would decry these happy gifts. But they are secular joys in her eyes, not spiritual. "The religion of the wife lies in serving her husband: the religion of the widow lies in serving God," say the women; and there is no doubt in their minds that the widow's call is the higher of the two.

While we talk of the seclusion of woman, however, as if it were a fact, we must be careful to guard against misconception. In society and in the streets of Indian cities, it is practically true that we see men alone. This fact makes it a possibility for the religious to pass his life without looking on the face of any woman, save such as he may call "Mother." Inside the house, if we penetrate so far, we shall probably meet with none but women. But if we live there day after day, we shall find that every woman has familiar intercourse with some man or men in the family. The relation between brothers and sisters-in-law is all gaiety and sweetness. Scarcely any children are so near to a woman as the sons of her husband's sisters. It is the proud prerogative of these, whatever be their age, to regard her as their slave. There is a special delicacy of affection and respect between the husband's father and his daughter-in-law. Cousins count as brothers and sisters. And from the fact that every woman has her rightful place in some family it follows that there is more healthy human intercourse with men in almost every Hindu woman's life than in those of thousands of single women, living alone, or following professional careers, in the suburbs of London and other Western cities.

It is an intercourse, too, that is full of a refined and delicate sense of humour. Indian men who have been to Europe always declare that the zenana woman stands unrivalled in her power of repartee. English fun is apt to strike the Eastern ear as a little loud. How charming is the Bengali version of "the bad penny that always turns up," in, "I am the broken cowrie that has been to seven markets"! That is to say, "I may be worthless, but I am knowing."

We are too apt to define the ideal as that towards which we aspire, thinking but rarely of those assimilated ideals which reveal themselves as custom. If we analyse the conventions that dominate an Indian woman's life we cannot fail to come upon an exceedingly stern canon of self-control. The closeness and intimacy of the family life, and the number of the interests that have to be considered, make strict discipline necessary, doubtless, for the sake of peace. Hence a husband and wife may not address each other in the presence of others. A wife may not name her husband, much less praise him, and so on. Only little children are perfectly untrammelled, and may bestow their affection when and where they will. All these things are for the protection of the community, lest it be outraged by the parading of a relationship of intimacy, or victimised by an enthusiasm which it could not be expected to share.

This constant and happy subordination of oneself to others does not strike the observer, only because it is so complete. It is not the characteristic of the specially developed individual alone, for it is recognised and required, in all degrees of delicacy, by society at large. Unselfishness and the thirst for service, stand out in the Western personality against a background of individualistic conventions, and convey an impression of the eagerness and struggle of pity, without which the world would certainly be the poorer. But the Eastern woman is unaware of any defiance of institutions. She is the product of an ethical civilisation. Her charities are required of her. Her vows and penances are unknown even to her husband; but were they told, they would scarcely excite remark in a community where all make similar sacrifices.

This is only to say that she is more deeply self-effacing and more effectively altruistic than any Western. The duty of tending the sick is so much a matter of course to her that she does not dream of it as a special function, for which one might erect hospitals or learn nursing. Here, no doubt, she misses a great deal, for the modern organisation of skill has produced a concentration of attention on method that avails to save much suffering. Still, we must not too carelessly assume that our own habit of massing together all the hungry, sick, and insane, and isolating them in worlds visited throughout with like afflictions to their own, is the product of a higher benevolence on our part.

Throughout the world women are the guardians of humanity's ethical ideals. The boy would not be so anxious to carry the dead to the burning ghat if his mother had not filled his babyhood with admiration of the deed. The husband would not be so strenuous to return home at his best if his wife did not understand and appreciate his noblest qualities. But, even beyond this, women give themselves as the perpetual illustration of the ideal. The words, "He that will be chief among you let him be your servant," fall on Western ears with a certain sense of sublime paradox. But the august Speaker uttered the merest truism of that simple Eastern world in which He moved. He roused no thrill of surprise in the minds of His hearers, for to each his own mother was chief, and yet servant of all.

Those who, knowing the East, read the list of the seven corporal works of mercy, may well start to imagine themselves back in the Hindu home watching its laborious, pious women as they move about their daily tasks, never questioning the first necessity of feeding the hungry, harbouring the harbourless, and the like. Truly the East is eternally the mother of religions, for the reason that she has assimilated as ordinary social functions what the West holds to be only the duty of officialism or the message of the Church, and to those who deeply understand it may well seem that Christianity in Europe is neither more nor less than the mission of the Asiatic Life.

CHAPTER VI

THE IMMEDIATE PROBLEMS OF THE ORIENTAL WOMAN

The student of Greek vases cannot fail to be struck by the frequent repetition of a single theme—the procession of women to and from the well. In ancient Greece, in Palestine, and in India up to the era of water-taps and street hydrants, that is to say till the other day, the women had an established social centre, the well from which the community drew its supply of drinking water. Hither, in the last hours before sundown, came the maidens of various households, young daughters-in-law, maybe, in charge of some elderly aunt or mother-in-law, or with each other's company for chaperonage, each bearing her shining metal vessels to be filled. And thence, their mutual talk and task being ended, went the girls to their homes, with towering loads some two or three pots high, and superb swaying walk. Sometimes, it is said, for a trial of skill, they would run and skip, and even dance, as they went along the road, and never a drop of water spilled the while. The hour was held in great esteem. The way was avoided by men, and the women proved, what all women know, that their real motive in dressing well is to compete with each other, not to shine in the eyes of the sterner sex. Showy silver anklets, the pearl-decorated pad or ring on which the water-pots rested on the head, saris draped as severely as in

Greek statues—all these beauties were arranged for the discriminating envy or sympathy of sister eyes, not for the enjoyment of a being who may be trusted to think his own wife and sisters beautiful, yet cannot do them the honour to remember what jewels and clothes they wear.

For a vanity not less than that which chooses a gown in Paris, can go to so simple a matter as the fitting of a dark-blue sari against a fair complexion, that the wearer may look "like the full moon in the midnight sky," the placing of opal or diamond on one nostril or the other, or the selecting of a glass bangle of white or green, according to the tint of the brown skin. The vanity may be no less, and the highest skill always desires the eye of the keenest connoisseur.

This picture of the women drawing water has its pendant in the cluster of men who gather for friendly smoke or chat at evening about the smouldering log, lighted on the outskirts of the village by any wandering sannyasin who may have taken up his abode for a few days beneath the local banyan tree. But this suggests a wider, more cosmopolitan relation. The men's talk is apt to be of other lands than their own, and the strange customs and lapses of customs prevailing there. Their interests are rather general, abstract, impersonal. For the yellow-robed guest of the village is, it must be remembered, a traveller of the ancient time. He has not journeyed in railway trains and lived in hotels. Rather, tramping his way from village to village, he has shared, at each halting-place, in its personal drama; has begged a meal daily from door to door; has eaten, therefore, the characteristic food, cooked and served according to the ways of each district. By such modes the geographical sense of this old-time wayfarer is developed far beyond that of a generation that lives on maps and learns from the schedules of facts known as newspaper reports and the journals of other men's travels. And it is his geographical knowledge that he shares with the men of the village where he eats and sleeps for a few days. In the old Sanskrit books, kings are represented as receiving such guests with the question, "What have you seen elsewhere?" and asking before they depart, "And what have you noted here?"

But amongst the women gathered about the well it was the civic life that found expression, the civic life of the village or small township. Here they could form a consolidated feminine opinion, of great weight in local affairs, and exchange the news of the day with each other. The better organisation of public convenience now deprives them of the laborious necessity of meeting in the old way; but it is much to be desired that, with the dying out of their ancient forms and institutions, new occasions of assembly and new subjects of discussion might spontaneously arise. At present Indian emotion spends itself more and more within the home. Woman, always dominant in private life, by her very affection is co-operating with the loss of public institutions to restrict the activity of Man. Surely, then, Europe has no right to grow contemptuous if rich men prove effeminate and poor men inefficient, or taunt India with the fact that she has not yet seized the *ethos* of the West, that her princes send out no expeditions to discover the South Pole, and her youth grow up with no consuming curiosity about rocks and stars; for the European organisation quietly defeats all through which the people are accustomed to find expression and yet fails to call them to new responsibilities, in which their mind and character could receive adequate scope and stimulus in a different form.

It is quite evident that if the centre of social

gravity is some day to be shifted, if the intellectual atmosphere of India is yet to be saturated with fresh ideals, not only must her womanhood participate in the results of the implied revolution, but they must contribute largely to bringing it about. For it is the home, not the factory, that fills life with inspiration; and the school, in British India, is no more than a mill or institution in which children master the reading and writing necessary to future clerkships, as they might learn the technical processes of any other industry. A census-taking, index-making age conceives that without literacy there is no education, as if to read the *Strand Magazine* were greater than to be the mother of Shakespeare. With such an age it is difficult to argue regarding the existing education of a Hindu woman. Yet if a thorough training in a national mode of living, and that extremely complicated, be an education, she has something; for the ordinary wife can act in any capacity, from that of cook or dairy-mistress to that of chief of commissariat and general administrator for a hundred or more persons. If a knowledge of language, poetry, and folk-lore, with all thereby connoted of logical and imaginative development, form an education, she has this, sometimes to the extent of understanding and reciting works in Sanskrit. More: poor women who may not be able to read and write are deeply, and even passionately, possessed of the spirit of the ancient culture. The philosophy of Maya, not seldom bewildering to the Western *savant*, has no difficulty for them. They understand to a hair the meaning of the word *Nirvana*. It is no one special command to deny oneself and take up a cross and follow, that has weight with them; but the bearing of the great law of renunciation on the personal realisation of freedom. Add to all this the inbred habit of life in community, and it will appear that under the old scheme women found not only a training and a discipline, but also a career.

It was a preparation and an opportunity fitted only, it is true, to the soil on which it grew. This limitation pervades the whole of the Indian civilisation. The Indian mind is more contented with the architectural and natural beauties of the home, more free from a desire for extraneous decorative detail, than any other taste in the world, perhaps, and in the same way it has devised a daily round of duty which belongs strictly to its place. The good mother-in-law occupies the position of the lady of the manor in English feudal days. But whereas the manorial household could be transplanted to any age or clime almost intact—Japan, Rajputana, Turkey, Scandinavia, and Spain furnishing parallels fairly complete—the same is not true of the Indian type. Here the girls gathered round its head are the wives of her sons, instead of her husband's vassals. And it is the care of babies, the treatment of animals, and all kinds of cooking and domestic offices, rather than deft spinning and dainty embroidery, with which they are busied under her. Caste equalises the dignity of beggar and king, and the form of work is merely a question of wealth.

At the same time, while every detail of the Indian domestic system is justified and justifiable, we cannot refuse to admit that some great educational readjustment is necessary at this moment, if only because long habit blinds the eye to the forest that looks much upon the trees; but when the trees grow too scanty it is the forest, as a whole, that demands our care. To-day every Indian woman can cook, and that well. But she cannot sew, and she has nothing but gossip and prayer when the afternoon siesta is over wherewith to occupy her leisure. The great-grandmothers of the present generation were as busy in spinning as our own ancestresses, and one of the chief domestic joys was to take the yarn to the weaver with the measure of grain for which he would make it into a web. To-day, alas, the weaver finds it difficult enough to maintain himself by the fine work, for which there is always some market, shrunken though it be, and the common sari of the women's daily wear is spun and woven by machinery, far away in Manchester or Glasgow. Here also, then, the modern revolution has narrowed her lot. A like destruction is being felt in all directions. Higher standards of comfort are rapidly arising. The days when the little boys in the village school wrote on the floor in sand are long past. Even the palm-leaf manuscript is little more than a memory. Steel pen, instead of wooden stylus, cheap paper, smooth writing fluids are everywhere. Soap* is becoming a necessity. European utensils for cleaning, for cooking, and even for eating, are coming into use. Certain kinds of furniture are growing familiar. Kerosene and tin and modern glass are to be found in every village. But this does not mean that the people are learning to provide these things for themselves, much less does it imply that they are mastering their use and incorporating their production under the old caste-crafts, bringing their Indian taste and intelligence to bear upon creating new modifications of Western forms. What it does mean is that the country has already become a host to the parasite of European trade. Absolutely and fatally obedient to laws of patent and copyright, the people accept any new convenience as it stands, allow the village craftsman to go by the door, cease

* Lest it should be thought that India had ever been a land of the unclean, let me point out here that the use of earths and oils for the bath has always been compulsory. There is, perhaps, no people in the world from whom the culture of the skin receives so much attention, or where it is so successful. But manufactured soap, as producing a chemical change on the epidermis, is theoretically disapproved.

to use the old-fashioned utensil, whatever it may have been, and allow the stereotyped ugliness of the new acquisition to corrupt taste and standards as long as it lasts. Even the brass-smiths have quietly accepted the fact that their metal is cheapest brought in sheets from Europe, and housewives mourn in vain that their beautiful brass cooking vessels are no longer fit to be heirlooms, as were those of their grandmothers. In all this India is not more careless or easy of corruption than European countries themselves. She has more to lose and is more defenceless, that is all, and she has not learnt to think of such questions on the national scale.

Orthodoxy does, of course, oppose some obstacle to this process of decay. It would still be accounted an act of vulgarity if a man of means gave a piece of English cotton as wearing apparel to a friend. Soap, kerosene oil, and the substitution of chairs for mats, are still regarded askance by the leaders of pious opinion. But this opposition savours too much of mere prejudice. Therefore it can only retard, it cannot overcome, the evil. What is wanted in this regard is a dynamic orthodoxy, capable of enforcing a decision that only what Indian people can make ought Indian persons to use. And such a canon, it is needless to point out, would have to find its root and strength in the women, who are buyers and consumers, reaching the craftsmen through constituted social and religious channels. Once having obtained a grip of the national conscience, no political or commercial cajolery would be of the slightest avail against this principle; but then, if the people were capable of understanding and carrying out such an idea—women, priests, pundits, heads of castes, and labourers—the whole problem would already have been solved, and there would be no disaster from which India must be saved.

It is clear that as the objective of the old education

of Indian women lay in *character*, the new cannot aim lower. The distinctive element, therefore, in their future training cannot be reading and writing—though these will undoubtedly grow more common—but the power to grasp clearly and with enthusiasm the ideas of nationality, national interests, and the responsibility of the individual to race and country. Even in Europe, habits and opinions tend to stereotype and harden themselves quite as much as in the Orient. But at present there is still a certain flexibility. This flexibility rather than any definite change is what the East requires. It is a form of freedom and mastery. European communities, in consequence of this mobility of structure, enjoy a power of intelligent co-operation towards new but agreed ends which is universally desirable. India has the power to act, but the end must be familiar. A few women will organise themselves at a moment's notice to cook for hundreds or even thousands of guests, without the least waste of energy or temper such as Western women would incur in organising a soup-kitchen. But if we call the guests "the unemployed," and refer to them as "a social problem," the Oriental becomes bewildered, as would we in like manner were it proposed to us to regard them all as visitors. It is clear that the Western mode of approaching such tasks can only be acquired by India, if it be necessary, through an enlarged idea of the public lfe.

When the women see themselves in their true place, as related to the soil on which they live, as related to the past out of which they have sprung; when they become aware of the needs of their own people, on the actual colossal scale of those needs; when the mother-heart has once awakened in them to beat for land and people, instead of family, village, and homestead alone, and when the mind is set to explore facts in the service of that heart—then and then alone shall the future of Indian womanhood dawn upon the race in its actual greatness; then shall a worthy education be realised; and then shall the true national ideal stand revealed.

Such a change, however, is only possible as a direct growth out of old conceptions. The national idea cannot be imposed from without—it must develop from within. And this will be in full congruity with the national religions. Islam, in the days of its power, rejoiced to establish itself as Indian on Indian soil. The architectural works of the Mogul emperors are full of enthusiasm for the Indian past, for the Indo-Saracenic style owes as much to Rajputana as to Mecca and Constantinople. Asiatic among Asiatics—there was no wide gap between Mussulman conquerors and Hindu conquered: no gap in taste, or morals, or style of thought and education. The newcomer settled down as a child of the land, in his own home. His children were first Indian, and only in the second place members of the Mohammedan confraternity. To-day, under the necessity of a secular expression, there is nothing whatever to prevent him from projecting himself upon the cause of his own people, both Hindu and Mohammedan, and working for them with that same power with which his fathers once made the deserts of Arabia ring. For the Hindu, the point should be still more obvious. His avatars have lived always for humanity. They have appeared in the hour of the national need. They have been followed by waves of popular and political rejuvenance. Neither Hinduism nor Mohammedanism has been weak in putting forward the claims of soil. The sacred texts go so far as to say that he who dies for his country at once attains the Beatific Vision. With regard to their fundamental duties, both faiths stand like converging artillery in the world of motive, ready to shoot forth individuals upon the great common task of remaking the motherland.

But for all this again, there must be a re-reading of orthodoxy, a re-discovery of essentials. Already the revolution has commenced that is to bring this about. Already India has begun to realise that if poverty is to be defeated, if national efficiency is to be achieved, she dare not continue much longer to glorify the element of blind refusal. Vital orthodoxy, however we define it, certainly cannot be the child of fear alone, always on the defensive, never becoming aggressive, its best courage that of endurance or resignation. He whose idea has ceased to advance is already in retreat. There was a time when everything in India was her own. In those days she went forward freely, welcoming the new as an advance in power and knowledge, not meeting it with terror as a defilement. Indian orthodoxy, then, must learn once more to struggle forward. But we are met by a host of questions. Amongst many conflicting paths, which is to be chosen? Towards what goal? By what methods? What is to be included? What eliminated? Here are the actual difficulties. Every one is agreed that certain things must be done, but no one can distinctly picture how.

Yet the weakness is easy enough to probe. The West conquers the East, as long as the East on the one hand shuns it as contamination, or, on the other, accepts it as a bribe. The idea of assimilating just so much of Western science as shall enable India to compete in the same market by the same processes as the West is as delusive as it is mean. The idea of refusing to participate in Western methods, and dying of starvation if need be, martyrs to national purity, is manifestly impracticable for the people at large, even if it had not long ago been carried out of reach of all on the high tides of economic disaster. What then?

Western Science must be recognised as holy. The idea of that Science must be grasped and pursued for its own sake. Modern astronomy must claim its "star-intoxicated" prophets in the East as in the West. Geology, physics, biology, and the sublime and growing sciences of man, history and morals, must be felt in India as new modes of the apprehension of truth, studied passionately without ulterior object, as the religious experience is now followed, at the cost of all.

Such an attitude is, indeed, of the very essence of the Asiatic genius. To it mathematics have never sunk to the position which they tend to occupy in Europe—a convenient means for the measurement of secular utilities—but have always been held as a sacred inviolable method of expressing the fundamental unity of phenomena. The learned man will mention this subject with the same throb in his voice that we may give to a great picture or a moving poem. The Indian imagination regards all knowledge of beatitude. Nor is any intellect in the world more keenly logical and inquisitive, or at the same time more disinterested and comprehensive in its grasp. A great Indian school of science is therefore no absurdity, but, under necessary conditions, one of the most attainable of all ambitions. The Hindu has but to realise that the world waits for the hundred and eight Upanishads of modern knowledge; the Mussulman needs only to understand that the time is again ripe for Averrhoes and Avicenna; and both will make, not only their own opportunity, but a new era in culture as well.

This is not merely an inspiration of defence. Oriental methods have had an unparalleled success in producing a widely extended amelioration of conduct and cultivation of mind. Any large country town in India may be observed, and the number of its saints and scholars counted. Not even the most favoured of London suburbs can boast, of its commercial or scientific order, so many men severely learned. But the old Indian learning is now complete. The task is done. There is nothing left for the common mind to add.

It is necessary, therefore, as a vindication of that great intellectual vigour which it has actually bred, that new worlds of mental conquest should be found, new subjects opened, and a new development initiated, in which the common people shall measure their strength against the modern world, and learn their power.

Out of such a revolution, but as an incident, not as its main goal, must inevitably arise a development of mechanical skill which, in the East, might steer clear of the demoralisation produced elsewhere by the worship of usefulness and privilege. It is certain that if India throw herself freely upon a mechanical era, she will restore to the factory hand those human qualities and ethical prerogatives which in the West he tends more and more to lose.

In order to make such changes possible, however, there would need to be a spontaneous appearance, in various parts of the country, of persons with the synthetic habit of mind and heart. India is actually a unity, but few of her people realise the fact, and fewer still feel the appropriate emotion. No parochial ambition can, at this juncture, save the motherland. The Mahratta may not seek the good of Maharashtra, nor the Sikh of the Punjab. There must be no revival of forgotten feuds. Not in such things lies the thrill of nationality. Rather, all must unite in a common glorification of India and the whole Indian past. Each must recognise what the others have contributed. There must be thinkers able to take advantage of every accident in local history, and to turn it to the advantage of the one great cause. The passion of nationality was so strong in the Punjab, in Rajputana, and under Sivaji, that it broke even the power of the Mogul Empire. Yet the fact that she has never had any definite and consolidated form of her own may be the critical element in the history of Bengal, to make her the welder and fuser of all the provinces to-day.

Such an inspiration as this is social as well as political. It is religious in the highest sense. It has to fill home, school, and market-place. There is no question therefore as to its requiring the co-operation of woman with man. For her, also, there is a new and greater orthodoxy. She must become of her own freedom that which custom now makes her. Eastern piety is often good bacteriology. Sitola, the Smallpox Goddess, is depicted as riding on the washerman's donkey, an unclean beast. But requiring to be worshipped with water and broom, and isolation of the patient. The myth is admirable. Europe can show nothing of its kind so good. But the next step is, obviously, facts at first hand. Woman must be enabled to know, think, and judge freely, on all questions such as those of food and the public health. The severe exigencies of modern labour make the old food and cooking entirely insufficient. Dyspepsia has become a national curse; yet this is certainly one of the difficulties that could be overcome. An extended choice of food-stuffs, and the alternative of simple methods of preparation, would be fully consonant with orthodoxy, which has always aimed at making the body the servant of man, and not his master.

With increasing poverty, and the tendency to break up the family into smaller groups, the career within the community-house is becoming limited. This will have to be counterbalanced by some increase of the power to consider national and communal responsibilities. The Mahabharata, the Ramayana and the Puranas, represent the culture of nationality popularised. Every ritual, every sacrament, is full of unwritten history. But the times demand a direct and simple knowledge of the fact even more than of the vehicle. To meet this demand, however, is not to attack orthodoxy, but to fulfil it, to carry it to its highest power.

There is no question here of educating an intellect hitherto left in barbarous ignorance. Only those can do vital service to the Indian woman who, in a spirit of entire respect for her existing conventions and her past, recognise that they are but offering new modes of expression to qualities already developed and expressed in other ways under the old training. Therefore the fundamental task of grasping and conveying the inspiration of the West must be performed by Easterns for Easterns, and not by foreigners.

Nor ought the result of such a process to be in any sense denationalising. To assimilate an ideal and make our own persons a demonstration of its power—this is not imitation. A merely imitative apprehension of the West—like that of the clerk in his office, the constitutional agitator in politics, the manufacturer who knows only enough of mechanical industry for a cheek-by-jowl competition with Manchester—is indeed the parent of death to the Orient. But to achieve a living, forceful, heart-to-heart appropriation of the Western energy and its immediate re-translation into Eastern terms, is not death but life.

The East suffers, as has been said, from the very perfection of its formulæ. "Tell the truth," says the commandment in the Occident; and again, "Be courteous in thy speech." How often have we not seen crude logic struggle blindly to co-ordinate these conflicting dicta, with how many degrees of ill-success! But in the East, for more than two thousand years, people have lived under the shadow of Manu's saying: "Tell the truth, but not that which is unpleasant: tell the pleasant, but not that which is untrue." Alas, its completeness leaves nothing to be added! That unconquered space which the mind needs to bring out its fullest potentiality; that strip of wilderness to be empirically observed and reclaimed, and finally annexed to the territory of prescribed law; that sense of personal adventure on the great ocean of truth, there to encounter tempests of doubt and negation and overcome by slowly gathered knowledge only,—all these are now most attainable in the view of the Universe which is presented by Western science.

Very little that deserves the name of Education has been attempted in modern India. A machine has been created; an organisation stands ready. But nothing in all this represents the work of the people themselves, for ends which they spontaneously perceive to be good in themselves. Moreover, liberal ideals of what Education means are wanting. It is obvious that no system can be complete till secular culture exists in all forms and grades as does religious culture now, from that of the child playing with sense-impressions, up to the solitary student, standing on mountain-peaks of knowledge where human foot before his has never trodden, and yet finding abundance of sympathy and understanding and new stimulus again, in the social matrix out of which he climbed, when he returns to recount his vision and his wandering.

The process of creating a great nation out of the rich civilisations and faiths of an Eastern land is by no means simple. Yet there is not a single weapon that is not ready to hand. Long ages of peace (for the trifling feuds of dynasties do not disturb the fundamental peace of agricultural peoples) have somewhat puerilised the military factors in the faiths.

Yet still the fencing is exhibited at the Mohurrum; still the weapons are carried in procession at the feast of Durga; still the great Kayasth* families of Bengal and the Kshatriyas of Rajputana practise the annual Worship and Tribute of the Sword. And still the women throng to the temples with lighted candles on the eve of the Birth-feast of the War-Lord in December, to make it the most imposing in the year. A still more extraordinary paradox lies in the fact that it is India the peaceful, the patient, the entirely submissive, which possesses the most militant and stirring of all the world's Evangels—the Gospel of the Blessed One, uttered from a war-chariot on the actual field of battle.

There is another feature necessary to the making of a great people—a sense of community among all classes. Sharp distinction of races and manners has made the pariahs of the South a byword among the nations, and the very name of India a synonym for caste as opposed to nationality. Yet even in the South, and amongst these same pariahs, the effort has been made. The whole life of Ramanuja, the great religious leader, was as passionate an offering to the despised and rejected as that of the Teacher of Galilee is represented to have been. Even here, then, the national consolidation sounds no new note in Hindu ears. Islam is nothing if not a great mission of fraternity. Guru Nanak in the North,† and Ramanuja in the South,‡ have preached the same doctrine in words and lives made ever memorable. And if once the mother-heart of India can

* Kayasth families.—The Kayasths are the second caste of Bengal. They claim descent from the old Kshatriya, or military caste, but the authenticity of this genealogy is disputed.

† Guru Nanak in the North.—Guru Nanak was the first of the ten leaders or Gurus who formed the Sikh nation—the people of the Punjab. He was born 1469.

‡ Ramanuja in the South.—A saint and teacher of marvellous love and mercy. He lived in the twelfth century.

grasp the meaning and necessity of these incidents in its own history, we shall see all barriers broken, all difficulties overcome, and a new age inaugurated that shall be at once the flowering-point and blossom of all the realisations of the past.

But how do we propose that Indian women shall grasp an idea of such vastness as this of Nationality? How are they to acquire the knowledge necessary to define it? And how are they to grow in clear and accurate mastery of essential facts? Is it to be expected that the conventional channels of their education—the Homeric singers who chant the epics from door to door—is it to be expected that these shall transform themselves at a stroke from pious rhapsodists into heroic bards, chanting of nationality? No, it is clear enough that such a change could only befall them as result, not cause, of some great upheaval, from which the nation herself had emerged radiant, victorious, impressing herself upon the imaginations of her own children for ages to come. But the spring of such an upheaval, where is that to be found?

In answer to such questions we can only assure ourselves that when the world is ripe for some epochal idea—as the Indian world is surely ripe to-day—that idea pours itself in from all sides upon the waiting consciousness. The very stones speak it, and the timbers out of the wall cry out and answer them; some immense struggle for the common good precipitates itself; idea and struggle act and react, each throwing the other into greater distinctness, till the goal of both is finally achieved.

This is the more true in these days of telegraphy and letter-writing, of a common language and cheap print. A process which in Asoka's India would have taken at least two hundred years, may now be accomplished in a single decade. And wherever a word of English goes, the national idea constitutes for itself the necessity of an apostolate. No one can say exactly how it will come to birth among the women. Some will catch it for themselves. Some will gather it from the men Some are possessed of it already. But it is certain that woman, with her determinately synthetic interests, will refuse long to be baulked of her right to consider things as a whole. The interest of the mother is ever with the future. Woman will readily understand that a single generation of accomplished defeat is sufficient to divorce a whole race from its patrimony; and she will determine, and effectively determine, that the lot of her own sons shall be victory, and not surrender.

And if once the Oriental woman seize the helm of the ship in this fashion, solving the problems of her whole country, whom is it suggested that she shall afterwards petition for the redress of her own grievances?

CHAPTER VII

THE INDIAN SAGAS

UNSEEN, but all pervasive, in the life of every community, is the great company of the ideals. No decalogue has half the influence over human conduct that is exercised by a single drama or a page of narrative. The theory of chivalry interests us, but the *Idylls of the King* help to mould our character.

The whole of history, in so far as it may be known, is the common possession of the race; but, in addition to this, every language makes its own contribution of literary creations, and national custom determines the degree in which these shall become available to all classes of the community, thereby reacting upon the national type. Few have considered how much might be done to ennoble and dignify common life in England by a wider dispersion of the love for Shakespeare. As it is, the Bible being the only book that is used in this sense, the careers and opinions of a few Syrian shepherds are apt to be more potent among us than that great Brutus, Desdemona, Horatio and their kindred, who are the offspring of the genius of our countryman, and in some sense therefore the fruit of English civic life itself.

It is said that in Greece the poetry of Homer and Euripides is known amongst the poorer classes to this day; and certain it is that the Catholic Church has done a great and little-understood service, in bringing the lives of the saints of all countries to bear upon the development of each. Every man habitually measures himself against some model, therefore every addition to the range of available types is to be welcomed. A king feels himself to be one of a class of royal persons who must be not only authoritative but also picturesque in their behaviour. And, whether he likes it or not, by this standard he knows himself to stand or fall. His very rank forces his pattern upon him. Amongst those of smaller place and greater personal freedom, capacity more readily shows its own complexion. Some of us, were our commonplace faculties touched with divine fire, would find our destiny in the qualities of the ideal merchant and administrator. That peculiar form of integrity, dignity, and wisdom that belongs to such a function would prove to be ours, or attainable by us. But although this is probably the commonest logical issue in English national life at present, it does not follow that every Englishman is fitted to achieve it. Here and there, especially perhaps among the Celtic contingent, we find one born for the quite different goal of perfect knighthood. Loyalty to leader and comrade, sympathy for the oppressed, far-shining fearlessness and love of freedom, are traits characteristic of an age of chivalry; and persons who embody them represent such a period, it being neither more nor less admirable than that of merchant-prince and caravan-chief. The potentialities of one man lead towards sainthood, of another to poetry, of a third to science or mechanics. One gravitates into leadership, another as naturally becomes disciple. One enjoys knowledge, another ignorance.

Were all of us developed to our own utmost we may take it that every place in life would be filled, every part in the world-drama played, but by men and women of such ripe and determined personality that we could no more confuse one with the other than we could mistake the conduct of Helen of Troy for that of Elisabeth of Hungary, or hers for that of Faust's Gretchen.

We have to notice, moreover, that in European life only the born idealist is deeply influenced by any of the miscellaneous characters of history and literature. Religion alone amongst us can exercise this compelling power on a large scale. And this is related to the fact that only religion gives ideals themselves as motives. Circumstances have in many cases offered such a setting that a life has been forced into brilliance and distinction, but the self-born intention of the saints could never be wholly fulfilled. Iphigenia could hardly have refused her sacrifice. Joan of Arc, on the contrary, must always have felt that the sword of Michael might have been held still more stainless and with a greater courage. It is this fact that gives to the ideals of religion their supreme power of individuation. We must remember also that they differ from others in making a universal appeal. The girl who aimed at becoming Portia would be guilty of vanity: she whose model is the Blessed Virgin receives the respect of all. To imitate Socrates would be a miserable affectation: to imitate the religious hero is regarded as a common duty.

It may seem impossible to dower the heroes and heroines of literature with this projective energy of the lives of saints; but in India, as to some extent in Iceland, the feat has been accomplished. For India is also one of the saga-lands. At every lull in her history we may hear the chanting of her bards, and the joy of her people in the story of their past. The long twilight of the North is no better adapted to the growth of such a literature than the deep and early night of the South. In verandahs and courtyards, with the women concealed behind screens at the back, it has been the Indian fashion for hundreds of years through the winter months to gather at dusk round the seat of the Wandering Teller, and listen hour after hour to his stirring theme. Surrounded by lights and flowers, gay carpets and burning incense, there is in his performance a mixture of reading, song, and story. It is something of opera, sermon, and literature all in one.

Ever since the commencement of our era the Hindu people have possessed in their present forms two great poems, the Mahabharata and the Ramayana.* The first of these is their Wars of Troy, their Heimskringla, their Morte d'Arthur. That is to say, it is the book of the Deeds and the Wars of the Heroes. Thanks to the long-established culture of the race, and the prestige which all literature enjoys as "sacred," the Mahabharata is to this day the strongest influence in the shaping of the lives and ambitions of Hindu boys.

The battle which it describes took place, if at all, very nearly fifteen hundred years before the birth of Christ. It lasted many days, and the field of combat was called Kurukshetra, being situated on that great plain near Delhi where critical moments in the history of India have been so often decided. For many a century after Kurukshetra the wandering bards all over India sang of the great battle; and when any new theme claimed their creative powers, it had to be recounted as if originally told by one of the heroes to another at some particular moment in the course of the main narrative. In this way the heart's heart of the whole poem, the Bhagavad Gita (a title translated by some scholars as "Gospel of the Bhagavats") brings an interesting instance of

* The theory of the dates of the Mahabharata and Ramayana put forward in this chapter is that of Mr. Romesh Chunder Dutt.

double drama with it. The Gita consists in itself of a dialogue between a young Chieftain and Krishna, the Divine Personage who is acting as his charioteer, at the moment of the opening of the eighteen days' combat. But the device which enables the conversation to be given in detail is the picture of an old blind king, head of one of the rival houses, seated some miles away, and attended in his anxiety by a man of what is called *yogic*, or hyper-æsthetic, that is, psychic sense, who utters to him every word as it is spoken.

The exquisite story of Savitri, similarly, is told by a *rishi*, or great sage, to Yudisthira, at the close of day, during the banishment of the five Pandavas to the forest.

On this plan, more than half the country-side tales of Northern India could be woven into the Mahabharata when it was first thrown into form by some unknown hand, three or four centuries before Christ. It underwent its final recension not more than two or three hundred years later—a possible fifteen hundred years after the occurrence of the events which are its central theme. It is easy to see that this saga fulfils thus all the conditions of great epic poetry. The stories that it tells have been worked over by the imagination of singers and people for hundreds of years. They have become simple, direct, inevitable. They are spoken out of the inmost heart of a nation not yet dreaming of self-consciousness. They are nothing if not absolutely sincere.

Comparing the Mahabharata with the Iliad and Odyssey, we find it less formed, less highly-wrought; more amorphous, but also more brilliant and intense. To quote a great writer on Indian thought—"Outline is entirely lost in colour."

These characteristics do not hold good to the same extent of the second Indian epic, the Ramayana, which has a closely-worked motive running throughout. This poem—the tale of the Exile of Sita and Rama—received its present form not long after the Mahabharata, early in the Buddhist period. It is supposed that under Buddhist influence the monastic life had come to be so honoured that the flower of the nation were drawn to it, rather than to the mingled responsibilities and joys of the home. The romantic reaction in ideals which was inevitable gathered itself about the ancient theme of a princely couple of the house of Oudh, in whom *all* that was precious in monasticism was found blended with all that was desirable in sovereignty and love. The strong and quiet story spoke straight to the heart of the people, and to this day there are no characters so beloved by the masses as those of the Ramayana, no one force that goes so far towards the moulding of Indian womanhood, as the ever-living touch of the little hand of that Sita who is held to have been Queen of Ayodhya thousands of years ago.

The Ramayana, then, is a love-story which grew up and came to its flowering in the beginning of the Christian era. But it is unlike all other romances of that early epoch in the subtlety and distinctiveness of its various characters, and in the complexity of its interpretation of life. For though humanity itseif may differ little from age to age, we have been accustomed to look for a definite growth in its literary self-reflection. We expect primitive poetry to be preoccupied with events, portraying men and women only in bold outline, as they move with simple grandeur through their fate. We do not look to it for subtle analysis of motive, or any exact mingling of the sweet and bitter cup of the personal life. The progress of literature up to this time has been largely, as we think, the intensifying recognition of human variation within a given psychological area. And in making such a statement we take pains to eliminate from the word "progress" all sense of improvement, since Homer remains for ever superior to Browning. Simply, we find in art a parallel to the physical process by which the race moves on from strong family and communal types to a universal individual divergence. An overwhelming appreciation of spiritual content is what we have been ready in Europe to call "the modern spirit." It is a question whether the name can stand, however, when the Indian Epics become better known; for, strangely enough, in spite of their age and the heroic nature of their matter, they are permeated with this very quality. In the Ramayana especially, as incident leads to incident, we have to realise that this is no story told for our amusement, but a woman's soul laid bare before us, as she climbs from steep to steep of renunciation.

Perhaps only those who are in touch with national aspiration can fully understand the roundness and plasticity of its drama, but even the most cursory reader must be struck with this insight and delicacy of the Ramayana.

It is more to-day than a completed work of art; it is still a means for the development of the popular imagination. Even amongst the written versions we find no two quite alike. All children are brought up on the story, yet those who can read the original Sanskrit are few in number. To meet this fact translations have been made into various vernaculars by great poets from time to time—into Bengali, for instance, by Kritibas, and into Hindi by Tulsidas. Special incidents again have been selected and worked up into great episodes in Sanskrit, by one and another, such as Bhavabhuti in his "Exile of Sita," or Datta in the "Epic of Ravana."

In these versions the story becomes more and more clearly defined. Pulsing through every Ramayana runs the Hindu reverence for Rama as man, husband, and king. This reverence may seek new modes of expression, but it can never admit that that which is expressed was at any time less than the ideal. Yet we must remember that that ideal is, in the ancient terms, Oriental rather than Occidental. It belonged to a conception of duty that placed Society far above the individual, and made the perfect king seek the good of his people without any consideration for his own or his wife's happiness. The fact that made his marriage perfect was its complete demonstration that it was as possible for two as for one to devote themselves first to the general weal. For the acquiescence of Sita is given in her twenty years of silent banishment. Once during that time, says one of the regional poets, she saw her husband as he passed through the forest where she was and kept silence still. And though the incident is an addition not found in the original, it only serves to bring out more clearly the intention of the first poem, where every dumb moment of those twenty years speaks louder than words the wife's acquiescence in her husband's will.

Behind the vernacular translators stand all those old nurses and granddams on whose laps the poets themselves first heard the great tale; and it is their perfect freedom to give their own versions of each episode—as must any of us in recounting actual happenings—that keeps it fresh and living and explains its changes of tint in the hands of genius.

Without the recognition of this working of the communal consciousness on the theme, there can be no complete criticism of the Ramayana, for of this are all new transcribings of the story born. It is more or less in this fashion that the old tale is told:

Long ago, in the age of the heroes, there dwelt kings in Oudh, of whose race came one Rama, heir to the throne, great of heart, and goodly to look upon. And Rama was wedded to Sita, daughter of Janaka the king, fairest and purest of all the children of men. Now Rama had been trained in all knowledge and in the sports of princes, living, as was the manner of those days, in the forest, with his brother Lakshman, in the care of a great sage. And it happened, after he was come home again and wedded with Sita, that there arose a trouble between the king his father, and one of the younger queens, Kaikeyi, who desired that her son Bharata should inherit the throne, and pleaded that her husband had once promised her whatever gift she should desire. And when one told Rama of this contention that was embittering his father's age, he replied at once by a vow to renounce the throne and retire to the forest for fourteen years. And gladly, he said, was this vow made, since it would give pleasure to Kaikeyi, his stepmother, and confer on Bharata, his younger brother, the kingdom and its wealth. And Sita, overhearing the vow, added hers to his, in spite of his entreaties that she should not quit her royal state. Lakshman also declared that he would not be separated from his elder brother. So all three fared forth together into the great forest. Thither, shortly after, followed Bharata, saying that the king their father was now dead of grief at the wrong done his eldest son, and imploring Rama to return and take his own place in his kingdom, for Bharata had mingled no whit in the scheming of Kaikeyi. But Rama refused till the days of his vow should be ended; after fourteen years, he said, he would return and reign. Then, very reluctantly, went Bharata back to Oudh, but he carried with him the sandals of Rama, declaring that these should hold the throne, and he himself sit always below them, governing in their name.

Left in the forest, the life of Sita, Rama, and

Lakshman, became that of gentle anchorites, and they grew great in all manner of woodcraft, so that the wild creatures answered to their call. But Rama and Lakshman never ceased to remember their knighthood, holding themselves ready with sword and bow for the service of all who were in distress. It was on one of their expeditions of knight-errantry that they offended a great ogress, and brought on themselves the enmity of her powerful kinsman, Ravana the Ten-headed, king of the island of Lanka or Ceylon.

It was inevitable that some of the skalds who chanted the deeds of Rama should attach themselves specially to the character of this mythical Ravana, elaborating all connected with him. Hence, just as Hector and Andromache are amongst the most beautiful figures in the Iliad, so, in the Indian poem, is Mandodari, the wife of Ravana, one of the strongest personages, at least from a literary point of view. To this day old wives tell of an incident that has crept into no published poem. When the time came, they say, that Rama had conquered and slain his ten-headed foe, Mandodari was inconsolable that she was now a widow. Then it was declared to her that, till her husband's funeral fire was dead she should be no widow, and that that fire should burn for ever. And so, sure enough, we have only to shut our ears tight, and we hear the roaring of the flames that are burning Ravana to ashes!

For so it was, that Rama had to defeat and slay this evil king in order to recover Sita, who had been stolen from him. The story of the Taking of Sita is as beautiful as Pluto's Capture of Proserpine.

It is the close of day in the forest, and Sita is alone. Lakshman—one of the most "perfect gentle knights" in the whole range of fiction—has left her, at her earnest entreaty that he should go to seek for

Rama, but he has first drawn three circles about her with the end of his bow, and warned her not to step outside. The sun is not yet set, however, when a Brahmin appears, ashen-clad, with matted locks, and begs for charity. Sita pleads that it is late and she is alone, imploring him to go. And this he promises to do if only first she will step outside and give him a little food. She is full of dim forebodings of evil, but pity at last gains the upper hand of fear; she steps out of her enchanted circles to bestow alms on him; he throws off the disguise of the Brahmin, appears as Ravana himself, and carries her off to his kingdom in his chariot. It is during the first terrible moment of the journey that Sita drops her jewels stealthily behind her, in order that those coming after may be able to trace her flight.

Surely this picture of the exiled queen, standing amidst the long shadows in her simple hut, lost in the struggle between her desire to aid and all the invisible safeguards of her womanhood, is one that deserves the brush of some great painter.

For years Sita is kept confined in Lanka, and Rama and Lakshman, in their progress through what is depicted as the wilderness of Southern India, owe her discovery and much of their success in finally releasing her, to the services of their great ally, Hanuman, the monkey-general. It is supposed that if there be any historical foundation for the legend of the Ramayana, this name of Hanuman may refer to the chieftain of some strong aboriginal tribe. In any case, he stands to-day for all that is great in discipleship. Filled with the worship of Rama, he brings to his service the unquestioning obedience of a child and the genius of a man. It is in his presence and that of Lakshman that Sita goes proudly, at her own request, through that ordeal by fire which is to prove her stainlessness, and he declares as he dies that the names of Sita and Rama will be found written on his heart.

It is now time for the return to the kingdom, and Sita and Rama go back to Oudh, reigning there in perfect happiness close upon a year. Then comes the great crisis of their parting, in deference to the people's doubt of Sita. She retires to a distant forest, to live the life of a nun, under the care of Valmiki, the old hermit; and Rama sits alone on the throne of Oudh for the rest of his life. Once only does he speak of his loss. His subjects desire him to take a new queen, for the performance of a state sacrifice that he cannot make alone. But here the wrath of the king blazes forth. No woman shall ever be put in Sita's place, but a golden image of her is made, and fills her part in the appointed ceremonies.

Shortly after her arrival in the forest, Sita had become the mother of twin sons, and Valmiki, their foster-father, brings these up as princes, only taking care to add to their education the knowledge of his own great poem, the Ramayana. He allows it to be supposed, also, that their mother is dead. When the boys are some twenty years of age, news goes about the country of a great religious festival to be held at the Court of Ayodhya, and the hermit makes ready to go up to it, taking his two foster-sons in the character of minstrels, and the queen.

The rest of the story is inevitable. The eyes of Rama discover his boys as they recite before him the deeds of his own past, and calling Valmiki to him, he speaks with hopeless longing the name of Sita. The old man draws her forward, and she unveils her face to her husband. At this moment, as the two look, each upon the face that has been present to every thought for twenty years, the murmur of the people's doubt is once more heard, and the cry rises from the crowd, "Let her be tried by fire!"

No woman's pride could brook this renewed insult. Sita, the proud, the silent, the stainless, cries out for death. At her words, the ground opens, a chariot appears, and in the arms of her Mother Earth she is withdrawn from the world of men. Rama waits only to bestow the kingdom on his sons, and then plunges into the forest, to be for ever lost to humanity.

The story of the Mahabharata would be less easy to recount. Mighty warriors, beautiful women, and great saints move to and fro across its scenes in a glittering *melée*. The local colour is rich to a fault. The poem abounds in descriptions of social customs, domestic comfort, the fashions of old armour and similar details. But it is in the conception of character which it reveals that it becomes most significant. Bhishma, the Indian Arthur, is there, with his perfect knighthood and awful purity of soul. Lancelot is there—a glorified Lancelot, whose only fall was the utterance of a half-truth once, with purpose to mislead—in the person of the young king, Yudisthira. And Krishna, the Indian Christ, is there, in that guise of prince and leader of men that has given him the name in India of "The Perfect Incarnation." One of the rival houses consists of a family of no less than a hundred children, so that the multiplicity of persons and incidents is best left to the imagination. Yet certain main features belong to the treatment of all characters alike. For the attention of the poet-chronicler is fixed on the invisible shackles of selfhood that bind us all. He seems to be describing great events; in reality he does not for one instant forget that he is occupied with the history of souls, depicting the incidence of their experience and knowledge on the external world.

One story is typical. The young princes are taking a lesson in shooting, and a clay bird has been set up as target. One by one they are asked by their master what they see. They reply, "A bird," "A branch supporting a bird," and so on. Till at last he puts the question to Arjuna, one of the youngest, and receives the answer, "A bird's head, and in that head only the eye." The moment of the telling of this story to an Indian child is tense with feeling. For it embodies the culminating ideal of the nation, inasmuch as "Concentration of Mind" stands among Hindus for the supreme expression of that greatness which we may recognise in honour or courage or any kind of heroism.

The central character of the Mahabharata fulfils a very subtle demand. Bhishma is intended for the type of king and knight. Now, knighthood implies the striking of many blows, and kinghood the protecting of manifold and diverse interests, but perfection requires that nothing shall be done from the motive of self-interest. In order, therefore, that he may display all the greatness of character that is possible to man in these relations, Bhishma is made, as heir to the throne, to renounce all rights of succession and even of marriage, at the beginning of his life, by way of setting his father free to marry a fisher-girl whom he loves, and make her son his heir.

From this point, having set aside the privileges of parent and sovereign, Bhishma is made to bear to the full the responsibilities of both; and finally, in the energy and faithfulness of his military service, life itself can only be taken from him when he with his own lips has given instructions for his defeat. In Bhishma, therefore, we have the creation of a people who have already learnt to regard detachment as a necessary element of moral grandeur.

It is strange to us, but perfectly consistent with

this point of view, that as long as Bhisma remains a militant figure in the battle of Kurukshetra he is acting as generalissimo for what he regards as the worse cause of the two. He has done his best to prevent the war, but when it is determined on, he sets himself to obey his sovereign, in the place that is his own. He is filled, as the Indian poet represents him, with supernatural assurance that his side must lose, yet he strikes not a single blow either more or less for this consideration. In like manner it is told of Krishna that after he has done his utmost for peace in the interests of justice, he is approached by both parties for his aid, and that such is the calmness of his outlook on life that he submits the matter to a moral test. To one claimant he will give his armies; the other he will serve in person unarmed, he says, leaving the choice to themselves. It is clear that the man whose greed and ambition are plunging whole nations into war will not have the spiritual insight to choose the Divine Person for his champion, rather than great hosts. And he does not.

Such stories illustrate the Hindu endeavour to understand every man's relation to a given situation, and to read in conflicting lines of conduct that same irresistible necessity which, acting from within, hurls each one of us upon his fate. In this endeavour lies the real secret of that tolerance which has so puzzled observers in the Indian people. Not only has there never been religious persecution among Hindus, but the sceptic, the atheist, or the Christian missionary is as free to preach on the steps of the temple as the believing priest. The European correlative of the trait is found in the dramatist or novelist of genius who can represent the motives of opposing sides so as to draw equally upon our sympathy; but this has always been an exceptional ability with us, and not a common attitude of mind.

In the Mahabharata itself the most perfect expression of such reconciliation of opposites is perhaps found in the story of Shishupal, the enemy of Krishna. Shishupal's mother had won Krishna's promise that her son might sin against him a hundred times, and yet be forgiven. But this cup of error was already full, when his crowning blasphemy occurred. The occasion was that of the offering of certain honours to the Chief of Knights. Krishna, in right of his divinity, had already been named, and the decision that to him should the sacrifice be made was spoken. To the deep-rooted hostility of Shishupal, however, this was unendurable. He broke out into indignant protest. In what sense, he asked, was Krishna greatest of the knights? Was not Bhishma present? Was not Yudisthira their liege? Let the honours be paid to one of these.

Shocked and outraged, every one looked to Bhishma to punish the impiety; but that aged clansman's face was turned towards the Avatar. Then, as all waited in suspense, from behind the Blessed Knight flashed forth the bright discus of Vishnu, and striking the helmet of Shishupal clove him through, even to the ground. And lo, before their eyes, the soul of that sinful one came forth like a mass of flame, and passed over and melted into the feet of Krishna. "For even the enemies of God go to salvation," says the old chronicler, "by thinking much upon Him." A later increment of explanation makes the point still clearer. It had happened in some previous age that a great and enlightened spirit had fallen under a curse—had strayed, that is to say, into those circles of destiny that would involve him in human birth. And the All-Merciful, being touched with pity, offered him the path of return through seven births as the friend of God, or three as His enemy. The second alternative was his instant choice, and he became in one life Ravana the foe of Rama; in another, a certain persecuting king; and in the third, this Shishupal, now once more absorbed into Eternal Bliss.

Few characters in literature can rank with the heroic figure of young Karna. Dark with anger, but perfect in chivalry, he resents to the death a slight levelled at his birth, yet turns in the midst of princely acclaims to salute reverently the aged charioteer supposed to be his father. Full of a palpitating humanity is Draupadi, the Pandava Queen. Beautiful and high-spirited as she is, she has all a woman's inability to keep a secret, and her foolish boastfulness almost betrays the heroes before their time is ripe. The strongest attraction of such figures is always the actuality. There is nothing incredibly exalted about them, but good and evil are entwined in their natures, strong and heroic though they be, as in us all.

The end of Bhishma is like that of some ancient Norseman. Lying on the field of battle where he fell, he refuses to be moved, and asks only for a bed and pillow such as are fit for knightly bowmen. One of the young chiefs divines his meaning, and, stepping forward, shoots arrows into the earth till what was desired has been provided. And on his bed of arrows Bhishma dies.

Such are some of the characters who form the ideal world of the Hindu home. Absorbed in her "worship of the Feet of the Lord," the little girl sits for hours in her corner, praying, "Make me a wife like Sita! Give me a husband like Rama!" Each act or speech of the untrained boy rushing in from school, may remind some one, half-laughing, half-admiring, of Yudisthira or Lakshman, of Karna or Arjuna, and the name is sure to be recalled. It is expected that each member of the family shall have his favourite hero, who will be to him a sort of patron saint, and may appear as the centre of the story, if he is bidden to recount it. Thus, when one tells the Ramayana, Ravana is the hero; another makes it Hanuman; only the books keep it always Sita and Rama. And it is well understood that the chosen ideal exercises a preponderant influence over one's own development. None could love Lakshman without growing more full of gentle courtesy and tender consideration for the needs of others; he who cares for Hanuman cannot fail to become more capable of supreme devotion and ready service. And justice itself must reign in the heart that adores Yudisthira.

The character of Bhishma in the Mahabharata as that of Sita in the Ramayana is a proof that Indian philosophy was completed before the Epics. But that philosophy itself, we must remember, was directly related to the common life of common folk. Only this fact can explain the recognition and welcome of such conceptions by the whole nation. Let us look at the love story of Sita. Her feeling is consecrated by the long years of poverty filled with worship, in the forest. When it is thus established, she undergoes the dreary persecution and imprisonment at the hands of Ravana. Every moment finds her repeating the name of Rama, her faith unshaken in her ultimate rescue. At the end she herself suggests the fiery ordeal, and goes through it with dauntless courage.

Then for one short year, as wife, and queen, and future mother, she tastes of entire earthly happiness, only to be swept away from her home again in the sternness of her husband's will for his people's good. Through twenty years of acquiescent silence she keeps now, in all its fulness, that love that sent her first to share Rama's exile in the forest, and yet the perfection of her pride of womanhood is shown when she dies of the insult conveyed in a spoken doubt.

We believe vaguely that the power to renounce distinguishes the human from all life known to us; but a conception of renunciation so searching, so austere as this appals us. It is clear that a commanding philosophy of self-discipline lay behind, or the poet's hand could not have been so remorseless; but it is also clear that that philosophy was living in the heart and effort of the people, or Sita and Rama could not have been so loved.

We ask in vain what can have been the life of India before she found refuge and direction in such dreams as these. For to-day it has become so one with them that all trace of the dawn before they were is lost. They penetrate to every part of the country, every class of society, every grade of education. Journeying in the mountains at nightfall, one came upon the small open hut of the grain-dealer, and saw, round a tiny lamp, a boy reading the Ramayana in the vernacular to a circle of his elders. At the end of each stanza they bowed their heads to the earth, with the chant, "To dear Sita's bridegroom, great Rama, all hail!" The shopkeeper in the city counts out his wares to the customer, saying, "One (Ram), two (Ram), three (Ram)," and so on, relapsing into a dream of worship when the measuring is done. Nay, once at least it is told how at the "Four (Ram)" the blessed name was enough to touch the inmost soul of him who uttered it, and he rose up then and there and left the world behind him. The woman terrified at thunder calls on "Sita Ram!" and the bearers of the dead keep time to the cry of "Rama Nama Sattva hai!" ("The name of the Lord alone is real!")

What philosophy by itself could never have done for the humble, what the laws of Manu have done only in some small measure for the few, that the Epics have done through unnumbered ages and are doing still for all classes alike. They are the perpetual Hinduisers, for they are the ideal embodiments of that form of life, that conception of conduct, of which laws and theories can give but the briefest abstract, yet towards which the hope and effort of every Hindu child must be directed.

We are in the habit of talking of the changeless East; and, though there is a certain truth in the phrase, there is also a large element of fallacy. One of the most striking features of Hindu society during the past fifty years has been the readiness of the people to adopt a foreign form of culture and to compete with those who are native to that culture on equal terms. In medicine, in letters, in science, even in industry, where there has been opportunity, we are astonished at the intellectual adaptability of the race. Is the mere beckoning of the finger of the nineteenth century enough to subvert predilections as old as Babylon and Nineveh? we ask, amazed. By no means. Such changes as these are merely surface deep. The hauteur of the East lies in the very knowledge that its civilisation has nothing to fear from the social and intellectual experiments of its youngsters, or even from such complete changes of mental raiment as amongst newer peoples would constitute revolutions of thought, for the effort of Eastern civilisation has always been to the solitary end of moralising the individual, and in this way it differs essentially from Western systems of culture, which have striven rather for the most efficient use of materials. If Alexander, capable of organising the largest number of his fellows most effectually for a combination of military, commercial, and scientific ends in that most difficult form, an armed expedition over hostile territory—if Alexander be taken as the type of Occidental genius, then, as the culminating example of the Oriental. we must name Buddha;

for clear and intense conceptions of perfect renunciation and inner illumination are the hidden springs of Hindu living, around which the home itself is built. These it is of which the Epics are the popular vehicles, these it is which give its persistence to Indian civilisation through the centuries, and this is why no examination syllabus, no alien's kindly inspiration, no foreigner's appreciation or contempt, can ever hope to have one iota of permanent influence on the national education at its core.

Reforming sects are very apt to reject what is much cultivated amongst the orthodox—the folk-lore that has grown up round the Epics in the Puranas and other literature. But to the poems themselves all cling fast. None fail to realise that they bear the mark of supreme literature, and so they remain a constant element, capable, like all great interpretations of life, of infinitely varied application, a treasure greater, because more greatly used, than any Anger of Achilles or Descent into Purgatory amongst them all.

CHAPTER VIII

NOBLESSE OBLIGE: A STUDY OF INDIAN CASTE

A GRAVER intellectual confusion than that caused by the non-translation of the word *Caste* * there has seldom been. The assumed impossibility of finding an equivalent for the idea in English has led to the belief that there is something mysterious and unprecedented in the institution. People become bewildered as to whether it is a religious or a social obligation. Every one demands of the reformer a conflict with it. The whole question grows obscure and irritating.

Yet all this time we have had an exact synonym for the word, and the parallel is the closer since our word connotes the same debatable borderland between morals and good taste. *Caste* ought to stand translated as *honour*. With Oriental quaintness, it is true, India has given a certain rigidity to this idea, but her analysis of the thing itself is as profound as it is acute.

Our conduct is commonly governed far more by social habit than by considerations of right and wrong. When the tide of the ethical struggle has once set in over some matter, we may regard ourselves as already half-lost. Why are my friend's open letters absolutely safe in my presence, though I am longing for the information they convey? Why

* The word *Caste* is of Portuguese origin.

can money given for one purpose not be used for another, when all the canons of common sense and expediency urge that it should? Who will confess to an effort in speaking the truth at any cost whatever? Why, when I am annoyed, do I not express myself in the language of Billingsgate? To each of which questions one would reply, somewhat haughtily, that the point was one of honour, or, that such happened to be the custom of one's class.

Yet if we examine into the sanction which honour can invoke there is nothing beyond a rare exercise of the power of ostracism. The Church excommunicates, the law imprisons, but society merely "cuts" the offender in the street. Yet which of these three inflicts the deepest wound? It is as true of London as of Benares that caste-law is the last and finest that controls a man. For it comes into operation at that precise point where tribunals fail. It takes cognisance of offences for which no judge could inflict penalties. It raises standards and demands virtues that every man will interpret according to the stringency of his pride, and yet that no one can feel himself to have wholly fulfilled. And it does all this without once permitting the sensation of merit. Having done all one remains an unprofitable servant. For no one would count the punctual discharge of debts (all debts are debts of honour), the hauteur that brooks no stain upon the name, the self-respect that builds the whole ethical code upon itself, as religious observances. These things were due, we say, to our birth or blood, or position before men. It is true that their non-fulfilment would leave a stain upon the conscience, and it is also true that the attempt to work out the obligations of honour must be the immediate test of the sincerity of one who proposes to lead a life of greater devotion and earnestness than common.

Still, caste is not the same thing as personal piety, and perhaps for this reason complete renunciation of its claims and benefits is essential in India to the monastic life.

There is another point about our Western conception of *noblesse oblige.* Few as the persons may be who could formulate their sentiment, the fact pervades the whole of the social area. Each class has its own honour. If honourable employers feel compelled to think of the comfort of their workers, honourable servants feel equally compelled to keep their lips shut on their masters' affairs, and either responds to an appeal in the name of his ideal. The priest may find the honour of his profession in conflict with that of the detective, but all the world will uphold the faithfulness of both. The efficient realisation of his ideals by the schoolmaster will involve an occasional pardon, even of a grave offence, if he conceives forgiveness to be the best formative influence which at the moment he can command. The very same effort in the merchant will require a distribution of punishment that is rigorous and just, since order, integrity, and unfailing promptitude—not the development of human character—are his ends. Thus every man, in every critical act of his life, calls silently for the judgment of his peers and refuses all other.

The weaknesses of caste everywhere are manifold. For society, like the individual, is always apt to insist upon the tithing of mint and rue, and to neglect the weightier matters of the law. But it is not usually the martyr who marks its worst failure. He is the white dove cast forth by crows, that is, a member of a higher tried by consensus of the lower castes. We have here a case of government usurping the functions of society, much as if the headmaster should exercise authority in a dispute among boys. For it is essential to the very idea of honour that every caste should be autonomous. The true failure of caste occurs whenever it establishes such an ascendency of social opinion over the individual's conscience that his power of advance is impeded and he becomes less of a man, or less really beneficent socially, by remaining more of a gentleman—a state of things which is not uncommon among ourselves. For we may postulate that all ideals are helpful only in so far as they subserve a man's manhood and freedom, and destructive the instant they render him less able to express his own inmost will. It is he, therefore, who ought to have been a martyr and chose ease who is the true caste victim, not the hero of an *auto-da-fé*.

That this is a real danger we all know. What Protestant has never exalted the creed of his sect over freedom of thought? What Catholic has never put comfort above spirituality? What politician has not preferred party above principle? What student of science has never been prejudiced against new truth? And if we look without, where do we not see the mere breaker of conventionality treated as outside brotherhood? Where do we not find persons conforming to usages that displease them, merely because they would be inconvenient to dispute?

A certain sweeping justification of such facts may be urged, inasmuch as there are circumstances under which the cohesion of the group is well worth the sacrifice of the liberty of a few individuals. And the habitual outrage of custom without reason is perhaps rightly held to be as anti-social as any felony. In the last resort, however, social pressure must be held in bounds, for nothing should interfere with a man's right to try himself, or sap the roots of his independence. And society is a vague and irresponsible magistrate, with so little illumination as to his own purposes and tendencies that he frequently mistakes the pioneers of his march for deserters and orders the stoning of prophets, whose sepulchres and monuments will be erected by his children.

The question of the inner trend or intention of the social movement must form the law in whose name all doubtful cases are tried. And, while it is never easy to determine the point accurately for one's own people, in the case of the Hindu race the supreme purpose of their past evolution is quite apparent. Even a cursory reading of the Laws of Manu displays Indian society as united in a great co-operation for the preservation of the ancient race-treasure of Sanskrit literature.

The feeling must have grown up when the Vedas alone required conserving, and the families entrusted with various portions were encouraged to become in all ways dependent on the community, that every energy might be devoted to the task in hand. This is the real meaning of prostration at the feet of Brahmins, of the great merit acquired by feeding them, and of the terror of the crime of killing one. It is not the man, it is race-culture that is destroyed by such an act.

As ages went on and the Upanishads and other things were added to the store, that which was hitherto memorised became entrusted to writing. The *Vedas* became *Scriptures*—and now the *methods* of psychology, of astronomy, of mathematics, made themselves felt as integral parts of the Aryan treasure, in common with Sanskrit literature. This widened the conception of culture without liberalising the social bearings of the question, and the Brahmin caste continued to be recognised as the natural guardians of all learning, the old religious compositions being still regarded as the type.

If we ask how it happened that the Aryan folk became so early conscious of their responsibility in the matter of Sanskrit letters, there can be only one answer. They found themselves in the presence of other and unlearned races. This point brings us to the question of the origin of strongly differentiated castes in general. In its nature caste is, as we have seen, honour; that is to say, an ideal sentiment by whose means society spontaneously protects itself from some danger against which it is otherwise defenceless. For instance, life in Texas having been for many years dependent on the possession of horses, and safeguards against the horse-thief being few and difficult, he came to be the object of unprecedented social abhorrence. Horse-stealing was the last crime a lost soul would stoop to. In a similar way, as some think, may have grown up the Indian feeling about cow-killing. If the cattle, in time of stress, were killed for food, agriculture would be unable to take a new start, and so a people accustomed to eat beef grasped the situation perhaps, and renounced the practice. But since these two sentiments pervade whole nations, they are not exactly what we are accustomed to think of as caste, inasmuch as in the latter there is a distinct gradation of rank connected with the sentiment. In the term "blackleg" applied by trade unionists to competing forms of labour, we have an instance of the kind we want. Here we have an occupational group giving birth immediately to the ideal which is necessary to its safety. Throughout the worlds of love, of war, and of work, indeed, honour is an instinct of the very greatest potency. How few men, after all, desert to an enemy as spies! How strong is the feeling of class-obligation amongst servants and working men! This element is very evident in the Indian industrial castes, which are often simply hereditary trade-unions. No Englishman is so powerful, nor is any Hindu so hungry, that one man could be bribed to take up the trade of another.

Nothing would induce the dairyman, for instance, to take charge of a horse, or a laundryman to assist the household.

But the very strongest, and perhaps also ugliest, of all possible roots of caste is the sense of race, the caste of blood. We have an instance of this in the animosity that divides white men from negroes in the United States, and we have other instances, less talked of, all up and down our vast British possessions. There is probably no other emotion so inhuman which receives such universal sympathy as this. For it is fundamentally the physical instinct of a vigorous type to protect itself from fusion. And both sides participate in the revulsion. Here we have the secret of rigid caste, for the only rigid caste is hereditary, and of hereditary caste the essential characteristic is the refusal of intermarriage.

Granting, then, what could not well be denied, that the Aryan forefathers found themselves in India face to face with inferior and aboriginal races, what may we gather, from the nature of the caste system to-day, to have been the elements of the problem, as they more or less clearly perceived it ?

Those elements we may infer to have been four in number.

1. They desired above all things to preserve the honour of their daughters from marriage with lower and savage peoples. Exclusion from marriage with any but one's own caste became the rigorous rule, the penalty fell on the father and the family that permitted a woman to go unguarded on this head. To this day, if a son marry beneath caste he degrades himself; but if a daughter be wrongly given, the whole family becomes out-casted.

2. They seem to have desired to preserve the aboriginal races, on the one hand from extermination, and on the other from slavery of the person—

two solutions which seemed later the only alternatives to Aryan persons in a similar position!

Those aborigines, therefore, who became dependent on the Aryan population, had their definite place assigned them in the scale of labour, and their occupations were secured to them by the contempt of the superior race.

We must not forget, in the apparent harshness of this convention, its large factor of hygienic caution. The aborigines were often carrion-eaters, and always uncleanly in comparison with their neighbours. It was natural enough, therefore, that there should be a refusal to drink the same water, and so on.

On the other hand, it is one of the mistakes of caste everywhere, that it institutionalises and perpetuates an inequality which might have been minimised. But we must not forget, in the case of the Indian system, the two greater evils which were avoided altogether.

3. The Aryans realised very clearly that it was not only their race but also their civilisation that must be maintained in its purity. The word *Aryan* implies one acquainted with the processes of agriculture, an *earer* of the ground, to use an Elizabethan word—accustomed therefore to a fixed and industrialised mode of living, evidently in contrast to others who were not.

Fire and the processes of cooking and eating food are easily distinguished as the core of the personal life and establishment in a climate where habits can at any time be made so simple as in India. It is these that can never be dispensed with, though they may be arranged for to-night in a palace, and to-morrow in the jungle under a tree.

In view, then, of the necessity of safeguarding the system of manners grew up the restrictions against eating with those of lower caste, or allowing them to touch the food and water of their betters. The fact that the Aryan could eat food cooked by Aryan hands alone, implied that the strictest preliminaries of bathing had been complied with.

By a continuous crystallisation, all caste laws—from being the enunciation of broad canons of refinement as between Aryan and non-Aryan—came to be the regular caste-barriers between one class and another of the same race. In this way they lost their invidious character.

It is undeniable that this caste of the kitchen, so wittily named "don't touchism" by a modern Hindu leader, lends itself to abuse and becomes an instrument of petty persecution more readily than the intermarriage laws. Some of the saddest instances of caste-failure have occurred here. Nevertheless, the original intention remains clear and true, and is by no means completely obscured, even with the lapse of ages.

4. It was, however, in their perception of the fourth element of the problem that the early Aryans triumphantly solved the riddle of Humanity. They seem to have seen clearly that amongst the aborigines of India themselves were many degrees of social development already existent, and that these must be preserved and encouraged to progress.

From such a comprehension of the situation sprang the long and still growing graduation of non-Aryan castes, some of which have established themselves in the course of ages within the Aryan pale. Marriage, for instance, is an elaborate and expensive social function in the highest classes. But as we descend it becomes easier, till amongst the Baghdis, Bauris, and other aboriginal castes, almost any connection is ratified by the recognition of women and children. This is a point in which Eastern scores over Western development; for in

Europe the Church has caused to be reckoned as immoral what might, with more philosophy, have been treated as the lingering customs of sub-organised race-strata.

As is the nature of caste, mere social prestige constitutes a perpetual stimulus and invitation to rise, which means in this case to increase the number of daily baths and the cleanliness of cooking, and to restrict to purer and finer kinds the materials used for food, approximating continually toward the Brahmin standard. For is it not true that *noblesse oblige?* This fact it is that makes Hinduism always the vigorous living banyan, driving civilisation deeper and wider as it grows, and not the fossilised antiquity superficial observers have supposed.

Such, then, is the historic picture of the rise of caste. The society thus originated fell into four main groups:

(1) Priests and learned men—the Brahmins;

(2) The royal and military caste;

(3) Professional men and merchants—the middle-class or *bourgeoisie*, as we say in Europe; and

(4) The working people, or sudras, in all their divisions.

(Of the second group only the Rajput branch remains now stable. For the military caste, finding itself leaderless under the Maurya dynasty, is said to have become literary, and is certainly now absorbed in the *bourgeoisie.*)

This functional grouping, however, is traversed in all directions nowadays by the lines of caste. In the mountains it is no uncommon thing to find the Brahmin acting as a labourer, impressed as a coolie, or working as a farmer, and in the cities he belongs largely to the professional ranks. Many of India's most learned and active sons, on the other hand, belong to the third and even fourth divisions. And the new castes, which are of constant growth, are less easy than the old to classify.

Every new community means a new caste in India. Thus we have the Mohammedan, the Christian, and the modern reform castes—of all of which one peculiarity is non-belief in the caste principle!—as well as others. And who shall determine, for instance, to which of the four main grades Mohammedanism, with its inclusion of peasant, citizen, and prince, belongs?

The fact is, if a man's mode of life be acceptable to his own caste-fellows, the rest of Indian society has no quarrel with it. And this autonomy of castes it is which is the real essential for social flexibility and fundamental equality. As bearing on this point, few utterances have ever been so misquoted as the great dictum of Buddha, that "he who attains to God is the true Brahmin." For this is misquoted whenever it is made to imply that the Brahmin holds in any sense a monopoly in religion. No possible statement could be more foreign to the genius of Hinduism. When we read that shortest and greatest of India's gospels, the "Bhagavad Gita" (a poem composed by Brahmins, preserved by Brahmins, and distributed through the length and breadth of the country, always by Brahmins), we find ourselves in the presence of the most comprehensive mind that ever contemplated Hindu life. The compassion of Buddha, perhaps, looms greater across the centuries, but in dealing with social problems his very tenderness and spiritual fire make him second to Krishna, who was always calm, broad, and consistently national in his outlook. We must accept the Gita as an authoritative pronouncement on Hindu society. And the Gita rings with the constantly reiterated implication that "he who attains to God is the true *man*," while it interprets all life and responsibility as a means to this end. Thus, "Better one's own duty, though imperfect, than the duty of another well discharged. Better death in one's own duty; the duty of another brings on danger." We have to remember, too, that the Gita is made up of the very best of the Vedas and Upanishads, and was specially written for the benefit of women and the working classes, who, as destitute of classical learning, had little chance of studying these great scriptures. But its contents were to depend upon Brahmin effort for promulgation. Another witness to the fact that spirituality has always been regarded in India as the common human possession lies in the Hindu word for religion itself—*dharmma*, or *the man-ness* of man. This is very striking. The whole weight of the conception is shifted away from creed, much more from caste or race, to that which is universal and permanent in each and every human being. And, last of all, we may remember that the greatest historical teachers of Hinduism—Rama, Krishna, and Buddha, besides many of the Upanishadic period—were men of the second, or military, caste.

No, the Brahmin was never in any sense the privileged monopolist of religion: he was a common *channel* of religious lore, because his actual function was Sanskrit culture, and Sanskrit happens to be the vehicle of the most perfect religious thought that the world ever produced, but "realisation" itself has always been recognised as a very different matter from this, and, Brahmin or non-Brahmin, has been accepted wherever it appeared. The advantage that the priestly caste did undoubtedly enjoy, however, lay in the fact that in their case the etiquette of rank led directly to the highest inspiration, as the scholar's life, even in its routine, will be nearest to that of the saint.

One peculiarity of the place of the religious life in the Indian system is that it is an inclusive term for all forms of higher individuation. Theoretically, to the Hindu mind, all genius is inspiration, the perception of unity; and the mathematics of Euclid or the sculpture of Michael Angelo would be as authentic an expression of the religious consciousness as the sainthood of Francis. Only the result of this method of interpretation is that sainthood takes precedence of all others as the commonest form of greatness. Scientific research, as in the astronomy of Bhashkar Acharya and the psychology of Patanjali, has not had sufficient opportunity of securing defined and independent scope. And literature has been yoked to the car of mythology as much as the art of mediæval Italy.

Nevertheless, India is too well acquainted with genius to forget that the caste of the spirit is beyond human limitation, often beyond recognition. It is held that the best lower men can do for that brotherhood which asserts itself in the consciousness of greatness is to give it freedom. Hence a man can always be released from social obligations if he desire to live the life of ideas, of the soul. Only, it is held that if he will not fulfil the law, neither shall he add to the burdens of the community. So he who claims to be one of the great spiritual beyond-castes must renounce family and property, relying upon the charity of men for his daily bread, and knowing well that for any work of scholarship —such as the observatories at Benares and Jeypore —a Hindu govsrnment at least would provide him ample means. It is only as long as one avails oneself of the benefits of the social structure that it is held not unreasonable to require conformity to its usages.

This renunciation is *Sannyas*, the Indian form ot monasticism, and Sannyas, theories to the contrary notwithstanding, has always been open to all castes. Indeed, it is held that when the responsibilities of life are over, a man's duty is to leave the world and spend the remainder of his days in that state; and in some parts of Northern India one meets with "Tyagi Mehtars," or monastics who were by birth the lowest of the low.

Theoretically, the monk is caste-fellow of the whole world, prepared to eat with any one; and where, by sheer dint of spirituality and self-discipline, such a feeling is realised, every Hindu in India considers the broken bread of this lover of mankind as sacramental food. It is usual, too, to eat from the hands of holy men without inquiry as to their standing when in the world.

One of the most interesting points in all this to a Western mind is the difference implied and established between the caste of priests or chaplains on the one hand, and the fact of spiritual realisation, outside all caste, on the other. Nothing in the Indian thought about life can be more striking than this. The family chaplain in Bengal may be the official teacher, but every man and woman discards his authority silently the instant they find some soul (in the world or out of it; it may be husband or child, or the holy man living in his garden; usually it is an ascetic), with a quickening spiritual touch upon their own. He or she then becomes the *guru*, or teacher, and this relationship is made the central fact of life.

The appearance of this new teacher, when he is powerful enough to be an important social phenomenon, is the historic origin of almost all new castes. The Sikh nation was formed in this way by a succession of gurus. Chaitanya welcomed all castes to Vaishnavism and made it possible for them to rise thereby. The scavengers, too low to venture to claim either Hinduism or Mohammedanism as their own, were raised in consideration and self-respect by Guru Nanuk and Lal Begi Mehtar—the last a saint of their own degree.

The preacher arises and proclaims the new idea. He gathers about him men of all classes: the educated won to the service of his thought, the ignorant swept in by the radiance of his personality. Amongst his disciples distinctions of caste break down. The whole group is stamped with his character and prestige. Eventually, if it contain a preponderance of Brahmin elements, it may take rank with the best, carrying certain individuals up with it. But if it be composed chiefly of the scum of society, it will remain little considered; and yet, in the strength of its religious and intellectual significance may certainly claim to have progressed beyond its original point. Such is likely to be the fate of the present Christian converts. Those who are recruited from the lowest pariahs may acquire a certain prestige from their new faith and take a better place in the social scale, consequently, in centuries to come. At the same time we must not forget that forty or fifty years ago, conversions were made that undoubtedly involved great sacrifices, and the descendants of these Christians may lose rather than gain in the long run.

Taking the history of Hinduism as a whole, we observe a great systole and diastole of caste, the Buddhist and the present Christian periods ranking as well-marked eras of fusion, while the intervening centuries are characterised by progressive definition, broken every now and then by a wave of reform which thought itself a movement towards caste abolition, but ended simply in the formation of a new group. For this is the fact in which all would-be reformations in India find at once their opportunity and their limit. It may now be taken as proved that in order to affect caste widely, the agitator would need to aim deeper than the external phenomena, at underlying spiritual impulses.

If this theory of caste be valid, then, we find that the word signifies not so much mere rank in society as the standard of honour which is associated with rank. And as the private's conduct may be governed as much as his officer's by enlightened self-respect, we have seen that honour is something which applies to the whole of society equally. Even Tennyson, it will be remembered, pictures the country youth as outvaunting Lady Clara Vere de Vere in her pride of birth. The word caste, therefore, is by no means that antithesis of *democracy* which has been so commonly assumed.

Neither, amongst a people familiar with the process of self-organisation, would it prove any barrier to efficient co-operation. For the one essential to this power is an established habit of ignoring all points of mutual difference not germane to the matter in hand. What we call good-breeding, or what India calls *caste*, ought to make this easier. For any group of men met together for a common purpose find their individual rights secured to them in this way, and are free, by age-long acceptance, from any suspicion of another's desire to interfere with them. This is a basis of strength and not of weakness; so that it seems, if Indian men and women are not at present capable of combined action to any great degree, it is a matter of their own neglect of the habit, and not a necessary consequence of their institutions. We need not too readily accept the statement of such weakness, either, as infallible. My own observation has been that the Hindu people are capable enough of vigorous co-operation along the lines natural to them, those of the undivided family, the village community, and others. That inability which Europeans would show to face these tests, they may be expected to display before ours.

To be absolutely just, however, we must admit that the observance of caste law has entailed many foolish and irritating losses upon society during the last fifty years. We have seen that there are definite reasons, not wanting in cogency, why a man of good birth should not eat in all companies, or of food cooked by hands supposed less cleanly. Such rules, however, cannot be kept by those who, for any reason, cross the seas to Europe. This fact, more than any other detail, makes it a matter of out-casting to take the journey, and persecutions have sometimes ensued which are shocking to contemplate. A man may care little about the loss of station for his own sake, but the shoe pinches when he finds himself unable to make worthy marriages for his daughters; hence he will often submit to a heavy fine in order to buy back his position. This rouses the cupidity of ignorant and conventional persons who happen to have authority with the stay-at-home community, and such are apt to be unscrupulous in bringing about the ruin or recantation of any who resist their power. This is a series of events which does occur occasionally; but it need not be supposed that every Europe-returning Hindu who is kept at arm's length is a martyr. There is an element of distrust for the moral results of a visit to the West in the situation; and this is not altogether unreasonable. It is chiefly with regard to possibilities of political, practical, or technical education that caste deterrence is to be regretted, and it is obvious that as communities progress in the power of estimating modern conditions, they must recognise the suicidal nature of such an attitude. Yet it is curious to note here how caste may become thus a very real instrument of equality, for the power of the individual to advance is by this means kept strictly in ratio to the thinking of the society in which he lives. This fact is characteristic. The good of caste, of race, of family stands first, and only second that of the individual man or woman in India. To take another plane. Let a man of the lower castes become wealthy, and he is compelled to educate men of his own rank to marry his daughters. Thus the group to which he owes birth, vigour, and development receives from him again the benefits of his life's work. This is the exact opposite of the European device, where the upper class absorbs money, talent, and beauty from the lower, while that is continually recruited by the failures from above.

The fact that every human force is polar in its moral activity needs little demonstration in the case of social pride. Every day we see this working on the one hand for the highest idealism, on the other for revolting egotism. Social exclusiveness may be condoned, it may even be robbed of its sting but, especially when coupled with personal exultation, it can never be made anything but vulgar-looking to the disinterested outsider. It is not to be supposed that Indian caste forms any exception to this rule of double effect. Nevertheless, it is well to understand the conditions of the sentiment, perceiving how inevitably this very thing repeats itself wherever two physically-distinguishable races are found side by side.

And it cannot be denied that great benefits as well as great evils have accrued from caste. It is an institution that makes Hindu society the most eclectic with regard to ideas in the world. In India all religions have taken refuge*—the Parsi before

* Parsi, Jew, Christian.—The Parsis took refuge in India a thousand years ago, fleeing before the Mohammedan conquest of Persia. There are ancient communities of Jews and Christians also from Asia Minor and Syria.

the tide of Mussulman conquest; the Christians of Syria; the Jews. And they have received more than shelter—they have had the hospitality of a world that had nothing to fear from the foreigner who came in the name of freedom of conscience. Caste made this possible, for in one sense it is the social formulation of defence minus all elements of aggression. Again, surely it is something that in a country conquered for a thousand years the door-keeper of a viceroy's palace would feel his race too good to share a cup of water with the ruler of all India. We do not easily measure the moral strength that is here involved, for the habit of guarding the treasure of his birth for an unborn posterity feeds a deep, undying faith in destiny in the Hindu heart. "To-day here, to-morrow gone," says the most ignorant *sotto voce* as he looks at the foreigner, and the unspoken refrain of his thought is, "I and mine abide for ever." Caste is race-continuity; it is the historic sense; it is the dignity of tradition and of purpose for the future. It is even more: it is the familiarity of a whole people in all its grades with the one supreme human motive—the notion of *noblesse oblige*. For though it is true that all men are influenced by this principle, it is also probably true that only the privileged are very conscious of the fact. Is caste, then, simply a burden, to be thrown off lightly, as a thing irksome and of little moment?

And yet, if India is ever to regain national efficiency, this old device of the forefathers must be modified in the process,—exactly how, the Indian people themselves can alone determine. For India to-day has lost national efficiency. This fact there is no gainsaying. Her needs now are not what they were yesterday. The Brahmins lose distinctiveness in these days of cheap printing and widespread literacy. But this only means that the country requires multiplied methods of self-expression as the goal and summit of her national endeavour. She wants a greater flexibility, perhaps, a readier power of self-adjustment than she has ever had. But it ought to come in an influx of consciousness of those great spiritual tides on whose surface all questions of caste and non-caste can be lifted into new and higher inter-relations. Chief among all her needs is that of a passionate drawing together amongst her people themselves. The cry of home, of country, of place is yet to be heard by the soul of every Indian man and woman in Hindustan, and following hard upon it must sound the overtones of labour and of race.

Then the question of whether to walk or not in the ways of the forefathers will be lost in the knowledge of the abundant power to hew out new roads, as those fathers did before them. Has India the possibilities still left in her own nature which can bring to her such an epoch ?

There are some who believe that there is no task beyond the ultimate power of the Hindu peoples to perform. The nation that has stood so persistently for righteousness through untold ages has conserved such vast springs of vigour in itself, as must ultimately enable her to command Destiny. The far-seeing wisdom and gentleness of her old constitution may unfit her for the modern world, but they are a sure proof, nevertheless, of her possession of sufficient sense of affairs to guide her to a full development once more.

For, after all, who were these old forefathers, with their marvellous cunning ? What inspired them so to construct the social framework that every act of rebellion and invasion should end henceforth only in contributing a new morsel of colour to fit into the old mosaic ? Ah, who were they indeed ? We may well ask, for have we not all this time been calling by their name one far greater than they, one infinitely more deserving of our reverence—the Communal Consciousness, namely, of a mighty patient people, toiling on and on through the ages up the paths of knowledge, destroying never, assimilating always, what they gain of truth and science, and hesitating only a little before fresh developments, because they are so preoccupied with the problems of the past that they do not realise that that stage is done, and that the sun is risen to-day on a new landscape, confronting them with fresh perils and unthought-of difficulties?

CHAPTER IX

THE SYNTHESIS OF INDIAN THOUGHT

When existence was not, nor non-existence,
When the world was not, nor the sky beyond,
What covered the mist? By whom was it contained?
What was in those thick depths of darkness?

When death was not, nor immortality,
When night was not separate from day,
Then *That* vibrated motionless, one with Its own glory,
And beside *That*, nothing else existed.

When darkness was hidden in darkness,
Undistinguished, like one mass of water,
Then did *That* which was covered with darkness
Manifest Its glory by heat.

Now first arose Desire, the primal seed of mind,
[The sages have seen all this in their hearts,
Separating existence from non-existence.]
Its rays spread above, around, and below,
The glory became creative.
The Self, sustained as cause below,
Projected, as Effect, above.

Who then understood? Who then declared
How came into being this Projected?
Lo, in its wake followed even the Gods,
Who can say, therefore, whence It came?
Whence arose this projected, and whether sustained or not,
He alone, O Beloved, who is its Ruler in the highest heaven knoweth,
Nay, it may be that even he knoweth it not!

RIG. VEDA: Hymn of Creation.

I

LIKE the delicate charm that is common to honourable women; like the distinctive greatness of saints and heroes; like the intellectual breadth of a university city; like all the finest things in the world in fact, Indian thought had remained till the year 1893 without a definition, and without a name. For the word *dharmma* can in no sense be taken as the name of a religion. It is the essential quality, the permanent, unfluctuating core, of substance,—the *man-ness* of man, *life-ness* of life, as it were. But as such it may assume any form, according to the secret of the individuality we are considering. To the artist his art, to the man of science his science, to the monk his vow, to the soldier his sovereign's name, to each believer his own particular belief—any of these, or all, may be *dharmma*. There is indeed another, and collective sense—somewhat akin to the English *commonwealth*, or, better still, perhaps, translated as *the national righteousness*—but even this does not connote a creed. It applies to that whole system of complex action and interaction, on planes moral, intellectual, economic, industrial, political, and domestic—which we know as India or the national habit. It was for this *dharmma* that the Rani of Jhansi fought. By their attitude to it Pathan, Mogul, and the Englishman, are judged, each in his turn, by the Indian peasantry. As head of this system, Judisthira, the Indian Charlemagne, received the name by which the people know him to this day, of Dharmma-Raja. And what this *dharmma* was, in all its bearings, is perhaps best laid down in the charge of the dying Bhishma to the future sovereigns of India, in the eighteenth book of the Mahabharata.

It is clear that such a conception is very inadequately rendered by the Engllsh word "religion." It is clear also that to dissect out and set in order the distinctively religious elements in an idea so definite at its centre, and so nebulous at its edges—claiming thereby to have defined the religion of the Indian peoples—would be a task of extreme difficulty.

It must have been in the face of just such problems that Max Müller exclaimed, "Ancient words are round, and modern square!"

As the forest grows spontaneously, of many kinds, each like all the others only in the common fact of the quest of light, and every plant having a complete right to regard its own as the chosen seed, so amongst the Hindu people, up to the twentieth century of this Christian era, grew faiths and creeds. Islam itself was scarcely an exception to this rule. For the spirit that makes a township, after learning English, differentiate itself sharply into Hindu and Mohammedan social cliques, is of modern growth. It appears to be a result of that false interpretation which reads the history of India as an account of the struggle between the two ideas. In the life of the villages there is no such strong distinction. In Bengal and Behar, the sons of Hindu and Mohammedan gentlemen grow up in the closest fraternity and fellowship. In the North-West Provinces they mingle their names. In the Moslem zenanas of the same districts the Hindu babies of the village are privileged guests. Every Hindu guru accepts Mohammedan as well as Hindu disciples. Every Mohammedan fakir is sought by Hindu as well as Mohammedan devotees. In the South, narrowly orthodox as the South is counted, the proudest feature of Trevandrum is the shrine dedicated to a Mohammedan princess, who forsook courts and palaces for the worship of Trevandrum's local god. Over and over again, in the political world, have the armies of Delhi and the nawabs been led to victory by Hindu generals; and in every Native State to this day will be found positions of responsibility and power assigned to men whose creed is that which the sovereign's is not. A more beautiful tribute was never surely paid than that spoken of the Mahratta queen: "she was peculiarly kind and considerate to such of her subjects as differed from her in faith." But indeed the intolerance of Mohammedanism itself has been grossly exaggerated by Christian observers, who seem curiously incompetent to grasp the secret of an Eastern attitude. This intolerance could never, for instance, be compared with that of theRoman Church. The necessity of making a strong and competent nation out of a few warring tribes led to the enunciation of a brief and simple religious thesis; but the Prophet did not fail, in true Asiatic fashion, to remind his people that "God is the God of all creatures, not of one section only," and to exempt especially from condemnation all the alien religions definitely known to him, namely, Christianity and Judaism, "the peoples of the Book." Truly the quarrel of that stern spirit of righteousness was with unfaithfulness, not with other faiths, however strongly, under unforeseen military and political exigencies, it might seem to lend itself to the contrary interpretation. The fact that Mohammedans have sometimes held another opinion is no argument as to the teaching of their religion in its purity, and it must be remembered that "dog of an infidel" is an expression hurled as freely against Spaniard and Crusader, as ever against what Christians called a Pagan. No. The feud between Delhi and Ghazni was no more a battle between *Din* and *Dharmma* than was that so long existing between France and England, the combat of the Catholic against the Protestant Churches. Even Sikh and Mahratta risings were only the psychological transfer of regional power-centres. The famous jewelled shawl of the Hindu State of Baroda was made quite naturally under the old *règime*, to be sent to the tomb of Mohammed at Medina!

Some air of the deserts, some tradition of the pastoral habit, some strong memory of Persia and Arabia, must indeed have come with the successful invader to make the stay-at-home invaded resenting and distrustful. But the talk about cow-killing can hardly be taken as sincere, since in that case the arms of chivalrous Hindus would to-day be turned against a newer power. It must be understood as purely symbolic of the strained relations naturally existing between industrialised agricultural communities on the one hand, and on the other the militant sons of the desert accustomed to live by keeping and killing flocks and herds. But the same process that tamed the nomad into a member of a peasant community, and converted boatmen and tillers of the soil into Mussulmans, minimised in course of time even these differences of association. The familiar sight of the Mohammedan *bhisti*, holding his goatskin below the hydrant-mouth for water, and the Hindu water-carrier with his earthen pot coming in his turn, is an instance of the contrast as it now exists. Two different civilisations stand side by side, but they are friendly castes, not rival nationalities.

In the religious consciousness of Islam there is nothing that is without analogy amongst the faiths that have sprung up on Indian soil. Every one is tolerant of the idea of "the one true church," for it is held by Hindus to be a necessity of the early stages of religious development. Allah is of course the Personal God: but then the worshipper of Vishnu has always had to admit his brother's right to offer praise to Siva, though the name left himself unstirred. Why not Allah, therefore, equally? The Hindu uses images: to the Mussulman the image is abhorrent. True, but every Hindu hopes to escape some day from the necessity of using images. Who is not touched by the devotional custom of Hindu women, bathing the reflection of the Holy Child in the mirror and saying, "This which we bathe is not the image: neither is the image He whom we worship!" Are not the saints for ever telling the idolater that even to name the Infinite Unity is sacrilege? And what Mohammedan saint has failed to say the same? The dispute about the image, in the light of such facts, becomes a mere difference of opinion as to the use of the concrete in the early stages of an education. Indeed, Hinduism itself has shown its power in modern times to throw out sects that decry the use of images as strongly as Islam.

Hence it would appear that the important points at issue between Hindus and Mussulmans are rather details of purification and domestic practice, than religious or doctrinal. This fact becomes increasingly evident as the higher phases of the two faiths are reached. For the more completely either is realised, the more perfectly is it fused in the other. Sufi-ism* leads the soul by love, and the Vedanta leads it by knowledge, love, or emancipated motive, as the case may be; but for both alike the theme is of a common goal, where all sense of difference shall cease, and the small self be swallowed up in the universal. Of each of the two faiths, then, it may be said, that it has nothing to lose and everything to gain by the more complete development of the other. Mohammed, Krishna, Buddha, Sankaracharya,† are not so many deplorable obstacles in each other's

* Sufi-ism.—A mystic set of Mohammedans. It rose in Persia, and at first suffered persecution, because the doctrine of the one-ness of the soul with the Divine sounded to the orthodox Mohammedan like a suggestion that a creature could be "partner with God." The Sufis now maintain secrecy as to their experiences and convictions. Their doctrines and those of Hindu Vedantism are practically identical.

† Sankaracharya.—"The father of modern Hinduism," often foolishly referred to as "a persecutor of Buddhism." A great saint and scholar. Born in Malabar, Southern India, 788 A.D. Wrote several famous commentaries, notably that on the Vedanta-Sutra, in which he formulated what is known as the philosophic doctrine of "Adwaita." He is said to have died at the age of thirty-two.

paths, but rather widely separated examples of a common type—the radiant Asiatic personage, whose conception of nationality lies in a national righteousness, and whose right to be a leader of men rests on the fact that he has seen God face to face. Such souls cannot fail to recognise each other, and the Prophet was not slow to salute Moses and the Christ, the only examples of his own order whose names he knew.

Thus it is easy to realise that as long as Hinduism remained nameless and vague, the sense of difference between itself and Islam was also obscure, subject to all the mitigating influences of a common Orientalism, intensified here and there doubtless by political ideas, but tempered again by manifold social and economic bonds. And if, with definition, the Indian religions are to take on a more sectarian character, is it not clear that this is only in order to be joined again with the faith of Arabia, in a new and deeper consciousness of that which is their actual ground of union—the Asiatic synthesis of life?

It is not difficult to understand the mental outlook that is expressed in the namelessness of Hinduism. An immense people, filling a vast territory, unconscious of the completeness of their boundaries, or of any sharpness of contrast between themselves and neighbouring nations, were necessarily incapable of summing up their thought, to give it a name. A knowledge of limits and of difference there must be, before there can be definition, and it is only when India sees herself reflected as a whole in the glass of a foreign administration and a foreign language that she can dream of limitation. Besides, in things religious, what was there that was not included within the Hindu area? If, crossing the Himalayas and reaching China and Mongolia, men came in contact with unknown rites and superstitions, they could always supply parallel or analogy from their home life and association. Strange and powerful goddesses were adored in China. But the worship of the Mother is so old in India that its origin is lost in the very night of time. What an age of common faiths that must have been that left us the Virgin Kanya (Kanya Kumari) as tutelary deity of Cape Comorin, and Kwannyon the Mother as the giver of all blessings, in Japan to this day! Who is to say which is older, *Kari*, the Mother-Queen of Heaven, of Chinese mythology, or *Kali* of Bengal? Even these conceptions, however, dating as they clearly must from the days of that matriarchate when nations and races were not yet differentiated—even these do not represent the earliest stratum of religious thought in India or in Asia.

All through the Old Testament, and throughout the story of the rise of Mohammedanism, we hear of "stones" as objects of worship. It is the black and mystic Kaaba, that is to this day the symbol of their unity to all the peoples of Islam. And throughout India still there are races of working folk who ask no better symbol of divinity than rude stones, selected with some care possibly, and then set up, singly or in a row, perhaps in an enclosure, perhaps not, to be regarded henceforth as objects of reverence. The people who use these emblems—for they cannot be regarded as images—may be anything, from sudras, or peasants, as I have seen them in the South, to Bhutias, or gipsy-like wanderers, as one meets with them in the Himalayas.

Everywhere in common life the miraculous elements are fire and light. And perhaps it is natural that oil, with its mystic power of leaping into flame, should be the characteristic offering in the worship of these stones. A Bhutia shrine will sometimes contain nothing but lamps. These are small and made of iron, like round-bowled dessertspoons at right angles to the handle, which is a spike stuck into the ground, and I have seen as many as sixteen or seventeen in one tiny temple. There was here neither image nor symbol other than the lamps themselves, and the pilgrim on leaving would tear off a shred of his garment, and tie it to a bush or a tree close by, there joining hundreds of tokens like itself of the wayfaring congregation whose spirits had met unseen in a common act of adoration. But the place, as is always the case with these peasant oratories, was where the view was finest, and the cry of the soul to commune with Nature most intense. Sometimes the sacred stones themselves are smeared with oil, for the very touch of the wondrous fluid that nourishes light seems to be holy.

To richer races in India only clarified butter is good enough for use in the service of the altar, and we of Europe require the great wax tapers. But can we not trace through all these a single common process of the sanctification of labour by the products of labour? "We worship the Ganges with the water of the Ganges, but we *must* worship," said a Hindu. Similarly does the peasant dream of the sacred oil, and the pastoral Toda* worship his cow-bells. Is it not true that if all could be blotted out in a moment from the human memory, the Eucharist and the sanctuary-lamp from Christianity, flickering light and fragrant flowers from the Mussulman grave, oils and fruits and incense from the Eastern worshipper, it would only be to spring forth fresh again to-morrow—corn, wine, and oil to the peasant, scented gums to the lover of gardens, the Good Shepherd the ideal of the herdsman, the ship of salvation the hope of fisher-folk? What are mythologies after all but the jewel-casket of humanity,

* Toda.—An aboriginal tribe in the Neilgherris.

by means of which its wealth of dreams and loves and sighs in every generation becomes the unperishing and imperishable treasure of the after-comers? The mystery of the birth of faith is about us always.

All the great Asiatic faiths—that is to say, the world-religions—would seem to have been born of the overflow of something that may be called tentatively the Aryan thought-power, upon the social and religious formations of earlier ages. Taoism in China, Zoroastrianism in Persia, and Hinduism in India, are all as three different applications of a single original fund of insight and speculation, and Islam itself has incorporated Sufi-ism after reaching the Aryan region. Doubtless of all these India developed her share of the inheritance with the greatest freedom and perfection, but we recognise common elements in all alike.

II

As the basis of Indian thought rests deep in the very foundation of human evolution, so it has not failed, at each new point in the historic development, to add something to the great superstructure. The whole story of India may be read in a philosophic idea. The constitutional ceremonies of the kingdom of Travancore contain clear indications of the transition from the matriarchate which was probably characteristic of the old Dravidian * civilisation, to the patriarchate, which was Aryan. In the yearly

* Dravidian civilisation.—The country of Dravida is that in the south of the Indian Peninsula, and includes Malabar. The languages of this region are non-Sanskritic, and the architecture peculiar and imposing. Some scholars are inclined to suppose a common origin for the Dravidian, Babylonian, and ancient Egyptian civilisations.

village-worship of the heroic figures of the "Mahabharata" which is common throughout the South, we have what may be the effort of distant peoples to include themselves in the "Great India" of Bhishma, Judisthira, and the national Epics.* The charge of country gunpowder which is fired off in the temples of the Southern Dekkan on festival days is sufficient evidence that orthodoxy was once aggressive, eager, absorbent of things new, fearful of nothing, and friendly to advance. It is a popular superstition that the East stands still. Children observe no motion of the stars. But the fact is that one generation is no more like another at Benares than in Paris. Every saint, every poet, adds something to the mighty pile which is unlike all that went before. And this is quite as true of the thought expressed in the vernaculars, as of the all-dominating culture contained in the classic Sanskrit. Chaitanya in Bengal, the Ten Gurus of the Sikhs, Ram Das and Tokuram in Maharashtra, and Ramanuja in the South—each of these was to his own time as the very personification of the national philosophy, relating it again in its wholeness to the common life. Each such great saint appears to the people as the incarnation, the revelation, of themselves and their own powers, and the church by him founded becomes a nation. Thus arose the Mahratta Confederacy. Thus arose the kingdom of Lahore. And far away in Arabia, Islam formed itself in the same fashion. For the law that we are considering is not peculiar to India; it is common to the whole of Asiatic life.

The Hindu world in its entirety, then, is one with

* In Southern India, rude figures of men and horses, of heroic size, are made of clay, hard-baked, and kept in enclosures outside the villages for annual worship. The illiterate worshipper explains these figures as likenesses of the characters in the Mahabharata.

the highest philosophy of Hinduism. The much-talked of Vedanta is only the theoretic aspect of that synthesis whose elements make up the common life. The most unlettered, idolatrous-seeming peasant will talk, if questioned, of the immanence of God. He recognises that Christianity is fundamentally true, because the missionaries are clear that there is but one Supreme. The question, What would happen could the nation be divorced for a single generation from the knowledge of Sanskrit ? is only another way of asking, What is the actual dynamic force existing at a given moment in the Hindu people ? What are the characteristic ideas that are now an inbred habit, past the reach of authority to substantiate, or disaster to shake ? It is given only to great events and to the imagination of genius to find the answer to such questions. Yet some indications there are, of what that answer might be.

Buddhism was the name given to the Hinduism of the first few centuries of the Christian era, when precipitated in a foreign consciousness. What authority did it claim ? What explanations did it give of the existence of the physical universe ? Of the soul ? Of evil ? What did it offer to humanity as the goal of the ethical struggle ? The answer to these questions will certainly have to be given in terms of ideas, or variants of ideas, derived from the pre-existent stock of Hinduism. And so, though the particular formulation may be regarded as heresy, the significance of its testimony on the point we are considering cannot be disputed. It must be remembered that there never was, in India, a religion known as Buddhism, with temples and priests of its own order. There was a tendency towards popularising truths that had previously been regarded as fit only for the learned, and there was an immense unofficial enthusiasm for a towering personality, doubtless, and for the interpretations which were identified with him, even as there is in Bengal to-day for Chaitanya. There came also to be a vast imperial organisation, highly centralised, coherent in all its parts, full of the geographical consciousness, uttering itself in similar architectural forms in the East and West of India, passionately eager to unify and elevate the people and to adorn the land. This Indian Empire was in full and living communication with China, Japan, Syria, and Egypt. It had traffic and commerce by land and sea. It sent abroad ambassadors, merchants and missionaries. And within its own territories it made roads, planted trees and orchards, dug wells, established hospitals, and insisted on the cessation of violence even towards dumb creatures.*

Just as the Protestant Reformation, releasing the mental energy of the people from thraldom to authoritative commentaries, has been the power within the rise of modern Europe, so the kernel and spring of the Asokan and succeeding empires was a similar assertion—not of the right of private judgment: this never required vindication in India: but—of the equal right of every section of society to enter the super-social, or monastic life. For we must not forget that in the East enfranchisement is always primarily religious and moral, not political. Power civic and national is there amongst the direct effects of the higher consciousness, never its cause. It is a man's right to renounce the world, and not manhood suffrage, which constitutes his equality with the highest. This sudden realisation of the spiritual life in all parts of society at once conferred on every man under Buddhism, whatever his birth or position, the right to make his opinion felt, the strength to exercise his full weight of moral in-

* Asoka's inscriptions on the Dhauli rock, Orissa, and a Girnar in Gujrat.

fluence. The result was an immense consolidation and blossoming of nationality. Men felt that they walked on air. They were born to receive and pass on the great message of human brotherhood. They were to go out into *all* the world and preach the Gospel to *every* creature. What must not have been the faith and enthusiasm of the common people, when merchants, traders, and caravan-servants could suffice to make a permanent contribution to the religion of the powerful Empire of China? It was a great age, and only those who have seen the colossal fragments which remain of it to this day can form any idea of its wealth and vigour.

And yet Asoka's conversion had not been to a new religion, but only into the piety of his time. "I, King Piyadasi, beloved of the gods, obtained true intelligence ten years after my anointing." Hence the thing that we call Buddhism ends its career in India very gradually. He who has first visited Ellora * is surprised, on entering Elephanta, † to find the Buddha-like figure on his left to be Siva, and the Triumph of Durga on his right. At Ellora itself there must be a gap of centuries between the cathedral-like caves of the Thin Thal ‡ and of Kailash. § Yet even there we see the solitary figure of the teaching or the meditating Buddha give place by degrees to a rich pantheon of devas and guardian kings. But the hope and delight that are expressed

* Ellora.—Buddhist cave-temples close to the north-western frontier of the Nizam's dominions. The town of Rosa, containing the tomb of Aurungzeeb, is close by; and the whole is a few miles from Daulatabad, the ancient Deogiri.

† Elephanta.—A series of cave-temples on an island in the Bay of Bombay, between the second and the seventh century.

‡ The Thin Thal.—A cave-temple at Ellora which consists of three tiers or storeys. Hence its name. The most perfect of the non-Brahmanical structures.

§ Kailash.—The most ornate and modern of all the cave-temples at Ellora. Cut with marvellous elaboration out of solid rock.

so freely in the architecture and sculpture, and in the cosmopolitan intercourse of the Buddhist period die away imperceptibly into the rich imagery of the Puranic age,* and the manifold social and political problems of Sankaracharya and the age of chivalry.

The common tendency of Brahmins and yogis had been to hold out the emancipation of the whole nature through self-discipline as the goal of endeavour. This doctrine came to be regarded in a loose way as characteristically Hindu. The Buddhist conviction was, on the other hand, that the same goal was to be reached, not so much by a gradual ripening of the self, as by ceasing from the illusion of egoism. Nirvana, not Mukti, became the watchword. The fact that these two ideas are related to each other as the obverse and reverse of a coin, cannot have escaped the contemporary mind. But its own generation must have given a more antipodal value to the divergence than is obvious to Western thought at the present day. It would seem to them to include all possible theological differences, and it is not unlikely that this fact contributed largely to the belief so explicitly stated in the Gita, and so markedly Indian, that all religions express a single truth.

In the period of the Upanishads, the conception of Brahman—the one real appearing as many—had been reached. This implies the doctrine of Maya, or the illusion of things, as popularised under Buddhism. It is clear that in this theory the whole question of the origin of evil is put aside. Evil and good are

* The Puranic age.—The Puranas are the third class of Hindu sacred literature, the first being the Vedas and Upanishads, and the second the national Epics. They consist of a series of books of very mixed character, of which the representative specimens were written between the sixth and twelfth centuries. Hence this period is spoken of as "the Puranic Age."

alike shadows on the wall, cast by our sense of personal convenience in magnified and distorted form. The saints recognise neither pain, insult, nor self-interest, being swallowed up in the joy of God.

The cyclic manifestation of the Cosmos—never created, but eternally self-existent, self-destroying, self-repeating—was another idea sown broadcast by Buddhist teachers. Here we have an interpretation that is significant of the immense scientific energy that has always gone hand in hand with Hindu religious speculation, making the spirit of research inherent in the spirit of devotion. Perhaps had orthodoxy offered the same resistance to science in the East that it did in the West, Indian investigation would have appeared more imposing to-day in the eyes of foreigners. But the only thing that the Indian priesthood has conceived itself set to guard has been the social system. It has opposed nothing save social aberrations. Knowledge has gone unhindered. And it will not be difficult to show that the much vaunted science of Moorish Spain was neither more nor less than the tapping of Indian culture for the modern world.

But perhaps the most significant of all points in the Buddhist propaganda is its assumption that the word of the Blessed One Himself is all-sufficient authority. Hinduism recognises only one proof, and that is direct perception. Even the sacred writings give as their sanction the direct perception of saints and sages, and the Vedas themselves declare that man must reach beyond the Vedas. That is to say, the books allege as their authority that realisation out of which they were written. The Jains refuse the authority of the Vedic texts. But there is less divergence between them and other sects of

Hinduism than would appear on the surface. Common language and the historic acceptance of the race alike, lead up to the last great pronouncement on the subject—"By the Vedas no books are meant. They mean the accumulated treasury of spiritual laws discovered by different persons in different times."

"It is Veda," we say in India of a statement which we perceive to be profoundly true. It is held in a general way that there are two classes of Scripture, one Vedas, the other Puranas. Vedas are eternal truth. Puranas are characterised by containing stories of the creation and destruction of the world, tales of the life and death of holy persons and avatars, accounts of their miracles, and so on. These elements are commonly mixed up, but can easily be disentangled. Thus, when the Christian Gospel says, "Thou shalt love the Lord thy God with all thy heart and with all thy soul," it speaks Veda; but when it says, "Jesus was born in Bethlehem of Judea in the days of Herod the king" it is only a Puran, and may contain some elements of error.

And so, if the word be rightly defined, it may be said that the Vedas themselves are the sanction of Buddhism, of Mohammedanism, of Christianity, and of Confucianism; but it may at the same time be claimed on behalf of India that there, and not in the West, has this fact been understood.

Some of the greatest of French and English thinkers hold that the history of the West is made into a unity by the evolution of science and its progressive application to life, from the sixth century before Christ to the present day. These thinkers maintain that Greece, Imperial Rome, and the Catholic Church have been the three integral formative influences of what we call the European mind. To the student of Oriental history it appears equally clear that the history of Asia is that of a single living organism, of which India may be taken as the heart and focus. Regarded thus, in relation to its surroundings, the culture to which we give the name of Indian thought becomes likewise a unity, as clear, as continuous, as consistent in its development as is the evolution of the scientific idea in the West. Considered as an appanage of Europe, India is meaningless; taken in and for herself, and for that to which she rightly belongs, it need not surprise us if we find her the essential factor of human advance in the future as in the past.

III

India is the heart of Asia. Hinduism is a convenient name for the nexus of Indian thought. It would appear that it takes some thousand to fifteen hundred years to work out a single rhythm of its great pulsation. For this is about the period that divides the war of the Mahabharata from Buddha, Buddha from Sankaracharya, and Sankaracharya from Ramakrishna, in whom the immense pile reaches the crowning self-consciousness. Of the long prehistoric evolution that went to the building up of Mahabharata, Great India, the heroic age, we can say little, for nothing is left to us, save the legend of Sita and Rama, out of the night of time. Yet we kow that this period must have been long. Three thousand years seems not too much, if enough, to allow. Behind this again loom up the millenniums spent on the tableland of Central Asia, that head-water of world-civilisation where Aryan man entered the patriarchate, and closed the account of his first combat with Nature, having tamed the beasts, learned the use of tools, domesticated corn and fire, produced the fruit-trees, and divided the week.* Of the sublime dreams, the poetry and song with which he consoled himself during those ages of herculean struggle, the fragments known as the "Rig Veda" still remain. And we learn therein how broad was his outlook upon Nature, even as that of the mind that declared "and the evening and the morning were the first day." How long did it last? Was it ten thousand years? Were there another five thousand before the war of Mahabharata . . . . However this be, the enthusiasm of succeeding periods strikes us as extraordinary.

There is no question that the characteristic product of the civilisation that succeeded the Great War was the forest-universities, notes of whose sessions have become the Sutras and Upanishads. But we must not forget also that during the same period the Vedas was written down, and the searching scrutiny of society initiated which was later to result in those accumulations of reverent and sympathetic interpretations now known to us as the Laws of Manu.

It is only with difficulty that we realise the sense of vastness to which the thinkers of this period strove to give expression. The Celt, it has been said, strives ever towards the infinite of emotion. The Hindu, in the same way, cannot rest content, short of the infinite of thought. We see this, even so early as the hymns of the Rig Veda. "When darkness was hidden in darkness, undistinguished, like one mass of Water," opens the great Anthem of Creation. Still larger is the sweep of the Upanishads—"they that see the Real in the midst of this Unreal, they that behold life in the midst of this

* That learned and fascinating book, "The Arctic Home in the Vedas," is destined to work a revolution in our ideas on this subject. If the author's theory be correct, it would appear that Aryan culture was not acquired in Central Asia.

death, they that know the One in all the changing manifoldness of this universe, unto *them* belongs eternal peace—unto none else, unto none else." The Vedas were the capital with which Aryan culture began its occupation of India, and these immense and subtle generalisations of the Upanishads represent the first achievement of the national mind in its new place. Surely this is the secret of the striking fact in Indian history that all great eras of rejuvenescence, such as Sankaracharya's, and even minor movements of reconstruction like Guru Nanuk's, and Ramanuja's, have had to go back to the forest sutras and place themselves in structural continuity with them. In this light we begin to suspect that the war of the Mahabharata itself represents the apparent exhaustion of Vedic inspiration at the end of the first period, and the restoration of pristine vigour by force of Krishna's personality.

The twilight of Indian forests in the pre-Buddhistic age is resonant, to the historic ear, with chants and prayers. But the succeeding epoch leads us into the busy life of villages and cities. For the ballads and songs of the people are crystallising now into the great Epics. Their religious activity—stirred by the sublime spectacle of a life that represents the whole of Upanishadic culture, the national dream in its completeness—occupies itself with gathering together, and weaving into a whole, all the religious ideas innate amongst the masses, and those peculiar to the Indian environment. There is a sudden accession of force given to such practices as pilgrimage and relic-worship, and Brahmin intelligence is more or less unconsciously preoccupied with the interpretation of images, symbols, and rituals, in relation to those truths which had been the first realisation of the race. The distinction and larger scope of this Buddhist period lay to a great extent in its political, commercial, and sub-religious elements, in letters, arts, and sciences.

Certain evils must have come in the train of the ideas then elaborated, essential as they were to prove themselves in the long run to the completed fabric of Hinduism. We can understand that monastic notions may have attracted too much of the national energy out of the safe paths of domestic virtue, with a tendency to bring about not only the depletion of family life, but the disintegration of morality itself. No doubt it was at this time, and to meet this error, that the song of the ideal sang itself so clearly, first through the lips of Kalidas,* in his "Birth of the War-Lord," and again, in the final recension of the Ramayana, as the love of Sita for Rama, the glorified wifehood, before which the renunciation and faith of the cloister grow pale.

From the point of view of purity of doctrine, we can believe, too, that the very breadth of the welcome extended to religious ideas of all kinds, especially in the closing centuries of this age, had led to the undue emphasising of the popular notions, to the inclusion of an unnecessary multiplicity of symbols, and possibly to the interpretation of symbols already existing in rude or gross ways.

But agitation against abuses has never been the method of Hinduism. Rather has the faith progressed by lifting repeatedly in moments of crisis the banner of the highest ideal. Already, in the era we are considering, this organic law of the national genius, the law of the avatars, was well known. "Whenever the dharmma decays, and when that which is not dharmma prevails, † then I manifest

* Kalidas—the poet.—One of the famous "nine gems" of the Court of Vikramaditya, of Ujjain. Kalidas may have lived in the sixth century A.D. or earlier. He wrote the play of "Sakuntala," which so deeply touched the poet Goethe.

† Literally, the a-dharma—non-dharma. The prefix is privative. See p. 138.

myself. For the protection of the good, for the destruction of the evil *for the firm establishment of the national righteousness*, I am born again and again." So says the Bhagavad Gita—and never was any prophecy more conclusively vindicated than this, by the appearance of Sankaracharya, early in the ninth century after Christ.

This wonderful boy—for he died at the age of thirty-two—was born at the end of the eighth century, and had already completed a great mission when most men are still dreaming of the future. The characteristic product of Oriental culture is always a commentary. By this form of literature the future is knit firmly to the past, and though the dynamic power of the connecting idea may be obscure to the foreigner, it is clearly and accurately conveyed to the Eastern mind itself. The whole of Confucianism is contained in a commentary on the Eking, or Book of Change, and European Protestantism might almost be described as a special kind of commentary on the Christian sacred literature. The Sanskrit *sutras* lend themselves to critical writing, and even demand it, in a special degree: for the word *sutra* means *thread*, and is applied to works which are only the main line of a given argument, and require expansion at the end of every sentence. This literary convention obtains in all Oriental countries, and must date from the period when the main function of writing was to assist memorising. Obviously, by writing a new commentary on a given sutra, the man of genius has it in his power to readjust the relationship between a given question and the whole of current opinion. Hence it is not surprising to find that the masterpiece of Sankaracharya's life was a commentary on the Vedanta-Sutra.

The problems which faced the Indian mind during his lifetime, with the single exception that the country was then rich and prosperous, must have been curiously like those of the present day, and it is difficult to avoid the conclusion that in his eyes they assumed national dimensions. Religious practices had lost their primitive simplicity, and also perhaps their compelling power. Ideas as to national and unnational (for the word "orthodox" was but the Asiatic word for "national") were conflicting and confused. Men lived much in the thought of the recent sectarian developments of the faith, and tended to lose sight of its austere imperative, pointing to the highest realisation, of its antiquity, and its close-knit continuity. Lukshmi, Goddess of Fortune, was one of the chief objects of worship. Sects and kingdoms alike had lost their sense of mutual solidarity. Never perhaps was an Asiatic people nearer precipitating itself on a purely secular development.

At this moment the whole of the national genius awoke once more in Sankaracharya. Amidst all the brilliance and luxury of the age, in spite of the rich and florid taste of the Puranic period, his soul caught the mystic whisper of the ancient rhythm of the Vedic chants, and the dynamic power of the faith to lead the soul to super-consciousness, became for him the secret of every phase of Hinduism. He was on fire with the love of the Vedas. His own poems have something of their classical beauty and vigour, and his books may almost be described as chains of quotations from the most piercing and comprehensive sentences of the Upanishads, to which he has contributed links and rivets.

Sankaracharya wandered, during his short life, from his birthplace in the South as far as the Himalayas, and everything that he came across in his travels related itself to the one focus and centre, in his mind. He accepted each worship, even that from which he was at first adverse, but always because he found that the great mood of One-without-a-second was not only the Vedic, but also the Puranic goal. This is the doctrine that he expresses in his twelve epoch-making commentaries, especially in his crowning work, the commentary on the Vedanta Sutra. And this idea, known as the Adwaita Philosophy, constitutes, for the rest of the Hindu period, the actual unity of India.

Western people can hardly imagine a personality such as that of Sankaracharya. In the course of so few years to have nominated the founders of no less than ten great religious orders, of which four have fully retained their prestige to the present day; to have acquired such a mass of Sanskrit learning as to create a distinct philosophy, and impress himself on the scholarly imagination of India in a pre-eminence that twelve hundred years have not sufficed to shake; to have written poems whose grandeur makes them unmistakable, even to the foreign and unlearned ear; and at the same time to have lived with his disciples in all the radiant joy and simple pathos of the saints—this is greatness that we may appreciate, but cannot understand. We contemplate with wonder and delight the devotion of Francis of Assisi, the intellect of Abelard, the force and freedom of Martin Luther, and the political efficiency of Ignatius Loyola; but who could imagine all these united in one person?

Subsequent critics have painted Sankaracharya as the persecutor of Buddhists. Inasmuch as he asserted a co-ordination of mythologies and doctrines, instead of preaching a single exclusive method of salvation; inasmuch as to him the goal was a positive, and not a negative affirmation, and in so far also as he insisted upon the worthlessness of ritual apart from philosophy, of worship without illumination, he may be taken as the enemy of one school or another. It is almost unnecessary to add that this enmity was purely controversial in its character, and to Buddhists of the Northern School, a clearer historic knowledge will reveal him as the very opposite of a persecutor, as, rather, another example of the race of inspired religious teachers to which their own apostle, Nagarjuna, belonged. *

Buddhism as a whole, with the succeeding Puranism, had been the creation of the lay mind, the creation of the people. The work of Sankaracharya was the relinking of popular practice to the theory of Brahman, the stern infusion of mythological fancies with the doctrine of the Upanishads. He took up and defined the current catchwords—maya, karma, reincarnation, and others—and left the terminology of Hinduism what it is to-day. At the same time, we must not neglect to remind ourselves that in all this, if he had been other than the expression of that which it was the actual tendency of the race to formulate, he would not have found the scope he did. The recognition of a great man is as essential a factor in his history as his own power and character. His complete appropriation by his nation only shows that he is in perfect unison with its thought and aspiration.

The two or three centuries immediately succeeding Sankaracharya are commonly known as the dark ages of Indian history. The application of the term is obscure. In what sense were these ages dark? They were centuries of chivalric dominance, and in many a Rajput line the bardic annals are still preserved that will one day enable a generation of Indian historians to read their record. Even the wars of such a period were never destructive; for, apart from their specially chivalrous character, Oriental

* Nagarjuna.—An Indian monk, whose name is well known in China and Japan. He followed in the wake of previous teachers, in the second century of the Christian era. He gave ultimate theological form to the first school of Buddhism.

military usage has always secured the safety of non-combatants. The lives of water-carriers and commissariat servants were scrupulously respected in Asiatic warfare. It is said, indeed, that the European gipsy is an example of this. These poor people were originally a tribe of petty merchants who used to accompany the march of armies. Wherever the camp was pitched, they could run up a bazaar in half an hour, and their caste-honour lay in telling neither side the secrets of the other. When Genghis Khan invaded Hungary, these particular clans were carried there, never to return.*

But it was not only camp-followers who were protected by a law such as that which now defends the Red Cross Sisterhoods of Europe. A like consideration prevailed, with regard to the peasant working in the fields, and the craftsman toiling at his anvil. The young crops were honoured in ancient combat, as would be Cologne Cathedral or Notre Dame de Paris in modern. Under these circumstances a battle became only a deadly form of tournament, involving in its peril none but fighting men.

But if such contests could not become destructive, neither could they succeed in educating the masses of the people to the common duty of military defence. This result could only be achieved when a religious idea should become the war-cry of whole regions, conferring on all men the right of struggle without distinction of caste. This right, so necessary to the completion of nationality, the Mohammedan invasion gave, and it is difficult to imagine any other way in which the lesson could have been widely learnt.

The great tide of vigour that emanated from Sankaracharya swept round India by south, west, and north, in a spiral curve. Ramanuja, Mad-

* In the year 1200 A.D.

havacharya,* Ram Das and Tukaram,† the Sikh Gurus‡ and Gauranga,|| were all in turn its products. Wherever it touched the Mussulman consciousness, it created, chiefly by means of contest, a well-centred nation. Where it did not come in contact with Mohammedanism, as in the extreme south, this spiritual energy did not succeed in evoking a nationality. And where it did not lead to definite fighting, as in Bengal under Chaitanya, the sense of national existence remained more or less potential. Thus the advent of Islam into India during the post-Sankaracharyan period cannot be regarded as a revolutionary invasion, inasmuch as under the new power there was no loss of Asiatic modes. New arts of luxury were introduced, but the general economic system remained undisturbed. India received a more centralised government than had been possible since the Asokan Empire, but no new forces came into operation, tending to reduce her own children to the position of agricultural serfs or tenants. And we have seen that even the wars which arose between contiguous populations of Hindus and Mohammedans must be regarded rather as those athletic contests between brothers and cousins which confer individuality, than as conquests on the one side or the other. The victor after victory attempts neither to exclude his rival's creed from

* Ramanuja and Madhavacharya.—Flourished in the South of India in the twelfth and fourteenth centuries.

† Ram Das and Tukaram.—Two Mahratta saints to whose inspiration Sivaji's passionate defence of his own people was due. Tukaram was born about 1605.

‡ The Sikh Gurus.—These were ten in number, Guru Nanak born 1469, was the first, and Guru Govind Singh, who died 1708, was the last. By the lives and teachings of these ten leaders was formed the Hindu nation of the Punjab, the Sikhs. Amritsar is still the sacred city of this sect of Hinduism.

§ Gauranga.—Another name for Chaitanya, born 1486, the saint in whom Bengal first begins to realise herself as a united consciousness.

office, nor to create invidious distinctions. "The great bankers and nobles of Bengal remained Hindu under the rule of the Nawabs, as naturally as the Mussulman maintained his face in the shadow of a Hindu throne."*

Nor have the clearness and self-consciousness that its definition has added to Hinduism in any way tended to impair its inclusiveness. For the personality that the nineteenth century has revealed as the turning-point of the national development is that of Ramakrishna Paramahamsa,† whose name stands as another word for the synthesis of all possible ideals and all possible shades of thought. In this great life, Hinduism finds the philosophy of Sankaracharya clothed upon with flesh, and is made finally aware of the entire sufficiency of any single creed or conception to lead the soul to God as its true goal. Henceforth, it is not true that each form of life or worship is tolerated or understood by the Hindu mind: each form is justified, welcomed, set up for its passionate loving, for evermore. Henceforth, the supreme crime for the follower of any Indian sect, whether orthodox or modern, philosophic or popular, shall be the criticism of any other, as if it were without the bounds of "the Eternal Faith." "Man proceeds from truth to truth, and not from error to truth," becomes in future the formula that constitutes belief.

At this point we could almost have prophesied, had it not already happened, that some great disciple of this master would declare, on behalf of the whole nation, that the final differentia of Hinduism lay in the acceptance of the doctrine of the *Istha Devata*, *i.e.*, the right of every man to choose his own

* Torrens' "Empire in Asia.'

† Ramakrishna Paramahamsa lived in a temple-garden outside Calcutta from 1853 to 1886. His teachings have already become a great intellectual force.

creed, and of none to force the same choice on any other.*

At last, then, Indian thought stands revealed in its entirety—no sect, but a synthesis; no church, but a university of spiritual culture—as an idea of individual freedom, amongst the most complete that the world knows. Certain conceptions, such as maya, karma, and reincarnation, popularised by Buddhism, and mukhti or the beatific vision, sown broadcast alike by Sankaracharya and the Sufis, are characteristic of large areas. But they are nowhere and in no sense regarded as essential. For it is as foreign to the genius of Hinduism to require an oath of conformity to any given religious tenet whatever, as it would be to the habits of an Oxford don to require adherence to the doctrines of Plato as against those of Aristotle. It would thus appear that the reforming sects of the Mohammedan period and of the nineteenth century itself, have to the full as good a right to call themselves Hindu as the most orthodox priest of Siva, or the most learned Sanskrit pundit.

We have seen then, that it is certainly a mistake to read the history of India at any time as the account of a struggle between Hindu and Mohammedan thought, though it is a mistake which is perhaps inseparable from the European conception of the influence of faith on politics. But it cannot, on the other hand, be too clearly understood that the problem which the Indian idea has had to face, during the period between Sankaracharya and the

* I desire to say that in thus referring to my own gurus, Sri Ramakrishna Paramahamsa and the Swami Vivekananda, I do not intend to imply that every one will or ought to be willing to assign them the same place in the evolution of Hinduism that seems to myself to belong to them. Whether their names be accepted or not, however, I believe that all Hindus will agree regarding the *ideas* which are here stated as constituting Hinduism.

nineteenth century, was the inclusion of the Mohammedan element in a completed nationality. From the nineteenth century onwards, it becomes the *realisation* of that single united nationality, amidst the vast complexity which has been the growth of ages.

It is said that nations and systems of culture fulfil special functions, as organs of humanity, just as individuals fulfil special uses in the community. If this be so, it would almost appear that within the bounds of India lies one of the focal or polar points of the race. The great task of the reconciliation of opposites would seem to devolve on the peoples within this pale. It is not enough that the Mussulman should inhabit the pastoral belt, the Mongolian rest secure behind the Thian Shan, and the Aryan and Dravidian dwell peacefully side by side in the Southern peninsula. It was decreed from the beginning, it lay unavoidably in the very nature of things, that sooner or later all these should meet in the land of the Indus, and learn their mutual significance and responsibilities. Buddhism may be regarded in one aspect as simply the synthesis of Eastern Asia. Neo-Hinduism (to borrow a term which has been coined in no friendly spirit) is equally indicative of a place found in Aryan thought for Semitic formulæ, and who shall say what is yet to be born of that conjunction between all these, in which Asia shall find herself to be—not, as she has so long been told, "merely a congeries of geographical fragments," still less a concert of rival political units, held in mechanical combination by a due admixture of mutual hopes and recriminations, but a single immense organism, filled with the tide of one strong pulsating life from end to end, firm-rooted in the soil of common origins and common modes? The value which we may attach to the prospect of this future will depend on the idea that we have already been able to form, of the place of Asia in the evolution of humanity, but to those who foresee a future moralisation of international relations it may well appear that this question is among the most important in the world.

CHAPTER X

THE ORIENTAL EXPERIENCE

THE spiritual intellect refuses to believe in any good tidings of dogmas and happenings. It is St. Thomas Aquinas himself who points out that prayer cannot avail to change the will of God, but may, in any given case, be the appointed means of its accomplishment. Truth is not something that is told of in books or stated in words. It is the self-evident, the ultimate. It is that of which all our modes of seeing and saying are but so many refractions through a falsifying medium. All the teachings of Christianity put together are but as a vase or form, within which is conveyed to us the central actuality, the beautiful myth of the Christian soul.

And rightly so. For what is the real stuff of the human tragedy, the hunger for bread, or the longing for salvation? The answer is not doubtful. And this, although it may be, more than half of us are without any conception of that which we seek to save, or what it is from which we seek to fly. The fact remains, the human race is dominated by an inexpressible desire for the well-being of a metaphysical something which it cannot conceive of, but calls the soul. And any scheme, even the wildest, that makes profession of accomplishing this object, will meet with some measure of welcome and approval, provided only that he who offers is sufficiently convinced of the efficacy of his own method.

Most beautiful, perhaps, of all those known to us, is the series of pictures in which Catholicism paints her promise of deliverance. The little bark of life, in which the soul puts out to sea, to be guided in its tossings and wanderings by a science that the Church names saving knowledge; the mysterious transition of death, by which it lands on the shores of purification; and, finally, the pain of sanctification exhausted, its being received up into heaven, and attainment of the Beatific Vision.

But, after all, are not the symbols somewhat crude? Heaven and hell, reward and punishment! Is it not possible for even a child to go beyond these? Can we attempt to describe what is meant by the moral sense, without implying that we would choose good, though we suffered countless ages for it, and refrain from evil, though it brought us Heaven? Besides, are there not amongst us parents who refuse to act out a melodrama of judgment every time a baby steals a sugar-plum? Is the whole universe, multiplied by eternity, only one vast kindergarten? Or are we somewhere to learn that in self-control itself is beatitude? How are we to believe in salvation that is expressed as an *event?* in unchangeable happiness conferred upon us from without? in a *process* of knowledge and praise?

Do we not feel within us an ungovernable protest against these artificialities, an irrepressible claim for something that is the Nature-of-things, and requires no stage-management; a desire to be done with vicissitudes, alike of heaven and hell, salvation and perdition, and find some fixed mean, some centre of enduring poise, which shall confer freedom from all perception of antitheses, and knowledge at last of That which is the thing in itself? Or are we so in love with the limitations of the personal existence, with the fact that our good is another's ill, that present joy is future pain, that we would, if we could, prolong the experience?

Some such protest, at least, is apt to be roused in the Oriental by Western dreams of a future life. It is all physical, all sense-impression, he says, and as such is necessarily subject to that law of change and decay which must sooner or later apply to all compounds. In the sublime imagination of the Beatific Vision, he catches a hint of a deeper reality, but why, he asks, this distinction between time and eternity? Can the apprehension of the Infinite Good be conditioned by the clock? Oh, for a knowledge undimensioned, untimed, effect of no cause, cause of no effect! Reaching That, and That alone, we could be sure of unchanging bliss, of existence ultimate. But if accessible at all, it must be now in the earth-life or never. It must transcend and still the life of the senses, when the senses are most active; it must absorb and transmute the personal, when personality is capable of every eager claim, or remain for ever incredible, save as one swing of a pendulum, some day to be reversed.

This is the illumination that India calls the knowledge of unity, and the gradual appropriation of it by the whole nature, so that it ceases to be mere words and becomes a living actuality, she names realisation. Thus every step, every movement in life is either dull and dead, or on fire with the growing knowledge that we know as spirituality. The highest genius becomes only an incident on the road to supreme blessedness. And the passionless desire of Pheidias that wrought Olympian Zeus, the love of Dante for Beatrice, the "glorious nothingness" of S. Teresa, and the light on the face of Faraday the physicist, are all alike and all equally beads on that rosary whereon the soul's experience is told. For the whole story in all its forms is summed up, to Indian thinking, in the struggle to pass from the perceiving of manifoldness to the perceiving of One, and every heightening of common knowledge is to be regarded as a step towards this. The kitten at play will pursue first one object and then another with all the bewilderment and disconnectedness of the animal mind, while even the youngest baby will show the superiority of human faculty by its greater persistence of purpose and pertinacity of desire. The man of low type is led hither and thither by every impulse of sensation, while Archimedes is so absorbed in thought that he never perceives the Roman enter his presence, nor dreams of begging more than time to finish his speculation.

It must be remembered that to the Eastern intellect man himself is the universe, for all differentiation is within the mind. India may accept as a working hypothesis the theory that sociology is the synthesis of all the sciences, but her own fundamental conviction is that psychology occupies this place. Hence to her, power is always lodged in personality. Mind is the lord of body, undoubtedly; but mind, like body, is only the tool of the great Self of Things that stands behind and uses both for its own purpose. Like a strangely complex telescope, one part of the instrument stands pointed to give reports of many kinds—of light, sound, weight, smell, taste, and touch; and by another we are led to conceive of vast ranges of these, outside the possibilities of our immediately perceiving, by which we can build up the conception that we call the Cosmos. But, according to Indian thinking again, perfect control over the apparatus has only been attained when every part of it can be directed at will to a common point—the whole power of investigation brought to bear on any object. When this is done, when the intensest vibration of the whole being is reached and every faculty is convergent on the point of attention, then declares India, we, being one, perceive oneness, the mind sees truth face to face.

How we shall interpret and express the vision is determined wholly by our own past language and discipline. The mother comes out of it to love and serve; Joan of Arc commands armies with unfaltering insight; Sir Isaac Newton gives us the law of gravitation; Mozart produces his *Requiem Mass*, and the Messiah comes down from the mountain side whispering, "I and My Father are One." That is to say, the self-limited joys of sense have given way to the pursuit of the good of others as an end in itself. The man is overpowered by a beauty and a truth that he must needs share with the whole world. Or the finite personality is completed, transcended, in union with the absolute and universal.

There are thus, as the East counts, two modes of existence—one the personal, or egoistic, and the other the impersonal, or supra-personal, where egoism and altruism are alike forgotten. The realisation of this illimitable existence is itself salvation, and is to be reached in life, not death. Concentration is its single secret, and real power is always power over oneself.

What, then, are the common hindrances to this centring of thought and feeling that we are not all constantly immersed in the Divine intoxication? And what are the paths by which we are ordinarily led to overcome such hindrances? For it is to be supposed that, if the experience be authentic, men first stumbled upon it by accident, and formulation of theory came afterwards.

The mind of man sweeps an infinite circle, and from every point upon the immeasurable circumference runs a life-path to the division of Unity as the common centre. Each man is, as it were, a new window through which all others may look upon the Infinite, each life a new name for That which we call God. The paths, therefore, are countless. No two methods can be exactly the same. Yet there are certain broad characteristics which are more or less general.

The soul that thirsts for service, gradually expunging from the area of motive even the subtler shades of selfishness—such as the preference for special forms of activity, exactingness on behalf of work, and desire for sympathy and affection as the result—this soul will more readily than another lose itself in the supreme intuition of the good of others. "The People" with Mazzini, "the fair realm of France" with Joan of Arc, the fulfilment of duty to his country with the great sovereign or statesman, are amongst the forms which this realisation takes. In such a mood of uttermost blessedness, some have even suffered death by fire.

The temporary experience, in which the subject becomes unconscious of bodily sensation, is called *samadhi*. The process by which he comes out of samadhi time after time, to work its volume of force, so to speak, into his daily life, is known as realisation. And the path of service in purity of motive, is spoken of as *karma-yoga*, or divine union by work.

Again, we can in some measure understand the development of a nature to whom everything appears in degrees of lovableness. This was undoubtedly the method of S. Francis, and after him of S. Teresa. It is called in India *bhakti*, or devotion. Gradually, in such souls—guided by the thought of reaching the Infinite in abnegation of self—the power of love becomes a fire scorching, burning, consuming the barriers of individuality. "One cannot understand," says S. Teresa, "what is meant by talking of the impermanence of worldly joys. For one would renounce them so much the more gladly, could they but be eternal." Then there is a fusing of all things in the one conception of the Beloved. Lastly, distinction ceases, self is forgotten, there is left nothing, save the Infinite Love. First the prayer of quiet, then the prayer of Union, last the irresistible rapture, says the great Carmelite. Such is *bhakti-yoga*, the road by which the vast majority of the saints have gone.

Highest of all, however, is Union by knowledge, or *jnana-yoga*. A life whose whole struggle is the passion for truth; a soul to which falsehood or superstition is the worst of sins; a mind clear as the black depths of a mountain-pool; an atmosphere of joy, all stillness, all calm, all radiance without emotion; to these comes the growing intensity of recognition, the increasing power of direct vision, and finally that last illumination, in which there is neither knower, knowing nor known, but all is one in Oneness. It is much to be regretted that we have in English no word corresponding to *jnana*. *Insight* has a certain affinity, but is not sufficiently intense. The fact is, the habit of thought that leads up to the conception is foreign to us: a true parallelism is, therefore, out of the question.

The greatest *jnani* that has appeared in human history was undoubtedly Buddha, for the calmness of intellect predominates in Him, living through a ministry of more than forty years, though it was the immense outburst of His love and pity (explained as the fruit of five hundred sacrifices of Himself) that drove Him forth on His passionate quest to serve mankind. Then He is also in a high degree a combination of the three types of realisation—by intellect, heart and work. Some measure of this amalgamation there must be in all who use their knowledge for the good of others, of whom the

Incarnations are the culminating type. For in *jnana* by itself, the personal existence is seen to be a dream, a mere illusion, and it is impossible for him, who has once received its overwhelming revelation, to believe that there exist outside himself other centres of illusion for whose emancipation he might work.

For *karma*, or service, again, there could be no sufficient motive, without the impulse of *bhakti*. And the madness of divine love, unlighted by knowledge, unawaking to compassion, is almost unthinkable.

Such are the three ways—truth, devotion, and good works—by which it is said that souls may reach their goal. He who has attained, and remains in life, is called a Paramahamsa, or swan amongst men. And of all such, Sukë—he to whom it was given while in mortal form to drink a handful of the waters of the ocean of super-consciousness—is ideal and head. For most men die, it has been said, having heard only the thunder of its waves upon the shore; a few come within sight: fewer still taste; to Sukë alone was it given to drink. Many Mohammedan saints have become Paramahamsas, and are equally loved and reverenced by all religions alike.

So far of the apprehension of unity when consciousness and self-direction have made it vital spirituality. The hindrance to our reaching it is always, it is declared, one, namely, under whatever guise, want of the power to give up self. "When desire is gone, and all the cords of the hearts are broken, *then*," says the Upanishad, "a man attains to immortality." And by "immortality," it should be understood, is here meant the quality of deathlessness. For this reason, all religions are a call to renunciation; all ethics negate selfishness of personality; all disciplines are a repression of individual impulse. In the Indian doctrine of One immanent in the many, all these receive interpretation. The scholar s austerity of study; the artist's striving to become the witness; the lover's desire to sacrifice himself; all speak, however unconsciously, of our longing not to be, that the infinite, the universal consciousness, may abide within us.

The fact that the final achievement is variously known as Freedom, Mukti, or Nirvana, the annihilation of the limited, requires, at this point, little explanation. The idea that the perception of manifoldness is *Maya* or illusion, that the One is the real, and the many unreal, underlies the whole theory. "They that behold the One in all the changing manifoldness of this universe, unto *them* belongs eternal peace—unto none else, unto none else."

Obviously, the final truth of the doctrine is capable of no other proof or disproof than that of experience. But the attitude to it of the common Indian mind is strictly scientific. We cannot prove, save by making the experiment, but we can point to the fact that the accumulated observation of life goes to establish the tenableness of the proposition, says India in effect. And when we are shown one morality that does not demand the holding of unity of principle against manifoldness of impulse; one science that does not grow by the correlating of apparent discrepancies in continually stricter unities; or one character that does not find perfection in surrendering the personal to the impersonal, the theory of Maya—real unity amidst apparent diversity—will fall to the ground, and must be acknowledged a misconception. Hitherto, it may be claimed, the whole history of the world has not sufficed to furnish the required exception.

Thus the beatific vision of Hinduism is not unlike that of Dante's Empyrean, only it is to be relegated to no distant future, but triumphantly vindicated within mortality itself. The name of God and the conventions of piety are as unreal as anything else in Maya, but they have the power of enabling us to break its bondage, whereas the delights of the senses only fasten it the tighter.

One point remains. The doctrine with which we have been dealing represents a national culture. Very few in the West can be said to have grasped the whole secret of that for which their country stands. Very few will be found to understand deeply any given idea or subject. The very reverse is the case in the East. Men who have no emancipation into the scheme of modern knowledge are emancipated into the sequence of renunciation and freedom. Though India is daily losing her grip on her own character, she is still the motherland of hundreds of the saints. And amongst that people of ancient aristocracies the realm of the ideal is so completely democratised that the poorest peasant, the meanest workman, comprehends what is meant by the great daily prayer of Hinduism :—

> From the Unreal, lead us to the Real!
> From darkness, lead us unto light!
> From death, lead us to immortality!
> Reach us through and through ourself,
> And evermore protect us—O Thou Terrible!—
> From ignorance by Thy sweet compassionate Face.

CHAPTER XI

THE WHEEL OF BIRTH AND DEATH

Reflection has taught me that there is nothing mightier than Destiny. . . . Zeus bows to her power. She surpasses iron in hardness.—EURIPEDES' *Alcestis.*

Heredity is a condition, not a destiny.—BJÖRNSON.

As a man casts off worn-out clothes, and puts on others which are new, so the embodied casts off worn-out bodies, and puts on others which are new.—*Bhagavad Gitâ.*

THE crucial feature of the Greek conception of life was the dramatic distinction which it made between will and the conditions with which will had to cope. Just as surely as our birth on the planet Earth gives us a place, definite, however infinitesimal, in the solar system, relating us in our degree to all that occurs within the orbit of the farthest satellite, so it is clear that our position, geographically, ethnologically, historically, upon that planet, places us from the beginning at definite points on lines of cause and effect, to which, as human beings, we can but exercise the function of acceptance. This Not-to-be-refused, which modern science calls natural law, was simply to the Greek an unexplained and unexplored Necessity or Fate.

To the ancients, a curse, for example, was no exercise of the volition of the speaker. It was in no sense a threat. Our own more frivolous use of the word is a case of degradation by the death of a conception. To the old Greek, as indeed to the

Hindu and the Norseman, a curse was entirely a prophecy. It was pronounced by way of warning or revelation that upon a certain act certain results would be found to follow. Apollo perceives that if Laios begets a son, disaster will result. He does not determine that it shall be so. Evidently, will is regarded as free up to a certain point, or we should not have the alternative imagined, of begetting no son. But to Œdipus and his children there is no alternative; he and they have been born in that circle of destiny where they can only fulfil the lot marked out.

This fact the Greek mind appears to accept without further inquiry. For it, overwhelming interest attaches, not to an analysis of the nature and conditions of fate, but to the spectacle of the human will in spiritual conflict with it. This spectacle is the theme of the whole of Hellenic tragedy. The Christian doctrine of grace introduces something confused and miraculous into the European idea of life, and for centuries the pursuit of the knowledge of things as they are is thwarted by a supernatural metaphysic of things as they ought to be, and are not. With the Renaissance, however, the intellect of Europe springs back sharply to the Greek position. *Macbeth* and *Othello* are in some ways as completely Hellenic as anything of Æschylus. Temptation is once more placed outside a man; true and false incentives are inextricably blended; and the will is shown as the mere plaything of its own blindness. On these points, and in the feeling of vastness with which he covers his subject, Shakespeare's delineation is all Greek.

In *Macbeth*, it is true, a sense of ethical suffering somewhat blurs the outline. But nothing dims the perfect beauty of *Othello*. Untortured by misgiving its heroic figures move from the dawn of their love to the noontide of supreme vindication of its purity in death. The particular problem is not antique. Its delicacy of tint is somewhat modern, but in simplicity and grandeur, in the conviction that life is a mere straw swept along on the current of necessity *Othello* is an ancient drama.

One great difference between the Hellenisms of antiquity and of the Renaissance lay in the fact that organisation was at the disposal of the modern. Isolated genius writes dramas, elaborates philosophies, or carves statues: organised genius produces scientific inquiry. In some sense modern science is nothing but the efficient development of the Aristotelian and Alexandrian elements of classical thought. The human will itself, however, is the one thing eternally baffling to human research. There is no crucible in which it can be melted. All science, therefore, resolves itself into the old problem of the Greek dramatist—the problem of due observation of the conditions which confront the will; and it is by a strictly logical development of the thought of the ancients—a thought which scarcely dreamt of any distinction between a man and his body—that we arrive at the modern conception of body-and-brain as the last and crucially important element of destiny.

Its *naïveté* is at once the strength and weakness of European thought. The springs of modern fiction are still brackish with the salt of our enthusiasm about heredity. Recent talk of degeneration is little more than the bitterness left within a cup. Like every single truth mistaken for the whole, heredity would impose as great a bondage on the human spirit as any system of fatalism. Of what use the fight against the weakness or ignorance of one's ancestors? What hope of victory over the taint that is in the blood? And yet, high over all law and all instruments rose, rises, and shall for ever rise, the human will, its brow bright with the sunshine of freedom, its foot on the foe that our subtle criticism had pronounced invincible, serene in the knowledge of its own power to defy alike heredity and the nature-of-things, and make for itself out of the web of failure the mantle of a supreme victory.

But this will so often seems asleep! Unaroused, or ignorant as a child, it has turned aside perhaps for every wayside flower, for any shining pebble, and in the hour of the crisis is simply missing. Or it may be that it suffers from some base intoxication of falsehood or desire, and has fallen down to kiss the feet of evil as though it were good, courting slavery and defeat as maidens to be caressed. Surely here, and here alone, is the crux of things, in the difference between the enlightened and the unenlightened will. Necessity is but the sum of the conditions. Heredity is but one, though the most critical, of those conditions. In the setting of the will itself towards bondage or towards freedom lies the secret of the unity of life.

There are thus three factors in the interpretation of human life, and it has been the distinction of Asiatic thought to have recognised all three. A profound certitude that cause must sooner or later be followed by effect, while effect has as surely been preceded by cause, gives to the Indian temperament an air of quiet resignation which is far from being the inactive fatalism so commonly supposed. For there is surely the difference of extremes between a dignified acceptance of things because they are unaccountable and not to be interfered with, and a similar dignified acceptance because they are so entirely accountable that events require no acceleration!

That India understands the doctrine of heredity is demonstrated by caste. There alone, amongst all the countries of the world, it has been held for ages an unpardonable social dishonour to allow the diseased or deformed or mentally alienated to marry. For such, the quietly enforced decree of caste has been always—no posterity. But more than this, the very meaning of the institution is, amongst other things, the attempt to develop still further the brain of the Brahmin, the hand of the toolbearer, and every form of expert faculty. It is true that it rejects the *crossing* of blood as a means to this end, but it looks to the cumulative influence of careful selection from generation to generation, to that of the occupational environment, and to the inheritance of the effects of clean-feeding. The last is held specially important to the user of the brain: hence the Brahmin represents more than any other the fibre produced by countless generations of care in this respect, and the lower we go in society the less do we find of such transmission.

But the Indian comprehension of the nature of things and of heredity as complementary elements in the scheme presented to the will has never meant blindness to the last and most important consideration of all—the efficiency of the will itself. If this were not the determining factor, India would say, it would not be possible, as it is, to watch two brothers, with the same inheritance, the same material opportunities, and the same moral environment, journey, one to glory and the other to shame, by a common road. And if it were not also the ultimate standard of success or failure, the Greek story of Aristides, for instance, would lose all its pathos. For we all know how, when an ignorant man asked his help in casting his vote for the condemnation of Aristides, the great man first complied with his request, and then, on mildly inquiring its reason, was answered, "I am tired of hearing him called 'the just.'"

Is it here, or in the story of Dives and Lazarus, that we catch a glimpse of inequality? Which is the crueller perplexing of our sense of justice—that one man receives wealth and another poverty, or that one cannot wish well, nor another ill?

The answer of India is not doubtful. There is one tool and only one, she says, that is finer than the most perfect human brain, and that is the tool of a noble intention. No more than other delicate instruments is this, she claims, immediately producible wherever we may wish to see it. Just as faculty grows from feeble and unrationalised to its perfection, just as organisms progress from minute and simple to large and complex, so must we suppose that will passes through all the stages of egotism till it reaches that illumination which we know as perfect charity. At each stage the possibilities of aspiration are limited, though they become less and less so as the goal is approached. The whole Hindu outlook is thus critical and scientific. There is no longer a vague horrible something called sin: this has given place to a clearly defined state of ignorance, or blindness of the will. Nor is this ignorance conceived of as a stationary or fixed quantity. So surely as trees grow and rivers seek the sea will it sooner or later give place to knowledge, in every human soul; and then a man's mere forgetfulness of his limited personality and its aims may look to others like nobility: to himself it will not even be apparent, lost in the larger yearning of more universal life. Thus a great and generous thought is like a position near the river-mouth to the water springing at the source, not by any means to be reached without traversing the complete distance. The supreme good fortune possible to man would consist of a noble intention, joined to a great brain, joined to an external position of mastery and freedom an advantageous point, that is to say, on some line of cause and effect. Such, we may take it, to Gautama the Buddha, was the opportunity of his birth. Most lives, however, represent every possible degree, and combination of degrees, of the three conditions. We see the great position made the background of stupidity and meanness. We see the kind wish rendered futile by feebleness of intellect. Very occasionally there is no discord between person and circumstance; but now and again the discrepancy takes the acute form of the lion caught in the net, or the common criminal wearing an emperor's crown. Whence have these anomalies arisen? In what firm order do they stand rooted?

The Hindu mind seems always to have been possessed of the quiet confidence that all phenomena will yield themselves to a rational explanation. Since "that which exists is one," it is absurd to suppose an ultimate contradiction between the human reason and the universe. The mind that is normal and right amongst its fellows is normal and right in its relation to things. If we see and hear and taste, it is because in primal vibration there is something correspondent to sight and sound and the rest, of which our human sense has been the necessary outcome. Our faculty, that is to say, may be feeble, but we must assume it to be true. If thirty years of life can impress us with a sense of terrible duration, utterly disproportionate to their relative importance, it is because in the Absolute there is no passage of time, all the infinite eternities of consciousness lying in the Now. If human love can oppress us with a vastness undreamed of, suddenly opened before us, it is because in it we have approximated to a state which transcends all limit and all change. Whatever be the nature of the Real it must include, not exclude, consciousness. This being so, we must take it that the order of things as we see them—time, space, and causation—applies to life itself as naturally as to all that within the limits of life we perceive. Our appearance here from birth to death is a simple case of the sequences that every moment of our stay brings to our notice. It is the effect of some cause which could no more have failed to find its fulfilment in time and space than the self-striking of a bird's wing could fail to be accompanied by flight. Everything, again, within the general effect, is a subordinate effect conditioned by its own subordinate cause. Physical, mental, and moral, are only terms denoting so many dimensions, as it were, within which the seed has germinated and come to its fruition. So much for the effect. Do things, as we see them, give us any hint as to the nature of the *cause?* Yes, there is one force—the force of desire—that we see at work daily, making, cherishing, gathering, action and its fruits. Without this as creative antecedent it will be found on examination that nothing that we know of comes to pass. Hence if life as a whole be regarded as but a phenomenon similar in kind to those which it encloses, we are impelled to the conclusion that of it also the efficient cause has been the human will. We dreamed of ourselves as bodies. Falling into some strange error, we longed for the sweets of sense. And we awoke and, without knowing it, found ourselves in prison, there but to continue adding to the energy of those desires, each of which was already a fetter binding us the faster. Such is the Hindu interpretation of our presence here. Of what led to our self-deceit he attempts no account, conceiving that his right to a rational theory applies only to the phenomenal, meaning those things that are perceived within the play of reason.

Thus, life is a harvest reaped at birth. It is also the sowing of fresh harvests for the painful reaping of the future. Every act is as a seed, effect of past cause, cause of effect to come—*Karma.* The unending wheel of birth and change and death. For the Hindu does not consider that a single life alone is to be accounted for. The very constitution of our minds forces on us the idea that phenomena are cyclic; that appearances recur; that the starry Universe itself blooms and will wither like another flower. Clearly then the causes that have placed us here to-day must bring us again; must, in the circling of infinite ages, have brought us infinite times before. This is the doctrine of Reincarnation. Our ignorance now tells of a deeper ignorance in the past. The desires that burn within us are but our subjective apprehension of what is yet to be. For that which we long for must come to our hand. The *Karma* of each birth is only the harvest of our ancient wishes.

What the victim of desire so constantly forgets, however, is the twofold nature of things, and their constant state of flux. Good brings evil; wealth is succeeded by poverty: love is but a messenger sent before the feet of sorrow. In fact, the seeming benefits of material things are in reality scourges, sooner or later to lash the very back of him who drew them to himself. None, for instance, could be so puerile as to declare palaces, jewels, and horses as good in themselves, so that their chance possession now and again should be any compensation for the suffering of requiring them. It is little more exalted, says the Hindu, to claim love, intellect, and salvation, as necessities. The world of Maya consists of the perpetual alternation of opposites. Every desire carries its fulfilment, its decay, and its retribution hidden within itself. That what we would have we must first give, is the lesson of austerity.

The *Karma* of an individual, then, consists of a given condition of taste or knowledge, a given physical equipment, and a given share of material fortune or misfortune. Taste sometimes rises to genius, or sinks to brutish appetite. The physical equipment may include a mathematician's brain, a violinist's hand, or a body tortured by perverse temptations. In any case, according to the theory, the will that has come to administer, earned exactly that endowment, and in this respect life is justly distributed. It is thought not unnatural that the soul of a Bach should seek incarnation in a family of musicians, since here it could best find the conditions it demanded. With regard to such matters, a vast lore has been accumulated, into which it is interesting to dip. There is a popular belief amongst Hindus that marriage is always contracted between the same two persons, and that the merit of either is divided equally with the other. However this may be, love at first sight—an occasional experience the world over!—is held a sure proof of past friendship and acquaintance. Very perfect relationships, by which is meant, amongst other things, those that are complex in their quality, would be considered in the same way, to be long-rooted. The religious life is one of the most fascinating subjects of speculation. It will sometimes happen that the stern ascetic in the midst of his austerities yields to, or at least harbours, some vain desire. This is enough to precipitate him once more into the world, where his position and power will be exactly equal to the severity of his past renunciations. He may thus very easily become a monarch, and it is believed that a faint memory of the religious habit often haunts the throne. The great Akbar of Delhi told of such a reminiscence in his own case. He had been a monastic novice, and had fallen in love! When sovereignty was exhausted, however, he would return to his prayers and gain freedom, without another fall. An impression of this kind about Queen Victoria was the real secret of the influence of her name in India—an influence, be it added, which would have been much deepened had she succeeded in abdicating some few years before her death, in order to devote the rest of her life to God.

We must remember, however, that the Oriental, born to the idea of re-incarnation, rarely becomes so infatuated with it as to make it his sole dependence in interpreting life. He does not lose his head over it, as may one who hears of it for the first time. He is well aware that, on his own hypothesis, we are engaged in the sowing of seed, as well as the reaping of grain. He will not therefore attempt to explain every new introduction from an imaginary past. This life is to him but one measure in a long passage of music. The great majority of its tones gain all their beauty and meaning from the fact that they were prepared beforehand and will be resolved after, but some nevertheless are new. That we do not, as a rule, remember our pasts is, he argues, no disproof of their existence, since neither do we remember our birth and infancy.

It is this clearness of logical speculation that lends its terror to the Indian notion of existence. To the wise man, frankly, life is a bondage, and the only question how to be freed from it. Suicide cannot solve the problem. The reasons for this act may be frivolous or weighty. It is an instrument as much within a man's own power as the tools of his calling or the weapons of self-defence. Only, it offers no escape from the misery of existence. Can the schoolboy make progress in arithmetic by wiping from his slate the sum he could not work? Will not that particular difficulty recur whenever he would take an onward step, confusing, taunting, blinding him, till it is conquered? Even so is the lot of the suicide, thinks the Hindu. He desired to escape the rope of justice? Then in some future incursion into life it will become his *Karma* to stand on the scaffold and undergo the extreme penalty, for a crime he has not committed. He would flee from a dishonour he had not strength to endure? No coward's self-banishment shall suffice to save him. Sooner or later the ordeal must be met and faced. Or was it the abstract hatred of life that used his own hand to slay the man? Fool! saw he not that the act was part and parcel of an extreme self-indulgence, and must bring its terrible consequence of exile from all that could make existence beautiful and blessed?

Desire, in short, is the ego-centripetal, the self-assertive, self-regarding force. The current must be turned out deliberately, not drawn inward. The passion for self must be destroyed in the thirst for service. Desire must be burnt to ashes in the fires of renunciation. Then, and then only, will there be escape from the incessant turning of the wheel. Then alone can the victim become the conqueror, and the slave master of the world.

This is the "cosmic suicide" of Schopenhauer, the much talked-of "pessimism" of the East. It is indeed a familiar conception to all Hindus, so familiar as to be an integral part of language. But it is hardly "pessimism." Does the prophecy of victory carry with it sadness? the certain promise of his freedom embitter the slave? There is a sense in which, if Hindu philosophy be not optimistic, it is difficult to know what the world means by optimism. Taking the doctrine of reincarnation as a whole, we find it so necessary to the theory of *Maya* that even the Buddhist formulation could not exist without some version of it. At the same time, a clear understanding of it is a valuable corrective of slip-shod misconceptions as to the philosophy of illusion. That this involves no lazy intellectual uncertainty regarding phenomena we have seen, since the whole doctrine of *Karma* is based on the Hindu's implicit conviction of the entire calculableness of law. It cannot be too clearly understood that the argument of *Maya* is compatible with, and tenacious of, the severest scientific research, and that to Oriental thinking, only that man who has in his own person, by some method of self-discipline, achieved a realisation, compared to which all that we know through the senses is unreal, has a right to speak of the phenomenal universe as, to him, fundamentally an illusion. The effort to reach this vision remains, nevertheless, to the Oriental mind the one end and justification of existence, the one escape from the wheel of life, and mankind is for ever divisible into those who see and struggle towards such a goal, and those who are engaged in sowing the wind, and reaping the whirlwind, of Desire.

The battlefield of Kurukshetra lies silent these many centuries, yet still to the ear of the wise man it echoes the doom of Humanity in the terrible words "of that which is born, death is certain: of that which is dead, birth is certain."

CHAPTER XII

THE STORY OF THE GREAT GOD: SIVA OR MAHADEV

Thou that art knowledge itself,
Pure, free, ever the witness,
Beyond all thought and beyond all qualities,
To Thee, the only true Guru, my salutation,
Siva Guru! Siva Guru! Siva Guru!

Salutation to Siva, as the Teacher of the Soul.

In India's great moments, the Himalayas have always been her highway, not her boundary. Those strings of pack-mules, with their sorry-looking rice-bags, that we meet on every hill-path, as we wander through the mountains, are the remains of a great continental traffic that once carried the religion into China. For beliefs, like diseases, do not travel alone. The pilgrim is accompanied by the pedlar: the begging-friar dogs the footsteps of the merchant; the faith follows the line of trade. It may be that if Chinese silk and turquoise had not found their way to India many centuries before the birth of Buddha, the news of the Great Nirvana could never have reached the remoter East.

To this day, we find ancient capitals and their ruins, old fortresses, royal temples, scattered up and down the heights from Beluchistan to Nepal, in regions long depopulated. And Himalayan shrines and cities have an art and architecture of their own, which is more severely beautiful, because more directly related to the common early Asiatic, than the later styles, to be found further south. For the first culture-area of humanity had these mountains as its rim. Long before a local prepossession had named the Mediterranean, Asia was. And of that Asia, Egypt, Greece, Etruria, were outlying provinces. The Saracen and Moor, with all that they brought of art and chivalry, with all the intellectual vividness they conferred on Europe, were but the relic-mongers of its past. In the West, even now, we admit a people to be civilised only if we can trace its intellectual descent from this ancient Asia.

Above all, it is the broken voices of its primitive consciousness that are hailed to-day in every civilised country as divine revelations. India herself is no exception to this rule. For all the migrations of Asokan and other periods pale beside the memory of the still more significant era when for the first time there came to settle on the Northern Plain those little communities of people, already agricultural and industrial in their habits, who carried with them the culture of Central Asia. It was not a regimented immigration. The Lall Kaffir, or pale folk, dwelling to this day in the Hindu Kuch, were not deserters, turning aside from the line of march. We must rather suppose a gradual overflow, through many centuries, of the Himalayan region. And yet, at some time or place, it must have been sufficiently consolidated and self-organised to become conscious of its great heritage of thought, to commit its knowledge to writing, and to give form and definition to the Aryan civilisation.

Wherever and whenever it may have happened, this was the moment at which long ages of accumulating reflection and observation precipitated themselves into form as the Vedas. Even so are all Scriptures born. The Tartar herdsman, facing his unknown future as a peasant, records at once his ideals and his memories, and we have the Eki, or Book of Change, of the Chinese people. The austere self-isolation of a few tribes of Syrian shepherds fronts with terror the degradation of Babylonian cities, and the prophets pour out their sublime woes. The Latin Church carries to the Norse peasant with one hand the waters of baptism, with the other the script, by means of which he is to write down his magnificent sagas. The old order blossoms into complete self-consciousness at that very instant when every petal trembles to the fall.

So passed the Vedic age, for the Aryans settled down in India, and became Hindus. The process by which this was accomplished must have been complex and gradual. In some directions towards a greater luxury, it must have been fundamentally a simplification of life. The builders of the Himalayas had used wood and stone. The builders of the plains used bamboos, mud, and bricks; and their architectural designs began to approximate to those of pottery. The weavers of Central Asia had worked in wool, doubtless of marvellous dyes. The craftsmen of the South were driven to cotton and silk. That system of ritual purification which was common to the whole of the Asiatic culture, and which is still retained by Europe in the form of sacraments and rubrics, must have been deepened and extended to meet the new climatic conditions. Natural metaphor underwent transformation. Coolness was exchanged for warmth as the qualification of friendship. Himalayan scenery was no longer present to give constant birth to grand myths and colossal imaginary. That gradual absorption of regional thought and worship began, which was to produce what in its latest phase would be known as Hinduism. But it was always to be absorption. It was always to be the play of the Aryan intellect upon the indigenous symbol; never the acceptance of a superstition that could not be rationalised. This wonderful continuity of thinking marks the solidarity of Hinduism as nothing else could. Every creed within its frontiers—and they are wide enough to include all types of religious thought—can prove the Vedas to be its authority. Even the image of the Goddess Kali is held to be foreshadowed in the sublime Anthem to Creation of the Rig-Veda:

> The Self sustained as Cause below,
> Projected as Effect above.

We find in India, then, a classical nation like Egypt or Greece, which has been allowed to develop freely on the mental plane, and has held the thread of its thought unbroken to the present day. It may be said broadly that great culture and subjective philosophies are almost always continental in their origin, while the sense of nationality and insistence on the beautiful are insular. If this be true, it would explain the greater sympathy between Hellenic and Japanese developments than between Greek and Indian.

For the Hindu imagination long ago detached itself from the cycle of physical beauty, to seek its fullest satisfaction in subtler realms. This fact is extraordinarily evident in Kalidas' poem of "The birth of the War-Lord," where he depicts the wooing of Mahadev by Uma, the Himalayan princess. Here the poet places his heroine at the very acme of maidenly charm, kneeling in worship to lay flowers at the feet of the Great God, and having as her background the forest of plum and cherry and almond, all suddenly burst into blossom, because to them comes Spring, as the comrade of Love. And then, with a single sweep of the brush, the picture is blotted out: the Great God has vanished from beneath his cedar; Eros is burnt to ashes; and the royal maiden kneels alone, while the bitter wailing of Desire, the beautiful wife of Love, fills the whole woodland. Uma's triumph is reached, and the Divine Spouse drawn to her side, only when, in the midst of unheard-of austerities, she gives supreme proof of courage and devotion as nun and worshipper instead of woman and lover. This touch lies far beyond the range of the Greek.

A similar tendency to use physical symbolism as a system of notation merely, instead of seeking in it the direct and adequate expression of spiritual conceptions, as did the classical genius of Europe, is to be found throughout the whole conception of Siva or Mahadev, the Great God Himself. The tiger-skin in which he is clad, and some of the names of this deity, induce Tod in his "Annals of Rajasthan" to regard him as simply a new version of the Greek Bacchus. It is a great deal more likely that behind the two, in the dim North, and in the distant past—in some Lake Mansarobar of thought, to quote Max Müller—there may loom up a common ancestor. But this probability only makes more significant the divergences between the two conceptions.

Any one who visits Northern India must desire to know the meaning of the little black stones under every conspicuous tree, which are so evidently set up for worship. They are said by Europeans to be of phallic origin; but if so, Hindus are no more conscious of the fact than we of the similar origin of the maypole. Wherever one goes, one finds them, by the roadsides in cities and villages, on the river-banks, or inside the entrance to a garden, if there is a tree that stands alone. For in such places one is glad to think that the Great God, begging His handful of rice from door to door, may have seated Himself to bless us with His meditation.

The small stone pillar, called the lingam—the

word *lingam* is literally *symbol*—may have been taken from the bed of a stream, and in that case is likely to be of a long egg-shape. But if it has been cut by the hand of man, it is short and slightly tapering, with a thimble-like top. Sometimes, in all good faith, the features of a human face have been more or less crudely marked on it, with white paint. In any case, it is only a question of time till some woman, passing by on her way from bathing, stops to pour a little water, or sprinkle a few grains of rice tenderly over the head of the stone, perhaps also to add bel-leaves, trifoliate like our clover; or a garland of white flowers; or, prompted by a heart more devoted and loving than usual, to touch it with a spot of sandal-paste, so cool and refreshing in this hot climate! Then the earth is touched with the head, and the worshipper passes on.

The simple act is not without its perplexities, and we seek for interpretation. At first in vain. Or the explanations given are more bewildering than helpful. Hindus are too conscious of the symbolistic nature of every faith, and too sensitive also to the scornful irreverence of most foreign inquirers, to speak out, or argue out, the heart of their heart with the passing stranger. Rather they will turn on one, with a strange pity. "Do you not understand," they will say, "that this is the Great God who is emblemed here? He can have neither visitor, nor history, nor worshipper. Such things are vain dreams of men. Only for our own hearts' ease, and to carry ourselves nearer to the inner vision, do we set up a stone whereon we may offer rice and water and lay a leaf or two!" It will be difficult in all India to find a woman so simple, or a peasant so ignorant, that to them worship is not, as some one has said, "a conscious symbolism, instead of a fragment of primitive personification." Yet by degrees the great myth leaks out. Little by little we learn the associations of the name.

The lingam, after all, is but a fragment of stone. Far better images of Mahadev are those who come and go yonder, amidst the passing crowd—the monks and beggars, some clad only in ashes with matted hair, others with shaven head, and clothed from throat to foot in the sacred yellow, but most of them bearing one form or another of staff or trident, and carrying a begging bowl. And finer still will these be, when, retiring into the forest, or climbing to the verge of eternal snows, they sit, even like this stone lingam, bolt upright in the shelter of tree or rock, lost to the world without, in solitary meditation.

About the whole conception there is a striking reminiscence of the Himalayas. Whether we will or not we are carried back, as we listen, to the great age of the Vedas, when the Aryan immigration was still taking place. It is a day of sacrifice, and at the forest-clearing people and priests are met, to heap the offerings on the mighty fire, chanting appropriate texts. Hour after hour, sometimes day after day, the mound of pure flame lasts, and long after it has ceased the hot white ashes lie in their immense bed, thrilling now and then to a faint trickling spark, sighing themselves out into the coldness of death. Who was it that first came and rubbed himself with those soft white ashes, in order to be clothed upon with the worship of God and separation from the world? Who was it that first retired into cave or jungle, and meditated, until his hair became a tangled mass, and his nails grew long, and his body emaciated, and he still pursued the sublime bliss of the soul? However the idea of such an exterior grew, the whole genius of India has spoken for many a century in just such a picture—the hermit clad in wood-ashes, with masses of neglected hair, piled on the top of his head, indifferent to the whole world, bent only on thought.

As the Aryans wandered in sight of the snow-mountains, with the fire-sacrifice for their central rite, an indissoluble connection arose in their minds between the two ideas. Were not the flames of the offerings white like the Himalayas, always mounting upward like the aspiring peaks, leaving behind them ashes for eternal frost? Those snowy heights, we must suppose, became the central objects of their love. Lifted above the world in silence, terrible in their cold and their distance, yet beautiful beyond all words, what are they like? Why, they are like —a great monk, clothed in ashes, lost in his meditation, silent and alone! They are like—like—the Great God Himself, Siva, Mahadev!

Having arrived at this thought, the Hindu mind began to work out all sorts of accessories and symbols, in which sometimes the idea of flame, sometimes of mountain, sometimes of hermit is uppermost—all contributing to the completed picture of Siva, the Great God.

The wood was borne to the sacrifice on a bull: Siva possesses an old bull, on which he rides.

As the moon shines above the mountains, so He bears on His forehead the new moon.

Like the true ascetic, begging food at the householder's door, He is pleased with very simple gifts. The cold water of the bath, a few grains of rice, and two or three green bel-leaves, are His whole offering in the daily worship. But the rice and water must be of the purest, for they are presented to a most honoured guest. Evidently the bel-leaf, like the shamrock, refers to the Trinity. For, as we all know, this doctrine is Hindu as well as Christian and Egyptian.

To show how easily Siva can be pleased, the people tell a pretty story. A poor huntsman—that is to say, one of the lowest of the low—once came to the end of a day's hunting without having snared or killed a single creature. Night came on, and he was far from home, in the jungle, alone. Near by stood a bel-tree, with branches near the ground, and he was glad to climb into it, to pass the night in shelter from wild beasts. But as he lay crouching in its branches, the thought of his wife and children starving at home would come to him, and for pity of their need great tears rolled down his cheeks, and falling on the bel-leaves broke them by their weight, and carried them to the ground. Under the sacred tree, however, stood a Siva-lingam, image of Siva, and the tears fell, with the leaves, on its head. That night a black snake crept up the tree, and stung the man. And bright spirits came, and carried his soul to Heaven, and laid it down at the feet of Siva.

Then, in that holy place, rose the clamour of many voices questioning: "Why is this savage here? Has he not eaten impure foods? Has he offered right sacrifices? Has he known the law?" But the Great God turned on them all in gentle surprise: "Did he not worship Me with bel-leaves and with tears?" He said.

Looking closer at the *flame*, however, one thing was very clear. It was white, but it had a blue throat—we see it even when we light a match!—and in order to bestow a blue throat upon Siva, the following story arose:

Once upon a time, all the splendour and glory of the gods seemed to be vanishing from them. (Are such tales, we wonder, a reminiscence of the period when the old gods, Indra, Agni, and the lords of the universe, found themselves growing unfashionable, because the Trinity, Brahma—Vishnu—Siva, was coming into favour?) What to do, the gods did not know, but they determined to pray to Vishnu, the

Preserver of the World, for advice. He told them, perhaps contemptuously, to "go and churn the ocean!" and the poor gods trooped forth eagerly to do his bidding.

They churned and churned. Many great and splendid things came foaming up, and they seized them with avidity, here a wonderful elephant, there a princely horse, again a beautiful wife for some one. Each was only greedy to be first in the handling of the next delight, when all at once something black began to come. Welling up and up, and then spreading over the whole ocean, it came. "What is it?" they asked each other in horror. It was poison—death to them, death to the world, death to the universe. It came to their very feet, and they had to retreat rapidly in fear. Already they were in the midst of darkness, and there was nowhere that they could flee, for this dense blackness was about to cover all the worlds. In this moment of mortal terror, all the gods with one voice called on Siva. He had taken no part in the receiving of gifts, maybe He would be able to help them now. Instantly, the great White God was in their midst. He smiled gently at their dilemma and their fear, and stooping down He put His hand into the waves, and bade the poison flow into the hollow of His palm. Then He drank it, willing to die, in order to save the world. But that which would have been enough to destroy all created beings was only enough to stain His throat, hence He bears there a patch of blue for ever.

Perhaps one of the most characteristic myths that have clustered round the name of Mahadev is the Legend of the Boar-Hunt. As we read it, we stand on the snowy heights of the third range of the Himalayas, and seem to watch a mighty snow-storm sweeping through the ravine before us.

Arjuna, one of the principal heroes of the Great

War, and the second figure in the dialogue of the Gîtâ, had gone up into the mountains, to spend three months in worshipping Siva, and invoking His blessing. Suddenly one day as he was praying and offering flowers before the lingam, he was roused by a wild boar, which was rushing forward to attack him. It was only an instant, and Arjuna, the practised archer, had seized his bow and shot the animal. But at the self-same moment a shout of warning was heard, and simultaneously with Arjuna's a second arrow pierced the body of the beast. The hero raised his eyes, and saw, coming towards him, a formidable-looking hunter and huntress, followed by an innumerable retinue of women, attired for the chase, and attended, at some distance, by a dim host of shadows—the armies of demons and hobgoblins. A second later, the whole hunt had come to a stop before him.

"The quarry was mine!" cried the Hunter—and his voice sounded like the winter-blasts, amongst the mountains—"the quarry was mine. Mine is the lordship of these forests! How dared you touch it?"

At this address, Arjuna blazed with anger, and picking up the bow and arrows that he had thrown aside before returning to his worship, he challenged the Hunter to a personal combat.

"Accepted," was the reply, and the duel began. But to the hero's dismay, he seemed to be attacking some terrible phantom, for, one after another, his good stout arrows disappeared into the person of his antagonist, working him no harm.

"Let's wrestle then!" shouted Arjuna, and casting aside his bow, he flung himself upon his foe. He was met by the quiet touch of a hand on his heart, and fell to the ground stunned.

"Well, come on!" said the Hunter, as he recovered himself a few seconds later, and turned aside from the contest. But he seemed almost intoxicated. "I must finish my worship first," he said, in a thick voice, taking up a garland of flowers, to fling about the Siva-lingam. The next moment the eyes of Arjuna were opened, for the Hunter towered above him, blessing him, and the flowers were about his neck.

"Mahadev! Mahadev!" cried the worshipper, flinging himself on the ground, to touch with his head the feet of the God. But already the hunt had swept on down the valley, and the Hunter and Huntress had disappeared, with all their train.

Such are a few of the stories told of Siva, so deeply loved by all his devotees. To them there is nothing in the world so strong and pure and all-merciful as their great God, and the books and poems of Hindus are very few in which he is not referred to with this passionate worship.

Sometimes He is entirely a personification of the Himalayas, as when the Milky Way is made to fall upon his head, wander round and round amongst the tangled locks, and issue from them at last as the Ganges. Indeed, the imagination of the people may be said to make of their northern ranges one vast shrine to Him; for it is far away, they say, across the frost-bound heights, where the Himalayas are at their mightiest and India passes into Thibet, that the Lake Mansarobar lies, at the foot of the great ice-peak of Kailash. Here is the reign of silence and eternal snow, and here, guarding the north, is the holy home that Siva loves.

He is the very soul of gentleness, refusing none. Up here have gathered round Him all those who were weary of earth, having found no acceptance amongst the fortunate. The serpents, whom all the world hates and denies, come to Kailash, and

Mahadev finds room for them in His great heart. And the tired beasts come—for He is the refuge of animals—and it is one of these, a shabby old bull, that He specially loves and rides upon.

And here, too, come the spirits of all those men and women who are turbulent and troublesome and queer, the bad boys and girls of the grown-up world, as it were. All the people who are so ugly that no one wants to see them; those who do things clumsily, and talk loudly, and upset everything, though they mean no harm, and the poor things who are ridden by one idea, so that they never can see straight, but always seem a little mad—such are the souls on whom He alone has mercy. He is surrounded by them, and they love and worship Him. He uses them to do His errands, and they are known as Siva's demons.

But Siva is more even than this. He is the Self-born, the eternally-existent postulate of freedom and purity and light. He is the great teaching soul of things. His function is to destroy ignorance, and wherever knowledge is achieved, He is. His name of "Hara! Hara!" ("The Free! The Free!") was the battle-cry of the Mahrattas. More yet, He is Rudra, the Storm, the Terrible; and it is under this aspect that Hinduism raises to Him its daily cry:

> Evermore protect us,—O thou terrible!—
> From ignorance, by thy sweet compassionate face.

For, after all, a human quality is always limited to one of two, the Divine must be lifted above good as well as evil, above joy as well as pain. We have here the Indian conception of same-sightedness, and perhaps its devotional significance is nowhere interpreted as in the Hindi song of Surdas, which is here repeated as a nautch-girl was heard to sing it in a Rajput Court:

O Lord, look not upon my evil qualities!
Thy name, O Lord, is Same-sightedness,
By Thy touch, if Thou wilt, Thou canst make me pure.*

One drop of water is in the sacred Jumna,
Another is foul in the ditch by the roadside,
But when they fall into the Ganges,
Both alike become holy.

One piece of iron is the image in the temple,
Another is the knife in the hand of the butcher,
But when they touch the philosopher's stone,
Both alike turn to gold.

So, Lord, look not upon my evil qualities!
Thy name, O Lord, is Same-sightedness,
Make us both the same Brahman.

* *Literally,* Make us both the same Brahman—*i.e.*, Let the Singer—low dancing-girl as she may be—become one with God Himself in the Supreme Essence, Brahman. The theological conception here is so difficult for Western readers that I have preferred to use the simpler alternative translation also furnished by my Master, the Swami Vivekananda.

CHAPTER XIII

THE GOSPEL OF THE BLESSED ONE

We worship Thee, Seed of the Universe,
Thou one unbroken Soul.
We worship Thee, whose footstool is worshipped by the Gods.
Thou Lord of the Saints,
Physician of the World-disease,
To Thy lotus-feet our salutation, O Great Soul!

Hindu form of salutation to a Divine Incarnation.

I

IT is told of a certain Bodhisattva that, all his struggles done and illumination reached, he was about to pass over into Nirvana. But as his feet touched the threshold of supreme blessedness there rose to his ears the sound of the sorrowful crying of humanity. Then turned that great soul back from Nirvana and entered again into life, declaring that till the last grain of dust in the universe had passed in before him, he would by no means go into salvation. And this Bodhisattva is he who sits on the throne of the Dalai-Lama in Tibet, watching the world of men with eyes of divine pity from afar off.

Called by various names, arrayed in widely-differing garb, we come constantly in Hinduism on the attempt, as here in the story of the Dalai-Lama, to express the idea that in the great Heart of the Absolute there dwells an abiding charity towards men. It would seem as if, to the religious instinct of humanity, the dream of "the pursuit of the soul by God" is a necessity; and the Hindu, well aware of the impossibility of giving it logical expression, veils his effort in mythology. Whence the stories of the Avatars. For our conception of the doctrine of reincarnation is only complete when we understand that now and again the Eternal Love is represented as projecting itself into the sphere of manifestation, taking shape as a man, in order to act as a lamp amidst the darkness of delusion, a counter-magnetism to the attractions of desire.

It is absurd, says the Hindu—whose imagination can never be charged with provincialism—to think that such an Incarnation, supposing it to occur at all, could visit the world only once. Is respect of persons a divine attribute? Or is the need of mankind at any time less than complete? Can we believe, again, that the power of creative energy to assume and throw off the shell of personality is exhausted in a single effort? Rather must the taking upon Himself of mortal form and limitations be to the all-pervasive "as the lifting of a flower's fragrance by the summer breeze," a matter of play; or like the shining of a lamp through the window wherein it is set, without effort—nothing more.

The orthodox Hindu is thus usually in no position to deny the supernatural character of the Babe of Bethlehem. He is only unable to admit that the nature of Christ stands alone in the history of the world, holding that his own country has seen even more than the three—Rama, Krishna, and Buddha—who were His brothers. Still more cogently does he claim sometimes that all these and possibly others of whom he has not heard, are but one soul, one expression of Godhead coming back at different times to lay hold on the hearts of men. And he quotes in support of this contention the familiar words of Krishna: "Whenever religion decays, and when irreligion * prevails, *then* I manifest myself. For the protection of the good, for the destruction of the evil, for the firm establishment of the *dharmma*, I am born again and again."

It is natural enough to the Hindu intellect that around each such forth-shining of the Divine should grow up a new religious system or Church. But each of these is only a special way of expressing the one fundamental doctrine of Maya, a new mode of endearing God to man. At the same time it is thought that every one, while recognising this perfect sympathy of various faiths for one another, should know how to choose one amongst them for his own, and persist in it, till by its means he has reached a point where the formulæ of sects are meaningless to him. "For it is good," say the people, "to be born in a church, though it is foolish to die there."

In this sense—somewhat different from the religious partisanship of Europe—the popular and growing belief of the Hindu masses consists of various forms of the worship of Khrishna. It is this creed that carries to those who need it, a religious emotionalism like that of the Salvation Army or of Methodism. In the hottest nights, during periods of "revival," the streets of a city will be crowded with men bearing lights and banners, and dancing themselves into a frenzy to such words as:

> Call on the Lord,
> Call on the Lord,
> Call on the Lord, little brother
> Than this name of the Lord,
> For mortal man,
> There is no other way.

* Literally, dharmma and a-dharmma. The prefix here adversative—dharmma and non-dharmma. See p. 276.

Khrishna, like Rama and like Buddha, is considered to be a special incarnation of Vishnu, God the Preserver. It is therefore pertinent to appeal to Him for the goods of life, for consolation in sorrow, for deliverance from fear. He is known as the Holy Child, born in humility amidst cowherds by the Jumna; the Gentle Shepherd of the People, the Wise Counsellor, the Blessed Lord, tender Lover and Saviour of the human soul; and by other names not less familiar to ourselves. It is an image of the Baby Krishna that the Indian mother adores as the Bambino, calling it "Gopâla," her cowherd. His name fills gospels and poems, the folk-songs of all Hindu races are full of descriptions of Him as a cowherd wandering and sporting amongst His fellows; and childish literature is full of stories of Him, curiously like European tales of the Christ-child. To the ecstatic mystic, He is the Divine Spouse.

If we dip into His history we shall think it a strange medley. So many parts were never surely thrust upon a single figure! But through it all we note the predominant Indian characteristics,—absolute detachment from personal ends, and a certain subtle and humorous insight into human nature.

His main spiritual significance for India does not, perhaps—with one exception—attach to that part of His life which is related in the Mahabharata, but rather to what is told of Him in the Purânas—works not unlike our apocryphal Gospels. But the one exception is important. It consists of no less an incident than that conversation with the chieftain Arjuna which comprises the Bhagavad Gitâ, or Song of the Blessed One. Of this little poem—only some three or four times the length of the Sermon on the Mount, and shorter even than the Gospel of St. Mark—it may be said at once that amongst the sacred writings of mankind there is probably no other which is at once so great, so complete, and so short. It provides the worship of Krishna—and incidentally all kindred systems—with that open door upon abstract philosophy without which no cult could last in India for a week. But it is by no means the property of the Vaishnavas exclusively. From Kashmir to Cape Comorin it is bone of the bone and flesh of the flesh of all forms of religious thought.

Its ideas are unmistakably Indian in colour: its *feeling* is just as unmistakably universal. The voice that speaks on the field of Kurukshetra is the same voice that reverberates through an English childhood from the shores of the Sea of Galilee. We read the gracious words, "Putting aside all doctrines, come thou to Me alone for shelter—I will liberate thee from all sins, do not thou grieve." "Fixing thy heart on Me, thou shalt, by My grace, cross over all difficulties," and we drop the book, lost in a dream of One who cried to the weary and heavy laden, "Come unto Me." We certainly now understand, and cannot again forget, that for the Indian reader the eyes of the Lord Krishna are most kind, His touch infinitely gentle, and His heart full of an exceeding great compassion, even as for us are the eyes and the hand and the heart of Him Who spoke of Himself as the Good Shepherd.

Like our own Gospels, the Gitâ abounds in quaint and simple metaphors. "As a lamp in a sheltered spot, not flickering," must be the mind. All undertakings are surrounded with evil, "as fire with smoke." The round of worship is "as a wheel revolving." So great is wisdom that though thou shouldst be "even the most sinful of all sinners, thou shalt cross safely to the conquest of all sin by the bark of wisdom alone." One of the most beautiful, referring to those perceptions which constitute the Universe as we know it, says, "All this is threaded upon Me as gems upon a string." Nothing is mentioned that would not be familiar to the poorest peasant, living on a fertile plain, diversified only by a river and an occasional walled city.

And indeed it was for these, labouring men, unlettered and poor, that the Gîtâ, with its masterly simplicity, was written. To those who had thought salvation and the beatific vision as far beyond their attainment as a knowledge of the classics—to these humble souls the Divine Voice declares that, by worshipping God and doing at the same time the duty of his station, every man may attain perfection. "Better for one is one's own duty, however badly done, than the duty of another, though that be easy." Again and again, as we read the Gîtâ, we are driven to the conclusion that we hear an infinite mercy addressing itself to a people who had imagined the knowledge of God to be the monopoly of priesthoods and religious orders, and bidding them be of good courage, for the true monk is he "who neither hates nor desires," the true worshipper any one who "offers to Me with devotion even a leaf or a flower or a cup of water." No wonder that the Indian people, saluting a Divine Incarnation, call Him *the Physician of the world-disease!* Never did speech know how to be more interior. "Those who worship Me, renouncing all actions in Me, regarding Me as supreme, meditating on Me with entire devotion, for them whose thought is fixed on Me, I become ere long, O son of Prithâ, the Saviour out of the ocean of this mortal world." . . . "For I am the abode of Brahman, the Immortal and the Immutable, the Eternal Substance, and the unfailing Bliss." We kneel in a vast silence and darkness, and hear words falling like water drop by drop.

Nothing is omitted from the Gîtâ that the unconsoled heart requires. There are even the tender promises of daily bread, so dear to the anxious: "They who depend on Me, putting aside all care, whatsoever they need, I myself carry it to them," runs one verse. Of this a beautiful story is told in the villages. The Brahmin sat copying the text, but when the word "carry" had been written, he felt a doubt. "My dear," he said, turning to consult his wife, "thinkest thou not it is irreverent to say 'carry' here? Did our Lord not mean 'send'?" "Beyond a doubt, beloved," answered his wife, "it is as thou sayest. Let the word be 'send.'" Then the man took his penknife and erased the word he had just written, substituting his own emendation for it. A moment later he rose up to go and bathe. But his wife stood before him with troubled face. "I told thee not," she said, "that there is no food in the house, and nought have I to cook for thee." The Brahmin smiled gently. "Let us call upon our Lord to fulfil His own promise," he replied quietly; "meantime, I shall go and bathe," and he passed into the next room. Only a few minutes had he gone, when his wife was called to the door by a beautiful youth, who stood there with a basketful of delicious foods, ready for eating. "Who sent me this?" the woman asked in amazement. "Your husband called me to carry it," said the lad carelessly, putting the basket as he spoke into her hands. But to her horror, as he lifted his arms, the housewife noted cuts and gashes above his heart. "Alas, my poor child, who hath wounded thee?" she cried. "Your husband, mother, before he called me, cut me with a small sharp weapon," was the quiet answer. Dumb with astonishment, the Brahmin's wife turned away to bestow the viands he had brought, and when she came back to the door the youth had gone. At that instant her husband re-entered the room, having returned, as she supposed from bathing. Her wonder about the food was forgotten in indignant sympathy. "Why," she cried, "didst thou so hurt thy messenger?" The man looked at her without understanding. "Him whom thou sentest to me with food, as thou didst go to bathe," she explained. "To bathe!" he stammered, "I have not yet been!" Then the eyes of husband and wife met, and they knew both who had come to them, and how they had wounded the heart of the Lord. And the Brahmin returned to the sacred text, and once more erasing a word restored it to its original form, for there can be no doubt that the true reading is, "They who depend on Me, casting aside all care, whatsoever they need, I myself *carry* it to them."

Such are some of the associations which cling to the little image of Krishna that the children about Calcutta can buy for a few farthings. It is made of lime, and painted blue—for just as white, to the dweller amongst northern snows, signifies purity, so blue, the colour of sky and ocean, to the child of the South, is the token of the Infinite. The left hand of the image holds a flute to the lips; the right carries a thin golden scroll, referring to the Gîtâ. The feet are crossed carelessly, like those of any strolling peasant-player, and the head is crowned. Simple toy as it is, there is hardly a detail of the composite figure in which a devotional system does not centre.

"O Thou that playest on the flute, standing by the water-ghats, on the road to Brindaban!" sing the lovers of Krishna, and their hearts melt within them while they sing, pierced as by S. Teresa's wound of seraphic love. Of all its elements, however, there is none which has the unequalled importance to the world of the scroll in the right hand, both as throwing light on Indian habits of thought and as an exposition of the science of religion. The questions, therefore, On what fundamental experience does the Gîtâ base itself? To what does it appeal? What does it single out in life as requiring explanation? What is its main imperative? are of singular interest. That place which the four Gospels hold to Christendom, the Gîtâ holds to the world of Hinduism, and in a very real sense, to understand it is to understand India and the Indian people.

II

It is believed by Hindus that when great forces are in action, on occasions such as those of battle and earthquake, a certain state of etheric vibration is produced, which makes it easy for minds trembling on the verge of supreme knowledge to vault the barricades of sense and find illumination. Perhaps this is because a great intensity of experience has to be found and transcended. Perhaps the conditions, apparently simple, are really more complex than this. At any rate, the story of the Bhagavad Gîtâ is of the coming of such beatitude to a young soldier named Arjuna, some three thousand years ago.

Incidentally, the opening of the poem presents us with an impressive picture of an ancient battlefield. On the great plain of Kurukshetra, already the scene of the prayers and austerities of saints and pilgrims for hundreds of years, two armies face each other. The leaders of both sides occupy chariots drawn by white horses; over each waves his personal ensign; and each carries a conch-shell, by way of trumpet, to enable him to give signals and enforce attention to his commands. Both armies are represented as great hosts, but indications are not wanting that that of Duryodhana, the usurper, under the leadership of Bhishma, is the larger and stronger. And this is natural, since Duryodhana, rightly or wrongly, is still suzerain of the whole country, while the five Pandava brothers, his cousins, are only bent on the recovery of their rights from him. We have to call to mind that this is an ancient battle, consisting of an immense number of small fights, before we are able to give our thoughts calmly to the narrative, for we are told that from all parts of the field and on both sides the white conch-shells have been blown, giving the signal for assault, and that already "the discharge of weapons" has begun, when Arjuna requests Krishna, who is acting as his charioteer, to drive him into the space between the two hosts, that he may single out those with whom he is to enter into personal combat during the fray.

The sight of the foe, however, has an extraordinary effect on the mind of the chieftain. Instead of looking on his enemies with an accession of faith in the justice of his own cause and a heroic determination to struggle to the last in its defence, he seems to realise for the first time the consequences of the attack. Amongst the foe stand all he has ever loved or honoured—Bhishma, the head of his house, the adored grandsire of his childhood; Drona, to whom he owes his education, and for whom he cherishes a passionate reverence; and cousins and relatives innumerable besides, of whom the very worst is an old playfellow or a gallant combatant in tourney. The path to victory lies through the burning-ghat of the dead! The ashes of all he loves are scattered there! As he realises this, Arjuna's great bow slips from his hand, and he sinks to the floor of his chariot in despair. We must remember that this is no mere failure of courage. The soldier has been tried and proved too often to be open for a moment to such an imputation. Neither is he represented as entertaining the slightest doubt of ultimate triumph. To the fortunes of war he gives not a thought, assuming, as do all brave men, that they must follow the right. He simply realises that for the sake of a few years of dominion he is about, with his own hand, to rid the earth of everything he loves. He realises, too, that this widespread slaughter will constitute an enormous social disaster.

This feeling of Arjuna's finds religious expression. "I desire not victory, O Krishna, neither kingdom nor pleasures. . . . It would be better for me if the sons of Dritarashthra, arms in hand, should slay me, unarmed and unresisting, in the battle." Surely the moral situation is finely conceived! A prince, of the proudest lineage on earth, is eager to be offered up as a sacrifice rather than accept empire at the price to be paid for it. On the battlefield of life does any case need better stating? Yet this thirst for martyrdom, which looks so like renunciation, is really quite another thing. "Thou art grieved for those who require no grief, yet thou speakest words of wisdom," says Krishna. For, instead of the actual indifference to the world and to his own part in it, of one who perceives that all before him is unreal, Arjuna is betraying that determination to maintain things as they are which belongs to those who hold that affection at least is a very actual good. It is on this distinction that the whole treatise is based.

At first, indeed, the charioteer affects to meet the chieftain's hesitation with all the contempt of knighthood for panic. "Yield not to unmanliness, O son of Pritha!" he exclaims. "Ill doth it become thee. Cast off this base weakness, and arise, O terror of foes." It is not till Arjuna, with a touching acknowledgment of grief and confusion, makes a supreme appeal for intellectual enlightenment, that Krishna, in the character of divine teacher, enters on that immortal pronouncement regarding the Real and unreal, which ends by sending the knight back to the duty of his birth, unshrinking, with the words: "Firm, with undoubting mind, I obey Thy word."

As the dialogue proceeds, the dramatic element disappears. The echoes of battle die away. We are standing alone in some chamber of the soul, holding that colloquy between human and divine, finite and infinite, which never ceases during life for any one of us, however little able we may be to disentangle it from the voices of the world. At the culminating moment of the interview, when the worshipper receives the sudden revelation of all existing in and by the Lord Krishna, as mere multiform expressions of His sole energy, even at this moment, and during the rapt and broken praise which follows it, we find nothing discordant in the *mise-en-scène.* A chariot of war has become, as only a Hindu pen could have made it, silent as any cell of meditation. The corner of a battlefield has grown as remote from the whirl of life as the inmost recesses of a heart at prayer.

The main argument is, as we might expect, that as all appearances are delusive, action is to the wise man indifferent, and should be performed, once he is sure that he is called to it, without fear of consequences. "Him the wise call a sage—the man whose undertakings are all devoid alike of objects and desires, whose acts have been burnt to ashes in the fire of wisdom." "Never did I not exist, nor thou, nor these rulers of men; and no one of us will ever hereafter cease to exist." Therefore, "Free from hope and from selfishness, without any anxiety of mind, plunge thou into battle!"

The words are addressed to one who is preeminently a man of action, a soldier—supposed, saving a due regard for his military honour, to be swayed by the passion for justice, and the impulse to defend it. These things being the stake, throw for them, and throw boldly, says Krishna, and as results, take whatever may chance to come. "Man has always the right to work: man has no right to the results of work," is as much the heart and core of the Gîtâ, as "Thou hast no right to success if thou art not also equal to failure," is of Stoicism. In application the two doctrines seem identical, but we have only to read, in order to see the advantage which the idea of Maya gives to the Indian thinker. Clear, sharp, incisive as chisel-strokes, are the utterances of Epictetus: like thunderbolts out of a tropical night the words of Krishna.

The Gîtâ, however, does not consist of a single chain of reasoning, moving in definite progression from beginning to end. Rather is the same thing said over and over again, in as many different ways as possible. Sometimes even a form of words is repeated, as if nothing mattered save to make the meaning clear. There is ample scope here for the digressive energy of ages, of which the outcome is the richly-woven texture, set here and there with those strangely-cut Oriental jewels, which must remain amongst the greatest recorded words of religion to all time.

But readers will completely miss the sense of the Gîtâ who permit themselves to forget its first ringing words: "Yield not to unmanliness, O son of Pritha! Ill doth it become thee. Shake off this base weakness, and arise, O terror of foes!" The book is nowhere a call to leave the world, but everywhere an interpretation of common life as the path to that which lies beyond. "Better for a man is his own duty, however badly done, than the duty of another, though that be easy." "Holding gain and loss as one, *prepare for battle.*" That the man who throws away his weapons, and permits himself to be slain, unresisting, in the battle, is *not* the hero of religion, but a sluggard and a coward; that the true seer is he who carries his vision into action, regardless of the consequences to himself; this is the doctrine oı the Gîtâ, repeated again and again. The book is really a battle-cry. Spirituality is with it no retreat from men and things, but a burning fire of knowledge that destroys bondage, consumes sluggishness and egoism, and penetrates everywhere. Not the withdrawn, but the transfigured life, radiant with power and energy, triumphant in its selflessness, is religion.

The Gîtâ is to-day the gospel of the Indian Revival. And never was book so well suited to such function. For its eighteen chapters are the expression of an overwhelming national vitality. It is as true of peoples as of individuals, that when the age is full and rich, living is apt to outrun knowing. It is then that large questions press for solution. Great areas of experience require to be related to their common centre and to each other. And so pre-eminently does the Gîtâ do this, that the Mussulman and the Christian can sit indifferently with the Hindu to gather its interpretations.

The nature of all faith, the relation of all worship to worshipped and worshipper, the dependence of knowledge on non-attachment under all its forms: it is with problems like these, and not with any particular *Credo*, that the Gîtâ concerns itself. It is at once therefore the smallest and most comprehensive of the scriptures of the world.

That indifference to results is the condition of efficient action is the first point in its philosophy. But there is no doubt that the action should be strenuous. Let every muscle be hard, every limb well-knit, let the mind sweep the whole horizon of fact; with the reins in hand, the fiery steeds under control, with the whole battlefield in view, and the will of the hero lifted high to strike for justice,

"Arise!" thunders the voice of Sri Krishna, "and be thou an apparent cause!"

It is the supreme imperative. Play thy whole part in the drama of time, devoting every energy, concentrating the whole force. "As the ignorant act from selfish motives, so should the wise man act, unselfishly."

Just as the child sees the sun above his head, and the earth beneath his feet, distinguishing himself from both, while to the man of science, sun, planet, and child are all single points in a great ocean of force-matter, absolutely continuous from its centre to its farthest bounds, so to us all, in the sense-plane of thought, God, soul, and relation exist. Having reached that truth, however, which is the Beatific Vision, any one of them will seem the whole, for all conception of limitation will be blotted out. As we ourselves are seen to be but light transformed; as thought and perception, life and motion, sun and planet, are all but different manifestations of a something that we call Solar Energy, so God, self, and universe, are now known to be only distinctions made by sense in that one, Brahman, "the immortal and immutable, the eternal substance, and the unfailing Bliss."

An account of such a vision gives us the culminating chapter of the Gîtâ. Krishna suddenly bursts forth on the sight of his astonished worshipper as the Universal Form, in Whom all that exists in one. Characteristically Indian in expression, full of the blaze and terror of the cosmos, this great scene can only perhaps be thoroughly appreciated by a Western mind if it has first understood something of the craving that it fulfils, caught some flash maybe of the radiance it describes. Yet if the rest of the Gîtâ were destroyed, this one chapter might take its place, for it makes all its logic actual.

Arjuna's single sight becomes the sacrament of a whole world's hope.

It was midnight when I reached Thaneswar. The fierce white light of a tropical moon bathed the great common in front, where only trees and bushes, with their coal-black shadows, could be seen, and not a single human habitation was in sight. Behind, the dâk-bungalow lay in darkness, and the train by which I had come had passed on long ago into the night. One was alone on the Plain of Kurukshetra with three thousand years.

But the silence did not remain unbroken. Clear and distinct on the still air rose the accents of the immortal dialogue. "Man has the right to work: man has no right to the fruits of work," said, once more, the divine Charioteer. Yet many a memorable battle has been fought, India herself has heard a thousand dialogues, preaching the truths of the Bhagavad Gîtâ. Why, asked my heart, does one come to this spot? For what thing, above all others, does the world remember Kurukshetra?

And then I saw why, never to forget. Kurukshetra was the place of the Great Vision, the field of the Divine Illumination of Arjuna.

CHAPTER XIV

ISLAM IN INDIA

I

The single continent of the Old World, outside the forests of Africa, is broadly divisible into the agricultural valleys of the East, the sands and steppes of the pastoral belt, and the countries of the European coast-line—and the geographical division is strangely correspondent to the history of its moral development. Civilisation and religion are born amongst peasants, become aggressive amongst sailors, and are passed from one to the other by the nomad races of the desert strip.

For adequate culture-histories of Venice, Genoa, and the Crusades, the world is still waiting. When they are written, men will be astonished to learn both how completely Europe is indebted to Asia, and also how far the Semitic races have been in modern times the stewards of that debt.

It has been administered through the Jew as well as the Mussulman. But the Jew was the spiritual heir of Egypt, and as such could not individualise the desert pure and simple. His religious ideas were too complex, his social system too exclusive, his national sentiment too unfixed. When he ceased to be a peasant in Syria, the world was before him as scholar and trader.

To the Arab, on the other hand, belonged the

shifting constancy of the desert sands. No luxury of cities could fire him with ambition to leave home and kindred, the scanty fare and hardy contests of his youth, that he might eat well and sleep soft amongst aliens. To this day the seamen in the Red Sea or the Indian Ocean will pass those curious, square-sailed boats known as Arab dhows, and will carelessly shout their bearings in answer to the inquiry of the navigators within, who are steering their way on the ocean as they would across the desert, by the position of the sun. But these boats are rude merchantmen merely, not emigrant vessels. They are going out, only that they may return and enrich their own people with the benefits of trade. When the Arab of old did set his eyes upon the capitals of the world it was to possess them. He went forth in his armies, taking his kindred with him, and seated himself in their palaces, upon their thrones. And yet the city where that idea of his own solidarity was born which enabled the Mussulman to ignore petty feuds for a great unifying idea, was the open port of its day and place, and the Prophet himself was more travelled than most of his contemporaries. It is always so. Behind the rise of a world-swaying idea there is always the sentiment of the advancement of truth, the impulse to assimilate all that is newest and best in foreign influences; there is always, too, the power of outlook in more than common degree. Mohammed had reached his burning tenderness for his own people, and his consciousness of a national perplexity, by direct contact with Syrian market-places and Byzantine townsfolk. Long talks beside the caravan fires at night with men of many different nations, had given him his education, setting dim thoughts and mighty longings vaguely astir within him. It is difficult for the modern world to realise the largeness of primitive thought and personality. We feel that we have triumphed mightily in the invention of the steam-engine and the railway train; and so, along one line, we have. We forget, however, that henceforth the leader of our travel is to be a mere mechanic, managing a few cog-wheels, and superintending water and coal. Once upon a time, in the same capacity, he was something of patriarch, savant, poet, and ship's captain all in one.

Similarly of the personal courage required in war, and the breadth of nature-painting in early literature. The progress of time and thought means the deterioration of these qualities. No modern poet can speak of the sunset like a Red Indian. No user of Maxim guns has the personal prowess of an old-time pirate. Strong individuality is demanded by undeveloped, unregimented conditions, and later civilisation is only a specialisation upon this, growing by degrees more subtle and detailed, in which the man has often lost in proportion as the institution has gained.

Depth of observation, vastness and nobility of hope, and wealth of assimilated experience—all, in short, that constitutes essential education—are often but inversely proportioned to literacy. Therefore there is no room for the library-and-museum learned of the twentieth century to refer to a camel-driver of the seventh as ignorant. The Prophet Mohammed can have been nothing of the sort. With rare beauty and sweetness of nature, he combined social and political genius, towering manhood, and an intellectual culture of no mean kind. As has so often been the case with the initiators of new faiths, he was in a special sense the blossom of the old, for not only were his family the guardians of the Kaabah, but his father had been intended in his childhood to be a sacrifice to the gods, and Mohammed was an only son, early orphaned. Indeed, had he belonged to any city but Mecca, the pilgrim-centre of the Arabian peninsula, he could not possibly have seen the Islamising of the whole Arab people within his single lifetime.

We think of the Prophet too much as the preacher of a religion, too little as the maker of a nationality. We hear the Name of God so frequently that we forget the love of humanity that is taught. We fail, in short, to understand the Asiatic character both of messenger and message.

In the name of God, the Compassionate, the Merciful.

But the word that follows argues little enough, at least in early days, about the Unity of God. After all, this is a fact that we recognise instinctively. No man, least of all the dweller in the desert, in his heart believes that God is two. The Prophet's first task is to give life and vigour to this supreme intuition by making it only the starting-point of a searching appeal to conscience, an authoritative condemnation of insincerity and evil custom, and terrible pictures of judgment and hell-fire. In all this he must only have uttered what was already in the air. Social life in Arabia must have been ripe for change. The sacredness of property, the protection of childhood, and the fixing of woman's status, had already doubtless been felt as necessities by good men of all tribes and cities. But the gigantic power of conviction that could use these very reforms as a means of welding the scattered and divided kinships into a single brotherhood, fired with a common purpose of righteousness and armed with the mighty weapon of a divine mission—this was the sole right of one whose boyhood had been spent among the sheepfolds, and whose manhood had known the solitary watch, with the awful trance of revelation, in the mountain caves.

From one point of view, Islam represents a transition between Asia and Europe. An Asiatic people takes on the consolidation, the mobility, and the militarism of a European State. It anticipates the West in so doing by many a century. It accomplishes the Napoleonic task of destroying the Persian and Byzantine empires, and setting itself up in their place; and yet, inasmuch as it does all this in the strength of an idea, inasmuch as its sanction lies in one man's superconscious inspiration, it remains at heart profoundly Asiatic.

The relation between the master and his disciples is always one of the most vital elements in the life of Asia. In this case, whole nations are the disciples of a single man. They are taken into his kindred. They form his family. They strive to approximate to his method of life—in dress, food, manners, even to some extent in language. Whenever they pray, they place themselves mentally in Arabia. Such facts make religion in the East a matter of enormous social consequence. The convert in India immediately changes his style of cookery. One can eat a dinner in that country, Hindu, Mohammedan, Parsi, Jain, Jewish, Christian, or Buddhist in kind; but assuredly without changing his food no man could be held to have sincerely changed his faith. It is inevitable, therefore, that communities which accept the creed of Islam should become Arabised in every possible way.

This does not mean, however, that they should remake the desert. Mohammed's whole polity made towards settled and industrial conditions. His last great speech, in which he gathers all his people together, knowing not if he shall ever again address them, reminds them of the sacredness of private property, and the rights of women, slaves and children. Nor was there any barbarism about the Mohammedan empires of the next six or seven centuries. Western Asia did not fail to build itself upon the arts of the Roman Empire, did not fail to assimilate Hellenic culture, and to display an original impetus in science, from the blending of Greek and Oriental elements. The history of the great Spanish schools is too well known to need comment. The splendours of the Abbasside Caliphs at Baghdad were well borne out by the Ommiades at Cordova, and an architecture that deserves to be the wonder of the world was the fruit of Saracenic civilisation. The blasting of Persia, Syria, and Asia Minor, would seem to have been the work of the Mogul invasions of Genghis Khan and Tamerlane, in the thirteenth and fourteenth centuries. These invasions sound through the pages of history like irruptions of subterranean forces. They were similar to, but incomparably vaster than, those which brought about the sack of Rome by Alaric and Genseric, and which left the city and Campagna, under the guardianship of monks, to the insidious decay of many centuries. The geographical position of the Eternal City and her surroundings was, however, some protection, whereas the Eastern provinces were exposed to the tramp and re-tramp of every hostile force. Gibbon says of Genghis Khan that he destroyed in four days what five hundred years had not sufficed to restore. The common statement that the blighting of Asia Minor has been the work of Mohammedanism may therefore be put down to historical ignorance and theological prejudice.

The utmost stigma that can attach to Saracenic governments has been that they have not had the energy and patience to bend themselves in such cases to the incredible task of beginning all over again the work of civilisation and polity. But are they peculiar in this? Would France, England, or Italy—were the past blotted out, and all sovereign and responsible persons removed, as at a single blow—show more courage, more persistence, than the Arab or the Turk? The very grandeur of the cities that had vanished would add to the hopeless inactivity of the generations that found themselves orphaned and despoiled. An additional factor in the case is—not the genius of Islam, whose purely destructive and desolating tendencies may at least be questioned by those who have seen its work in India, but—the nature of all conquests. The whole opportunity of a conqueror lies in the loyal submission of himself to the past of the conquered. Failing this, the structure that he rears must be, if not destructive, at least evanescent. No power remains at its height for ever; and in this decline, the ability to guard with decency and stability what it has created, preserving the hope and possibility of resurrection, will depend exactly on the amount of force that was put into that creation.

It is a curious fact that from the Parthenon to the Taj Mahal, the appearance of a memorable national art has always been coeval with the existence of a powerful centralising consciousness. Pericles adorned Athens with the tribute of the Greek States. Ancient Rome was decorated with the trophies of the world. Mediæval cathedrals and town-halls grew out of the vigorous craft and municipal solidarity. Florence and the Vatican were the blossoms of the Church. The commercial nexus of Venice was an empire wide as the planet. The diggers of Buddhist cave-temples in India, and the builders of Indo-Saracenic palaces and tombs, alike worked under the shadow of imperial thrones, which articulated for them the enthusiasm of the wholeness of things.

But what of a flower without leaf, stem and root? Times of blossom are few and far between, at least equally sacred and important is the task of maintaining and increasing the common life. Even so with the growth of nations. The humble, mole-like work of developing civilisation through the daily life and the simple home, is still more important than the ephemeral glory of an age of exploitation, and the persistence of a nationality is assuredly proportionate to the degree in which it represents the utmost of such unseen, steady, and joyous co-operation amongst its members.

It may be charged indeed against the flying squadrons of the desert that of such slow-accumulating toil they brought too little to the making of Baghdad, and the ruling of Damascus. It may be urged that in the stimulating union of Chinese, Hindu, Persian and Hellenic elements, over which the Arab there reigned supreme, there was too little intensity of culture and research; that the regal race was content to furnish its universities with translations only of the foreign texts on which so much of their learning was based; that there was too marked a tendency to despise the associations of its subjects; too great a readiness to build its own mosques out of the ruins of their palaces; and finally, that to a struggle so easy, an end was inevitable, a decay as long and inglorious as its triumph had been brilliant and short-lived. Such arguments may be true, but their truth constitutes a reproach against all conquests, not a stain on the Arab faith.

II

No one can stand and face the ruins behind the Kutb-Minar * at Delhi, no one can realise, even dimly, the beauty of Persian poetry, without understanding that Arab, Slav, Afghan, and Mogul came to India as the emissaries of a culture different

* Kutb-Minar, a famous tower or minaret, about eleven miles from Delhi.

indeed from, but not less imposing than, that of the people of the soil. The arches in the broken screen of Altamish, as it is called, which are all that remains of a mosque of the twelfth century, are as perfect in taste and devotional feeling as anything in the Gothic. The complete building must have lacked somewhat in weight and solidity, but it was not the work of ruffians and barbarians, nor were the men who thronged to it for prayer, mere lovers of wanton destruction.

A Hindu historian would have the first right to chant the pæan of the Mussulman faith, for it was upon Akbar, a sovereign of that creed, that the inspiration dawned to make a nation and a nationality out of the peoples of modern India.

The sixteenth century in Europe has been known as the era of great kings. Leo X. of the Papacy, Charles V. of the Empire, Henry IV. of France, and Elizabeth of England, are amongst the strongest personalities to whom thrones were ever given. And if we take the English Tudors alone, we shall find four notable figures, with strong policies of their own, out of the five members of that dynasty. About the last two, there is, however, one peculiarity. Even those who sympathise most strongly with the Catholic Queen would probably recognise that it was well for the country that Elizabeth reigned after her, and not before. Few would dispute the greater statesmanship, and more synthetic character of the policy, of the latter of these two sovereigns. Indeed the fact is well enough proved by the loyalty and enthusiasm with which her Catholic subjects united with the Protestant to repel the Spanish Armada.

The history of India, from the middle of the sixteenth to the end of the seventeenth centuries, displays a curious parallelism and contrast to this of England during the sixteenth. The reign of

Akbar was contemporary with that of Elizabeth, and, with a still greater statesmanship and breadth of mind and heart, he undertook to inaugurate a vast national, as distinguished from a sectarian policy. Few indeed of the world's monarchs have ever used so marvellous an opportunity with such wisdom and magnanimity as this Emperor of Delhi. An almost equal sympathy with the speculations of all religions, a deep understanding and admiration of the old Indian system, with a desire only to complete and extend, never to nullify it; a love of everything that was national, with a habit of striking swiftly and pardoning generously—all these qualities gave Akbar a place in the hearts of his subjects which makes "Secundra, the Great," a sufficient name for him to this day. He had been born in a Rajput household, and his greatest act, after the modelling of his administration on the ancient "dharmma," was the marrying of a Hindu princess, and making her the mother of the heir-apparent. Aurungzeeb was the first of his successors who was not Indian in this complete sense, of having had a Mussulman father and a Hindu mother.

Akbar's three immediate descendants—Jehangir, his son, Shah Jehan, his grandson, and Aurungzeeb, his great-grandson—were all men of marked ability. They retained intact the empire which his genius had consolidated. But unfortunately, of them all, Aurungzeeb's was the sectarian and somewhat narrowly devotional temperament of the English Catholic queen, better fitted to make him a saint of Islam than welder of the Indian nationality; and Shah Jehan alone had a genius of administration comparable to his grandfather's of initiation. In other words, India had the misfortune in her own case to see Elizabeth succeeded, not preceded by Mary.

Such were the four great Moguls, whose united

reigns began two years before the accession of Elizabeth, and ended at the date of the Parliamentary union of England and Scotland, scarcely yet two hundred years ago. Their Tartar blood, for they came of the race of Tamerlane, gave them unflagging energy and perseverance. Their Mohammedan faith gave them strength and simplicity of creed, unexhausted by the three hundred years' adhesion of their tribes. Their soldierly origin gave them the power to adopt the ruder side of military life at a moment's notice, while, at the same time, all their habits and associations imposed on them the power and means of unequalled splendour. Such were they all; but of them all, Akbar stands unrivalled in liberal statesmanship, and Shah Jehan in personal genius.

In the hands of this last monarch the unity of India became a visible fact, symbolised by the dazzling beauty of his building, and even Leo X. must give way to him for taste. Now it was the Taj, raising its stately head above its jewelled walls and lace-carved windows of white marble, in inconsolable love and sorrow. Again, it was the Pearl Mosque of Agra, vast in proportion and almost unadorned, in severity of creamy stone, of sun-steeped court, and shadowed aisles and sanctuary. Yet once more some dainty palace or exquisite oratory, the baths of an empress or the hall of audience of a king, testified to the fact that a lord of artists sat upon the throne. But it was not only in white marble that Shah Jehan gave the reins to his pride in the Indian soil and the Indian people. He built the modern Delhi, with her red walls, her broad streets, and her magnificent fortress. He made the peacock throne, of gold and jewels, which was removed to Persia by Nadir Shah a hundred years later. He and his court and household were collectors of choice books and pictures. And, like all the

Moguls, he was himself a past master in the art of illuminating manuscripts.

Not the least part of the beauty of his buildings lies in the acoustic properties of their domes, which act as bells, taking up every whisper and groan that may sound below them, and making it into music in the height above. There is no voice so harsh or vulgar that it is not in their presence made rich and harmonious; and if any poor old Mussulman be asked why every mosque is domed, he will answer in bewilderment that he can only suppose that it is to make the name of Allah resound again and again.

In all this Shah Jehan proved himself the monarch, not of some section, but of all his subjects, and as such he is regarded by India to this day. He might not be in active sympathy with every phase of the popular creeds, but there is none who is cut off from sympathy with him. The enthusiasm that spoke in his works is deeply understood. His addition of a third style to the architectural glories of the country is never forgotten. And it is still remembered by the people that, according to the unanimous voice of history, India was never so well administered as in his day.

The Mohammedan brought roses into India. "They are of the caste of the emperors," said a Hindu, sitting near, as two beggars came into my verandah in a southern province and offered me these flowers, "they are of the caste of the emperors. Even their begging is that of kings!"

The remark is significant of a liberalising influence upon social usage wherever the Mogul Empire has penetrated; for orthodox Hinduism is perhaps a little too barren of all luxury, a little too much hemmed-in by strict requirements and consideration of the highest motives. "The West," it has been said, "has mastered the knowledge of the ways and means of life, and this the East may well accept from her." Mohammedanism is much more than a half-way house towards the point at which such knowledge becomes possible. It is even said sometimes by Hindus that no gentleman can fulfil the requirements of modern life unless he have a Mohammedan servant.

The very courtesy of Mohammedan bearing speaks of palaces and of military life. Were India an independent country, her most important embassies would doubtless be filled by Moslems. The act of salutation is almost as a devotion amongst the sons and daughters of Islam. The pause of reverence, the evident depth of feeling with which the hand of the elder is lifted by the younger to the forehead and then kissed, the beautiful words, "Salaam alaikum!" ("Peace be unto you!"), which accompany a bow—all these things are the tokens of a culture of humanity which produces a depth of sympathy and tenderness not unworthy of that Prophet whose burning love of God found no adequate expression save in the love and service of man. It is a humanity in which still breathes the fragrance of that great pastoral peace of desert and steppe which is the living force and unity of the whole Moslem world, however the accidents of time or place may seem to betray it. The patriarch seated at his tent door welcoming strangers, loving and just in his dealings with wives and kindred, trusted and revered by all his tribe, and giving his very heart, as is the fashion of the men of Islam, to little children, is an integral imagination of the race. There is nothing in the world so passionately tender as a Hindu mother, unless it be a Mohammedan father.

It is this human aspect of the Arab faith that prepares us for its proselytising power in India. It represents to the low-caste Hindu what the Buddhist orders once represented—a perfect democracy, in which stains of birth, of blood, of occupation, are all blotted out by the utterance of the formula of fraternity, "There is no God but God, and Mohammed is his Prophet." However low and degraded was a man's past, he may now be and do whatever he desires and can. The word "Sheikh" prefixed to his name indicates that he comes of a family so adopted by conversion; and the vast majority of Mohammedan cultivators, boatmen, and builders in India, are thus Hindu by blood and instinct, and Moslem by creed. The gods of the old faith become the saints or "pirs" of the new. They pray at their tombs *to* the dead, as well as *for* them, and are regarded indulgently by the orthodox and learned of their new faith as illiterate, and therefore superstitious. That brotherhood which is talked of by Christianity is realised by Islam. The message of the Prophet is a message of humanity and freedom to the whole race of man.

Most religions have two phases: one the Puritan, and the other the ornate. The Puritan side of Islam finds expression in the Sunni sect, and the ornate aspect in the Shiah. It is the Shiahs who commemorate the Caliph Ali and the deaths of Hassan and Hussain. They carry the tombs of the martyrs in procession at the Mohurrum, and whenever they are bereaved they mourn for the family of Ali instead of for their own. Geographically, the Shiahs are Persian, and in India are most numerous in Bengal and round Lucknow. The sterner and narrower teachings of Sunni-ism formed the royal faith of Delhi and Hyderabad. Besides these, there is a third sect of Mohammedans in India, known as the Wahabi. This is described somewhat satirically as the religion of those who had one parent a Shiah, and the other a Sunni. It is in fact a modern reform. As amongst Hindus, however, his particular shade of religion is a matter of the individual's own choice, and the women are even more pronounced than the men, regarding personal doctrinal conviction.

The influence of the Indian environment is felt, further, in many of the social developments of the Islamic community. It is not unnatural that there should be a great aptitude for the formation of castes, and a stern refusal to break bread with those who are not of the chosen group. In other directions also there is an approximation of custom. Many Mussulman families in Bengal would turn with horror from the eating of beef. The wife insists that her own hands and no others shall cook the food eaten by the husband. The re-marriage of widows is discountenanced by the highest standards of taste, and in the royal family of Delhi the life of a widowed princess was spent exactly like that of a Hindu woman who had lost her husband—in austerity, prayer, and study. Finally, that hymn to the Ganges which is among the first things learnt by a Hindu child, was written three or four centuries ago by a Mussulman.

On its divine side, ignoring those dim reaches of Sufi-ism which only the saints attain, and where all saints, of all faiths, are at one, ignoring, too, all sectarian differences as between Sunnis and Shiahs, Islam stands in India as another name for *bhakti*, or the melting love of God. In the songs of the people the Hindu name of *Hari*, and the Mohammedan *Allah* are inextricably blended, and as one listens to the boatmen singing while they mend their nets, one cannot distinguish the hymn from the poem of love.

It was Mohammed's realisation of God's love for man, however little he may have put it into words, that thrilled through the Arab world, and drew the tribes as one man, to fight beneath his banner. His was no triumph of the fear and majesty of God. Five times every day, after his ablutions, does the pious Mohammedan turn towards Mecca and say:

> Praise be to God, the Lord of the worlds,
> The compassionate, the merciful.
> King of the day of judgment!
> Thee we worship, and Thee we ask for help.
> Guide us in the straight way,
> The way of those to whom Thou art gracious;
> Not of those upon whom is Thy wrath, nor of the erring.

And again:

> Say: He is one God;
> God the Eternal.
> He begetteth not, nor is begotten;
> Nor is there one like unto Him.

The prayer and creed, for all their ring of pride and awe, are not the words of beaten slaves, but of loved and loving children, confident of the depth of that mercy whereto they appeal. Something there was indeed in the fierce ethical passion of Mohammed, the basis of his piercing appeal to the conscience of his people, which might look like terrorism. If all men knew of hell and judgment, he said, what he did, there would be little laughter and much weeping amongst them. But all this is on behalf of conscience and the voice of righteousness. A nature itself so radiant in compassion for women, for the poor, for slaves, and for dumb beasts, could not long remain in contemplation of the terrors of the Divine. Throughout the creation he sees one law writ large, "Verily my compassion overcometh my wrath," and Mohammed, who believes in austerity, but not in self-mortification, feels all the passion of the Flagellant, as he utters the word *Islam*, or uttermost surrender of self to the Truth that is in God.

CHAPTER XV

AN INDIAN PILGRIMAGE

THE old roads of Asia are the footways of the world's ideas. There is a camel-track that crosses the desert from Egypt into "Sooria," broken at the Suez Canal by a ferry. What road in Europe, Roman or barbarian, can compare in charm and pathos with this sandy path? On it we might yet see a woman carrying a child on the back of an ass, and an old man leading them, even as the legends picture the Flight of the Holy Family. By it long ago marched the armies of Egypt to meet those of Assyria in destructive conflict on the borders of Israel. By it Judea sent the streams of her burning thought and fierce ethical emotion to Alexandria, before Christianity was born.

Similarly, all over India, away from her ancient high roads, and thrown like a network across her proudest Himalayas, are little thread-like paths like this—ways made indeed by the feet of men, but worn far deeper by the weight of impelling ideas than by the footprints of the toil-stained crowds.

Such roads must once have connected China with Kashmir. Afghanistan, always a province of India, must by just such paths have sent its wandering merchants with nuts and raisins to the South, as long ago as the days of Solomon. Even now it is by ways unpaved, deep-trodden, that the long-haired goats scramble down with their loads through the snowy defiles from Bokhara and Thibet, to be sheared in the sunny valley of the Jhelum, and furnish wool for its famous shawls. Which comes first, we wonder, commerce or pilgrimage, the trade route or the palmer's path? Would it not appear that the utilities of exchange draw men from their homes to points organically related, and does it not seem reasonable to believe that associations of beauty, arising spontaneously at place after place on the line of march, give birth to the notion of religious privilege and obligation in making a return to particular spots?

At any rate, it is certain that behind sanctity of pilgrimage lies admiration of place, of art, even of geographical significance. Benares in the North, and Conjeeveram* in the South, are loved and visited in India for the same reason as Durham or Cologne amongst ourselves. They are cathedral cities, rich in architecture, in treasure, and in the associations of saints and scholars. Jagannath † is placed where it is, for sheer beauty of the sea, and perhaps a little also for the old cosmopolitan grandeur of the port through which flowed the Eastern trade. Allahabad is sacred, because there two mighty rivers join their waters, making her the strategic key to two vast basins, inhabited by different races, with diverse traditions, hopes, and folk-lore. It is the solemn beauty of the Himalayas that makes them the refuge

* Conjeeveram.—A town in the Madras Presidency, which contains some of the most beautiful specimens of Dravidian architecture. Often called the Benares of the South. Ramanuja lived here, and Sankaracharya visited it.

† Jagannath.—Or Juggurnath—Lord of the Universe. The famous place of pilgrimage, and the "Car of Juggurnath," on the coast of Orissa, at Puri. This temple is distinguished for the fact that all castes eat together of its consecrated food. The oneness of all men is the religious idea which is associated with it.

of holy men. The four most meritorious pilgrimages* of the Hindus are the four extreme points of India —North, South, East, and West—knowing which the country must be known. The worship of the Ganges, and the reverence that makes a Dekkan villager journey, as an act of piety, to look on the face of one who has seen any of the seven sacred rivers, amongst peoples less poetic, would be simply called the love of place. How large an element in Hinduism is the folk-lore of the country! To the student who is looking for this, it appears to be past all computing. The Mahabharata, the Ramayana, and the Puranas are to a great extent the outpouring of passionate fancy in local interpretation. In the story of Sati, the perfect wife, who can miss the significance of the fifty-two places in which fragments of the smitten body fell? "And one finger fell in Calcutta, and that is still the Kalighat. . . . And the tongue fell at Kangra (Jowalla Mukhi) in the North Punjaub, and appears to this day as licking tongues of fire, from underneath the ground. . . . And the left hand fell at Benares, which is for ever Onnopurna, the Giver of Bread." No foreigner can understand the crowding of associations into these few sentences.

Even the Pole Star has its Indian myth in the legend of the child Dhruwa, whose heart was the steadiest point in all the universe.

Nor is the historic element lacking, in this unconscious worship of country. Like that of some Indian Bernadette is the story told at a beautiful Southern temple of a cowherd who had one cow that gave no milk. He followed her into the jungle, and found a natural lingam in the rock, over which she poured her offering freely, of her own devotion.

* "The four pilgrimages," which constitute the Hindu counsel of perfection, are Kedar Nath in the Himalayas, in the extreme North; Dwarka Nath in the West; Rameshwaram in the South; and Puri, or Jagannath in the East.

And, in proof of the occurrence, does the temple altar not consist to-day of that same lingam set in rough living rock? Of such stories the villages are full. Assuredly, a deep and conscious love of place pervades the whole of the Indian scheme. It has never been called patriotism, only because it has never been defined by boundaries of contrast; but the home, the village, the soil, and, in a larger sense, the rivers, the mountains, and the country as a whole, are the objects of an almost passionate adoration. And nowhere are we more impressed by the completeness of Eastern idealism, than in this, its relating of itself to Nature. Norway, with her broken crags and azure seas and sombre pines, her glacier-crowned mountains, and her island-dotted fjords, is surely beautiful. But Norway's memories are always of the heroes, and we miss those voices of the saints that greet us at every turn in every part of India. Brittany, windy and grey, storm-tost and boulder-strewn, is beautiful. Here too the miles are marked with rude *Calvaires*, and the tales of the saints lie like her own moorland mists across the whole Breton land. But this Catholic sainthood never reaches the stern intellectual discipline of Hinduism, and we long in vain for that mingling of mystic passion and philosophic freedom, where holiness merges into scholarship, that at once distinguishes the Orient, and weds its races and all their dreams to their own soil. It might almost have been S. Francis, but it is actually a Bengali poem of the people, that says:

> Oh, Mother Earth, Father Sky,
> Brother Wind, Friend Light,
> Sweetheart Water,
> Here take my last salutation with folded hands!
> For to-day I am melting away into the Supreme,
> Because my heart became pure,
> And all delusion vanished,
> Through the power of your good company:

Beauty of place translates itself to the Indian consciousness as God's cry to the soul. Had Niagara been situated on the Ganges, it is odd to think how different would have been its valuation by humanity. Instead of fashionable picnics and railway pleasure-trips, the yearly or monthly incursion of worshipping crowds. Instead of hotels, temples. Instead of ostentatious excess, austerity. Instead of the desire to harness its mighty forces to the chariot of human utility, the unrestrainable longing to throw away the body, and realise at once the ecstatic madness of Supreme Union. Could contrast be greater ?

It is commonly said that Hindus derive the idea of pilgrimage from the Buddhist worship of relics. But the psychological aspects of the custom make this appear unlikely. Doubtless the great commercial nexus of the Buddhist period made transport easy, and thus strengthened and stimulated the tendency, just as railways have in modern times opened up the country, and created the possibility of a geographical sense amongst classes who in older days could not have aspired to travel far or often. But in its essence, the institution is so entirely an expression of love for the Motherland, that it must have been anterior to Buddhism by at least as much as the Aryan occupation of India. If one visits the Kennery caves, hidden amongst the jungles to the north of Bombay, this fact is brought home to one. Here are a hundred and eight cells, cut out of the solid rock. They are grouped in pairs; each pair has its own water-supply; and, wherever the view is finest, wherever a glimpse can be caught of the meeting-line of sea and forest, there a staircase and seat will be found specially carved in the stone, for purposes of contemplation. For Nature is the eternal fact, and the landscape from this point a thousand years ago was as beautiful as it is to-day.

Ellora shows at a glance that through century after century it has been a holy place. The Buddhist found it already so, and in due time the Mussulman confirmed the ancient choice, by bringing his illustrious dead to lie in the mighty fane on its hilltop. But why was it first selected? None who has wakened to the dewy freshness of its morning, none who has gazed thence across the sea-like plain, can ask. To all eternity, while the earth remains what she is, Ellora will be one of the spots where the mystery of God is borne in, in overwhelming measure, upon the souls of men, whatever their associations, whatever their creed.

But we are dominated more by the idea that is behind us than by the spontaneous impressions of our senses. To the nomad of the desert, accustomed to the shifting of hot sands, and ceaseless moving of the camp, with what coolness and refreshment must rise the thought of death! Mussulman piety has three motives—the glory of man, the charm of woman, and the holiness of the grave. In very early times we see the august pastor Abraham seeking out a cave in which to place the body of his wife. Death, the fixed, the still, the cold, must be shrined within the steady and imperishable. "The long home," a great rock in a weary land, endless rest, eternal cold and silence, all these are to be found in the grave. Is it not easy to understand that while the peasant, from the banks of the Ganges to the banks of the Tiber, turns naturally to burning of the dead, the wilderness-dwellers bury him deep in mother earth, or build him about with unyielding granite, and thenceforth make this dwelling-house of the beloved as the centre of their own wanderings?

Hence, what the sacred place of pilgrimage is to the Hindu, that the Taj Mahal or the tomb of Aurungzeeb, or the ever-memorable grave at Medina, is to the pious Mussulman. Almost every Mohammedan village in India, too, has its sleeping-place of some "pir" or saint; and I have seen a poverty-stricken God's acre, where the sole treasure of the people was a gnarled and scarcely-living stump, that marked the last home of a long-remembered holy man. For it is the ideal of the desert—rest from their wanderings and shadow from its scorching sun—it is this ideal, and not the natural dictation of their own birth-place, that has become the guiding-power behind the life and choice of these Moslemised Indian folk. And yet all their old poetry of soil comes out in the spot they choose! The tomb in the village-grove; the Taj at the river-bend; the iris-covered graves on the riversides and hillocks of Kashmir; what pictures do these make at dawn and sunset, or through the long Indian night, with its mysterious voices sighing and whispering about the dead! Surely, by thus adding the pastoral tradition to her own, India grows rich, not poor, in the things that form the true wealth of men.

A pilgrim's camp is like some scene taken out of the Middle Ages. Or, rather, it would be like it, but that is so largely depleted of militant elements. The Nagas, or armed friars, are no menace to anything in the modern system, which indeed at this moment they do not understand; and the authority that actually protects and keeps order amongst the pilgrims is to be sought rather in the unarmed district officer, or *tehsildar*, than in anything that could be recognised as forceful by the naked eye. In the South, which is the home of orthodoxy, pilgrimage has gone out of fashion since the advent of railways. Fewer people, certainly fewer widows, visit Benares, since it became easier to do so. And those who have seen a genuine crowd of shrine-farers, in some place remote from steam, cannot wonder at the shock which the pious imagination suffers at the sight of a locomotive. Amongst other things that the religious traveller has a right to expect is the opportunity of a flight from the New India to the Old, as an actual environment. From any point where many ways meet, and various streams of pilgrims converge upon each other, the road to the sacred place will be divided into regular stages of a day's journey, and at each halting-place a camp will be pitched for the night. Even these rest-camps will be situated as far as possible at spots peculiar for their beauty or interest. Is there a cluster of springs? The place is said to be "holy," and we must halt there for worship. Originally, this referred only to beauty and convenience; but in process of time one cannot doubt that a certain atmosphere of insight and devotion has really thrown its halo about the dust and water of the locality, and in the place where so much simple faith has spent its rapture, the highest love and prayer have become easier to all comers.

But the temples are all visited, the bathing is performed, evening worship is over, and silence and sleep fall upon the pilgrims' camp. The moon grows to the full, for we must arrive at the goal on the fifteenth day. And again, it is the simple beauty of the world which determines the law, that under the young moon shall be the going forth, and with her wane the return home. The moon is near the full, and weariness sleeps sound. At what hour is the first tent struck? When does the first sleeper rouse himself, and take again to the road? Who can tell? Certainly not one who has never been able to rise so long before dawn that others were not up and afoot before her, their tents gone, and little heaps of white ashes from the cooking-fires the only sign of their twelve hours' tenancy of tree-shadow or stream-side.

On go the pilgrims, singly or in groups. Old women, bent double with age and toil, hobbling along by the help of the pointed alpenstock. Monks of all descriptions are to be seen. Some of them are covered with ashes, have long reddish-looking hair, wear only the yellow loin-cloth, and carry curious tongs and begging-bowls. These may be Yogis, of the order that believes in the mortification of the flesh; or Nagas, the militant monks, who were once ready to defend the Faith at any moment, and who to this day are powerfully organised to meet the shock of a world that has long ago, alas, passed away like a dream. The *sannyasin*, often a man of modern education, decently clad in the sacred salmon-yellow, accepting no alms save food, refusing the touch of any metal, is here, doing the distance cheerfully on foot. Next comes an ascetic, with withered arm held aloft and useless this many a long year. Again, a proud *mahunt*, abbot of some rich foundation, master of elephants and treasure uncounted, is borne past. Or, as one climbs, having abandoned the open dandy that costs such intolerable labour to the bearers on a mountain march, one may be joined in kindly chat by some one or two of the "Naked Swamis"—men who wear neither ashes nor clothing beyond the necessary scanty rag, who wander amongst sunny deserts and snowy mountains alike indifferent to heat and cold, and of whom, when one talks with them, one remembers nothing, save that here are friends of the culture of scholars, and the breeding and rank of gentlemen.

But the crowd is still more motley. In camp, the strips of yellow cloth that so often do duty as a shelter for the religious, stand side by side with tents of all sizes and conditions. And here now are zenana-ladies carried in scarlet-covered palkees; other women, again, on horseback; men and women alike on foot, or in open dandies; householders, widows, sannyasinis in beads and yellow cloth; there are even some, too weak for walking or climbing, who are borne in straw chairs, strapped to the back of a man carrying a stout staff. On and on presses the irregular host, mixed up with Mohammedan baggage-carriers and servants, cooks, and food-vendors of all sorts.

Here the road is broken by a glacier. There it becomes a mere goat-path, running across dangerous crags. Here is the lake into which an avalanche, brought down by their hymn of triumph, once precipitated thousands of returning pilgrims. Now we have reached the heights where the ground is carpeted with edelweiss instead of grass. Again, we are wandering amidst wildernesses of flowers, while every few yards the dominant note in the composition is changed imperceptibly: first the yellow wallflower, then flame-coloured Iceland poppies, again the long-stalked single-headed Michaelmas daisy of the Himalayas. When the journey began, almost the only blossoms were the orchids on the tree-trunks in the region of maiden-hair fern. Now we have passed the last of the pine woods. Even the white birches, like smitten silver veining blown sharp and twisted against the mountain sides, are gone: and to-night, when the tents are pitched over purple and white anemones, there will be no fuel save the juniper scrub that clings to the face of the rock in sheltered niches. On the edge of the last glacier, growing beside the gentian, we find an evergreen forget-me-not, unknown to us hitherto, and making the third or fourth new species —from a large crimson and purple myosotis onwards —which our pilgrimage has bestowed.

Our neighbours in the tents about us are not amusing themselves by botanising, probably, but they are communing with Nature none the less truly than ourselves. On the last day, drawing near to the shrine, we shall see them risk their lives to gather the great nodding columbines and the little Alpine roses growing on the rocks. Their talk is all of Siva. As they are borne along, they are striving, doubtless, to fix their minds on the repetition of His name, or the contemplation of His form. But the awesome grandeur and beauty of the heights about them will always be remembered by them as the Great God's fit dwelling-place. They are in a church. Rocks and glaciers form the sanctuary. Snowy passes are the pillared aisles. Behind them stand the pine-forests for processions of singers carrying banners, and overhead are the heavens themselves for cathedral roof. It is the peculiarity of Eastern peoples to throw upon the whole of Nature that feeling which we associate only with the place of worship. But is their love less real, or greater, for this fact ?

The day of the full moon comes, the last and most dangerous points are surmounted, and the Shrine is reached. Happy the man or woman, who, on this journey to God, is snatched out of life ! One false step, and the soul that was struggling to see may be carried up at once in a swift sure flight. Or death may come in other ways. " It is so beautiful ! I must be one with it ! " sighed a man who stood on a precipice, looking down at the valleys. And before any one could stop him, he was gone. Such things are not premeditated. There is a genuine ecstasy of the soul in which it hears the voice of the Eternities calling to it, and the prisoning body becomes suddenly intolerable. Is it a stain upon Hinduism that it has never called this " suicide while of unsound mind " ?

But the Shrine itself—where is it ? what is it ? Perhaps a temple, placed above some gorge, on a beetling rock, with sister snows in sight. Perhaps the source of a sacred river. Perhaps a cave, in which continual dripping of water makes a stalagmite of ice, a huge crystalline lingam that never melts.

One can picture how such a place would first be discovered. Some party of shepherds, losing themselves and their flocks amongst the ravines on a summer day, and entering the cavern by accident, to find there the presence of the Lord Himself. Men and beasts, awed and worshipping, how dear is such a picture to the Christian heart!

Worship! Worship! The very air is rent with prayer and hymns. From the Unreal to the Real! From the Many to the One! Lord of Animals! Refuge of Weariness! Siva! Siva! the Free! the Free!

Hours pass, and ere dawn next day the descent to the valleys is begun. Wonderful is the snowy stillness of the lofty pass, when, with our faces set homewards, the moon fades behind us, and the sun rises before. The pilgrims march with less regularity now. All are anxious to return, and some push on, while others break off from the line of route. We reach our own village, and say farewell to the acquaintances of the pilgrimage, adding what comfort we may to the provision for their further journeying. The nights grow dark now, and the great experience becomes a memory, marked always, however, in the Hindu's life, by some special abstinence, practised henceforth as the pilgrim's thank-offering.

It is easy to believe that the scenes in which we have mingled are nowadays denuded of half their rightful elements; that once upon a time as many of the travellers would have been Tartar or Chinese as Indian; that the shrine represents what may have been the summer meeting of great trading caravans; that Nagarjuna and Bodhidharmma, going out to the Further East with their treasures of Indian thought, were in the first place pilgrims on some such pilgrimage as this. Even now, many of the functions of a university are served by the great gathering. Hundreds, or even thousands, of religious men meet, in a manner to eliminate personal ties of friendship and affection, and emphasise and refresh the ideal and intellectual aspects of their lives.

At the vast assemblies of *sadhus*, which occur once in every twelve years at Hurdwar, at Nasick, at Ujjain, and at Allahabad, there are fixed halls of learned disputation, where, for hundreds of years, Hindu philosophy has been discussed, determined, and expanded, something in the fashion of the Welsh Eisteddfod. Here come the wandering monks from every part of India. Here the householder finds himself in vigorous and renewed relation to his faith. Here fresh voices of learning and devotion are able to win for themselves ecclesiastical authority. Such opportunities must have been the means by which Sankaracharya asserted his undisputed mastery of the world of Hindu scholarship. Did it, we wonder, occur to Alexander that learned Greeks might be sent to such wandering colleges in order to hear and to tell new things?

Sanskrit is the *lingua franca* of this ancient learning. To this day the visitor to a Calcutta *toll** may hear the boys dispute with each other on time-worn themes in the classic tongue, and may picture himself back in the colleges of Thebes or Athens in the long ago. But here in the great *melas* are the crowning achievements towards which are directed the hardier ambitions of those Brahman boys. And we need not wonder at their enthusiasm for such distinction. The great open competition, with its

* Toll.—A toll is a Sanskrit school, in which a Brahman lived with his disciples, studying and teaching. The ideal *toll* consisted of a series of mud cottages with wide verandahs, built round a small lake or "tank," with its cluster of bamboos, palms, and fruit-trees. Poverty and learning weie the inspiration of the community. These tolls formed the old Indian universities.

thousands of years of the prestige of learning, is like all the learned societies of a European metropolis thrown into one. The canvas city of a few weeks at Nasick or Allahabad serves all the purposes of Burlington House to London. But the system of culture to which Nasick belongs is no longer growing, it will be said. This is, indeed, its defect. The statement is not entirely true, for even now the test of a supremely national personality would still be, for the Hindu world, his power to add to their philosophy. But it is true to the extent that there is nothing left for collective thought to discover. The common mind of India has now to sweep great circles of intellectual exploration in worlds that as yet are virgin as the Polar ice, or India will die. Of this there can be no doubt.

Far away from the noisy throng of learned saints, or taking a humble place in white cotton garb as visitors amongst them, are the men whose lives are passed in the libraries of kings. For the system of patronage is part and parcel of Indian scholarship, and as the Japanese *daimio* or the Italian prince maintained his artists and artificers, so, under the old *régime*, did every Indian palace possess its staff of palace-pundits—men whose lives were made free of anxiety in order that they might heap up knowledge and pore over ancient texts.

The supreme privilege of the great is to foster piety and learning. But, on the other hand, Manu does not fail to point out that there is no crime for the Brahman like the acceptance of gifts from one who is not the lawful king. And it is not royal persons alone who are charged with the duty of supporting scholars. Never a wedding or a requiem can take place amongst the higher ranks of society without the distribution of money to tolls and pundits. For it is one of the postulates of ethical, and therefore of Eastern, economics, that all great accumulation is for subsequent great distribution.

It is a strange world that has been revealed to us in this camp of pilgrimage, and it is not easy to reach its full significance. Scarcely in any two tents do they understand each other's language, and we shall do better to ask for bread in Sanskrit than in English. Malabaris and Bengalis, Sikhs and Madrasis, Mahrattas and even Mussulmans, dwell side by side for the nonce. Could incongruity and disunion be more strongly illustrated?

Yet it was unity and not disunity that impressed us as we looked. From one end of the camp to the other the same simple way of life, the same sacramental reverence for food and bathing, the same gentleness and courtesy, the same types of face and character, and, above all, one great common scheme of thought and purpose.

The talk may be in different languages; but no matter at what tent door we might become eavesdroppers, we should find its tone and subject much the same—always the lives of the saints, always the glory of the soul, always fidelity to *guru* and *dharmma*. By two formulæ, and two alone, renunciation and freedom from personality, is all life here interpreted.

Other countries have produced art, chivalry, heroic poems, inventive systems. In none of these has India been altogether wanting, yet none is her distinguishing characteristic. What, then, has she given to the world that is beyond all competition? To-day her gifts are decried by all men, for to-day the mighty mother is become widowed and abased. She who has held open port to all fugitives is unable now to give bread to her own children. She with whom Parsi, Jew, and Christian have been thankful to take refuge, is despised and ostracised by all three alike. She who has prized knowledge above all her treasures, finds her learning now without value in the markets of the world. It is urged that the test of utility is the true standard for things transcendental, and that an emancipation into modern commerce and mechanics is a worthier goal for her sons' striving than the old-time aim of knowledge for its own sake, the ideal for itself.

And the modern world may be right.

But, even so, has India in the past given nothing, without which our whole present would be the poorer ?

Who that has caught even a whisper of what her name means can say so ? Custom kept always as an open door, through which the saints may dance into our company, thought sustained at a level where religion and science are one, a maze of sublime apostrophes and world-piercing prayers ; above all, the power to dream rare dreams of the Word becoming flesh and dwelling among men that they may behold His glory—are these things nothing ? If, after all the higher transformation of man be the ultimate end of human effort, which has more deeply vindicated its right to exist, the modern nexus of commerce and finance, or that old world on which we have gazed in the pilgrims' camp ?

CHAPTER XVI

ON THE LOOM OF TIME

THE essential differences between countries of the Asiatic and European types are as yet but little understood, and a main difficulty in the growth of an understanding is the absence of elements in the English language, embodying any wide power of social survey. The disciples of Auguste Comte have done much to popularise certain important words and conceptions, but the hearts of angels and the tongues of poets would be too little to meet all the necessities of the task.

The word *theocracy*, for instance, which is essential to an understanding of Asia, either territorial or historic, has but an ambiguous sound in English. To the learned Positivist it means "the social system built up on theism"; to the vulgar, it indicates some fabulous scheme of divine monarchy, such as is popularly attributed to Israel before the days of Saul, or to England in the dreams of Oliver Cromwell.

To persons thinking in the latter fashion, the two statements that India is a theocracy, and that it is at present occupied by the British raj, seem incompatible. It is clear that only detailed and penetrative knowledge of concrete examples can build up in our minds such a conception of the essentials of a theocratic system as shall give us the power of handling the term as confidently and intelligently as we now feel capable of using more purely political expressions. And of such examples it will be found best to take the nearest first.

In the history of the world, the city of Rome occupies a unique position, as the Occidental cradle and battle-field of two opposing forces, the Imperial and the Theocratic, or, as one may prefer to call them, the European and the Asiatic ideas. For it was Rome that first imposed upon the West that notion of organised force which is almost all that is at present meant by the state-empire. And through all the feuds and disorders of the Middle Ages, it was the Roman impulse that was working itself out by the energy of barbarian peoples, to its perfect triumph in the nineteenth century. Cæsar conceived, Napoleon completed, the imperial scheme. Alexander as an individual may have seen what they saw: but Greece was far too near to Asia, and his military designs could but evaporate before their time into mere learned observations and the exchange of interesting thought.

It was left to Rome to elaborate into fixity of precision that destiny which could not perhaps have been avoided by the peoples of a coast-line, kept militant by the daily conquest of Nature, tempted to aggression by the very habits of their life. For empire in the European sense is a very different thing from the marauding hosts of the East going out to warfare headed by a commander of brilliant prowess. Rome instituted, and modern Europe has inherited, the idea of one *people* exploiting another, under rights strictly defined by law, with an appearance of order which would deceive the very elect.

The Cæsars failed by the strength of the unassimilable elements which their Empire had to meet. Napoleon failed because those whom he temporarily subdued were as strong to re-act in imitation as to be assimilated. To-day the Roman Empire is represented by some eight or ten emulous peoples and princes, all armed to the teeth, all bent on appropriating the world. But it is the Roman Empire still.

And yet Rome herself is the one character whose part in the drama is completely transformed. For no one yet thinks of her as the metropolis of the juvenile kingdom of Italy. To the imagination of humanity she is still the city of the Church. St. Peter's and the Vatican still form her central point. The Pope still rules. This contrast between her first and second selves is much more startling than the transition by which the brigand-chief becomes the sainted ancestor. Before it happened, it would have seemed far more absurd than it would be to-day to propose to make the name of Oxford or Benares a synonym for the vulgar competition of trade. For Rome, the supreme, the invincible, has actually been conquered by the ideas of the East. The poor and the lowly have taken her by storm. Henceforth is she to be in Europe not the voice of domination, but of renunciation; not the teacher of aggression, but of self-sacrifice; royal in her rank and her prerogatives certainly, but far more deeply and truly the friend of the people than of kings. Henceforth, those who are in a special sense her children will live sequestered from the world, pursuing after poverty instead of riches, after self-mortification instead of self-indulgence; men and women apart, as in the Eastern household. Every simple act that she enjoins will possess a sanctity out of all proportion to its intrinsic value. Her customs will become rituals. Her journeys will be pilgrimages. The simplest ordinances of life, administered by her, will now be sacraments. The expression of her forgiveness will be absolution; of her affection, a benediction. Her very rulers will claim no personal right to their high places, but will declare themselves simple executors of the divine will. "Servant of the servants of God" will be, to the thinking of the world, their proudest title.

In the eyes of the Church, henceforth, all men are to be equal, at least until one has made himself a saint, and another Judas. The differences of rank established by the world are to be as nothing before her, and even ecclesiastical gradations are to be merely as conditions on which grace can work. Many of the saints will be humble and unlearned. Many a bishop will reach the lowest hell. Rank, at least theoretically, is nothing to Rome. Her children are all to be the sharers of a common supernatural life, of which a religious banquet is the token. A great responsibility is to rest upon them, of living worthily of the name by which they are called. Their life, as related to each other and to her, can be expressed only in terms of the exploration and manifestation of certain ideals, laid down broadly in authoritative writings, known as *Scriptures*, and with less clearness and power in secondary writings and teachings, called *traditions*.

In other words, the Imperial city has transformed herself into a pure theocracy. If we blot out the idea of birth by a sacramental rite, and substitute that of a chosen place and race, keeping everything else approximately the same, the Church is re-transmuted into any one out of half a dozen Eastern countries—ancient Egypt, Judæa, Arabia, modern India—under the government of the religious idea. Here, too, the priesthood dominates all classes equally, and the priestly interpretation of life prevails—the very gifts one brings home from a journey are explained as temple-offerings. Here, too, the political system is extraneous: custom is sacred, so that a grammar of habit takes the place of legislation; men and women live apart; merit is the sole real condition of social prestige; and so on.

It is due to the purely natural character of the great complexus, that we have in India the—to-us so extraordinary—spectacle of a society handed over to the power of a priesthood, without in any way losing its sense of the universal sacredness of learning and freedom of thought. In the case of Rome, where an artificial system was created on the basis of a foreign experience, the crude temper of the old imperialism betrayed itself primarily against mind and thought, which it conceived as the legitimate sphere of its authority. In Catholic Europe, a man might scarcely venture to believe that the earth moves; must apologise for enjoying the cosmic speculations of La Place; could hardly study Plato without grave suspicion. In India, atheism itself might be preached on the very steps of the temple. All that the people would demand of the preacher would be sincerity.* In Christendom, knowledge has been so much feared that men have again and again suffered torture and death for no other crime. In India, knowledge has always been held to be beatitude. Abundance of words, in every Indian language, testify to the honour paid to scholars. Persian and English books are held as sacred as the Sanskrit. And we should seek in vain, throughout history and language, for any trace of limitation imposed, or suggested to be imposed, upon the mind of man.

Even the vexed question of the right of literature to reveal more than is permitted to conversation, was

* The Charvaka system of philosophy, one of the orthodox schools, is a purely agnostic formulation. I have myself met a Charvaka on a pilgrimage. His statements of belief sounded like mockery of the people about him. The word "orthodox" here only means that by adopting Charvaka doctrines, a man did not cease to be called a Hindu.

foreseen long ago and settled in a flash of wit by the legislator who, writing of defilement by the touch of the mouth, makes three exceptions, in favour of "the beaks of birds, the lips of women, and *the words of poets.*"

In fact opinion is so free that religious propaganda is actually discouraged by Hinduism, lest zeal, outrunning discretion, prove mischievous to society. "A man has a right to hold his own belief, but never to force it upon another," is the dictum that has made of India a perfect university of religious culture, including every phase and stage of thought and practice, from that of the kindergarten, where all is concrete, to that of the higher research student, who has direct visualisation of the solutions of problems which most of us cannot even understand.

But freedom of thought in the East has not been the prerogative of religion alone. The deeper we go into the history of Hindu philosophy, the more perplexed we are that with its obviously scientific character it should never have created a scientific movement of the prestige and *éclat* of that of the West. Patanjali,* who wrote his great psychology in the second century B.C., was obviously a physiologist, studying the living body in relation to that nervous system which in its entirety he would call the mind. The action and inter-action of the living neuro-psychosis is a question which modern science, content with a more static view of human structure, has hardly yet ventured to tackle, and students of Patanjali cannot be controverted if they hold that when it is reached, it will only be to corroborate the ancient investigations step by step. But a still more interesting feature of Patanjali's work lies in the fact that

* Patanjali wrote "Yoga Aphorisms." "Raja-Yoga" by the Swami Vivekananda is a translation of this work, with a compilation from some of Patanjali's commentators.

it is obviously the final record of a long research, carried out, not by a single individual, but by a whole school, experimenting continuously through many generations. Each man's labour was conditioned by the fact that he had no laboratory and no instruments outside his own body, and there can be no doubt that life was often sacrificed to the thirst for knowledge. The whole, therefore, is like a *résumé* of two or three centuries of the conclusions of some English Royal Society, or some French Academy of Sciences, dating from two to three thousand years ago. And we must remember that, if the terminology of this old science has a certain quaintness in our ears, this is probably not greater than that which our own talk of forces and molecules, of chemical affinities and sphygmographic records, would have, if it were suddenly recovered, after a lapse of two thousand years, by a new civilisation, stationed, say, in Mexico.

What is true of the psychology is equally true of Indian mathematics, astronomy, surgery, chemistry. The Oriental predilection for meditative insight is an advantage in the field of mathematics, where deduction is a necessity. But at the same time its fundamental solidity and originality are shown by the fact that highly abstruse problems are stated by Hindu thinkers in concrete, and even in poetic terms. And it will be remembered that less than a hundred years ago, De Morgan* celebrated the solution at sight of certain hitherto uncompleted problems of "Maxima and Minima," by a young Hindu called Ram Chândra.

The law of gravitation itself was enunciated and discussed by Bhashkar Acharya in the twelfth century. And the antiquity of the Sanskrit word

* De Morgan died 1871. Père Gratry and George Boole were other distinguished mathematicians deeply aware of their indebtedness to Eastern systems.

shunyo, for *nought*, together with the immemorial distribution of the system all over the country, conclusively proves that our decimal notation is Indian, and not Arabic, in origin.

How is it, then, we repeat, that a more imposing scientific activity has not been the result of a faculty so undeniable? Many considerations may be adduced in explanation. There is a vast international organisation of scientific effort in Europe to-day, operating to make an incomparable sum of results. Ancient India knew what was meant by scientific co-operation, but by organisation scarcely. And no one nation, working alone, could have produced the whole of what we know as Modern Science, or even one division of it. Ancient Greece gives us the first word on electricity. What a leap from this to Volta and Galvani! Where, again, had these been without the German Hertz, the French Ampère, the Hindu Bose? And then Italy for a second time takes up the thread of inquiry, and produces the apparatus for wireless telegraphy.

Again, we must remember that in Europe to-day we have renounced almost everything for science. Art and letters are almost at a standstill. In these departments—at least, in every country outside France and Russia—we are living almost entirely on the treasures of the past. In religion we see the same superficial eclecticism, the same absence of genuine contemporary impulse. But India never was in this position. Side by side with the learned man, speculating or experimenting on the secrets of Nature, the builders were raising the village temple, the shuttle flew to and fro in the loom, the clink of the tools was heard in the brass-smithy, the palace pundits busied themselves with their collection of ancient texts, the saints poured forth the rapture of their souls, the peasant waked and slept in the good company of Nature, rice-field and palm-tree, cattle and farmstead. Faith, art, and industry lived on undisturbed.

After all, is it not possible that we deceive ourselves? The true secret of our elimination of every other intellectual activity in favour of science, is it really the depth of our enthusiasm for knowledge, or is it not rather our modern fever for its mechanical application? How far is the passion for pure truth unimpaired by commercial interests? How far is our substitution of specialisms for synthesis conditioned by finance merely? When our utilitarian ingenuity draws nearer exhaustion, when the present spasm of inventive ability has worked itself out, then, and not till then, will come the time for estimating the actual profundity and disinterestedness of our scientific ardour. Will our love of knowledge continue to drive us on to a still deeper theoretic insight, or will our investigations languish in our hands, lingering on as a mere fashion in learning, even as Aristotle lingered on through the Middle Ages? Till such questions are nearer finding their answer we are in no position to assume that the present period is, or is not, ultimately scientific.

Meanwhile, in India this danger of a mercenary science was always foreseen, and viewed with perhaps an exaggerated horror, so that from the beginning the disciple has been required to seek knowledge for its own sake, renouncing all ulterior motive. The value derived at the present stage of development from incorporating a progressive science in a progressive civilisation was thus lost; although we must remember that in a very real sense such a transition, shorn of its lower elements, has occurred in the East from prehistoric times, whenever new plants and animals were to be domesticated, or new tools invented. On the other hand, it is still open to India, facing the actual conditions of the modern world, to prove that the innate capacity of her people for scientific work and inquiry has been in no way lessened by this long abstention from its vulgar profits.

In spite, nevertheless, of the relative non-development of natural science in India, it is the perfect compatibility of the Hindu religious hypothesis with the highest scientific activity, that is to make that country within the present century the main source of the new synthesis of religion for which we in the West are certainly waiting. Several nations cannot suddenly come into contact by the use of a common language without a violent shock being given to their prejudices in favour of local mythology. Such an occurrence was inevitable in English-speaking countries under present circumstances, and has been accelerated, as it happens, by the agnosticism born of scientific activity. Christianity, moreover, has been further discredited by the discovery that its adherents possess no ethics sufficiently controlling to influence their international relations, and finally by that worship of pleasure which an age of exploitation necessarily engenders. Thus neither the sentiment of childhood, the reasoning of theology, the austerity of conscience, nor the power of idealism, has been strong enough to maintain the creed of the West against the assaults to which the age has seen it subjected. Everything seems to be going through a transition. Social morality, intellectual formulas, legal and economic relationships, all have broken loose from their old moorings, and are seeking for re-adjustment. The first agony of the loss of belief is now over, but it has only given place to a dreary hopelessness, a mental and spiritual homelessness, which drives some in whom heart predominates into the Church of Rome, while others in whom the faculties are more evenly balanced, try to forget their need in social service, or in the intellectual and artistic enjoyments of an era of *résumés*.

Protestantism has at last delivered herself of a genuinely religious product of the highest order, in that love of naked truth which finds its voice and type in modern science. For all other forms of non-Catholicism are more or less compromises, mere half-way-houses on the road to this. But, even in this, the environment of spirituality and the communion of saints are apt to be left behind with the Mediæval Church. Is there no way to combine these things? Can the devotional attitude receive no justification from the clear and unbiased mind? Does religion, which has made so much of *faith*, want less than absolute conviction as its basis? Is that sentiment which has produced all the greatest art, and almost all the greatest conduct, to be relegated to the mental lumber-room, as, after all, only a superstition? Surely, if so, there is an eternal inharmony and divergence between the creative and the inquiring faculties of man.

But the very constitution of our minds forbids us to accept this paradox. It may be that we are no longer able to believe in the exclusive authenticity of any single religious system. But we are fast inclining to the opinion that even here there must be some observable sequence; that creeds and mythologies must be as genuine a product of the Unity-of-Things as the animals and the plants; that order and meaning there must be, in the one case as in the other. Instead, therefore, of a contemptuous disregard of all faiths as equally untrue, we are beginning to adopt to all alike an attitude of respect as equally significant.

Only in India has this recognition of law in religious conceptions ever been held in its completeness as a part of religion itself. Only in India have inspired teachers been able to declare that the name of God, being also an illusion, differed only from worldly things in having the power of helping us to break our bondage to illusion, while they, on the other hand, increased it. Only in India has it been counted orthodoxy to believe that all is within the mind, that the forms of gods are but objectifications of our own sense of what is best to be attained, that prayer is only the heightening of will. And therefore it is from India that we shall gather that intellectualisation of belief which is to re-establish, in the name of a new and greater synthesis, our confidence in our own past. In this new synthesis every element of our own thought must find a place—the conception of humanity and the worship of truth, of course, because without these it would have no *raison d'être.* But even the emotionalism of the negro must not go unplaced, uninterpreted, any more than that wondrous mood in which the explorer of knowledge finds himself launched on a vision of Unity that he dare not name. Neither the Catholic organisation of monasticism nor the Protestant (taken from the Mohammedan) inspiration of common prayer can be left out. There must be a religious consciousness strong enough to recognise the anguish of denial as its own most heroic experience, and large enough to be tender and helpful to the ignorance of a child.

In that other synthesis which grew up under the Roman Empire, all the Mediterranean peoples and those originally related to them found a part. The doctrine of immortality came from the desert; resurrection, mediatorship, and personal consciousness of sin from ancient Egypt; many elements from Persia and Syria; purity and asceticism from the Asokan Essenes; the basis of ethics to be transcended from Judæa; the spirit of inquiry and the necessary feeling of an intellectual void from Greece, or at least from the Greek elements in

Mediterranean society; the instinct of organisation from Rome; and the all-absorbing renunciation and compassion for the world that alone can give sufficient nucleus for a new religion from one sweet central Personality, in whom each of these various hungers found its own Bethlehem—its house of bread.

Similarly, in the new up-growth of our own days, many preparatory influences now at work are to find fulfilment. All who have felt the love of the disinherited and oppressed, all who have followed truth for its own sake, all who have longed to lose themselves in a paradise of devotion and been refused by the armed reason standing at the gate, all who have felt out for a larger generalisation, as they saw the faith of their babyhood falling away from them,—all these have helped and are helping to build up the new consciousness, to make the faculty that is to recognise and assimilate the doctrine of the future. But the evangel itself will be mainly drawn from India.

And then, having thus renewed the sources of the world's inspiration, we may be pardoned if we ask, What of India herself? The Egyptian delivered up his whole treasure, and where is he now? Buried under many a layer of foreign invasion; tilling the soil as patiently and hopelessly as one of his own oxen; scarcely remembered, even as a name, by those who make so-called plans for the country's good, and are wakened only to a stupid wonder, as at the sound of something familiar from books, when they hear that to kill a cat to-day in the bazaar in Cairo would almost cost a man his life. The Jews produced Jesus, and what have they become? Pariahs and fugitives amongst the nations of men. Who remembers them with any feeling of gratitude for that which they have given? A miserable formula, "the Jews who crucified Him," has taken the place amongst the devout of any memorial of the fact that they created the language, the thought, the habits of life, and the outlook of righteousness, in which He assumed the garb of humanity.

Is something of this sort to be the fate of India? To give a religion to the world may be a sufficient proof that one's past was not in vain, but evidently it is no sort of safeguard for the future. The process by which the peoples of a vast continent may become mere hewers of wood and drawers of water has already begun, is already well afoot. Their indigenous institutions are all in decay. Their prosperity is gone. Some portion or other of the immense agricultural area is perpetually under famine. Their arts and industries are dead or dying. They have lapsed into mere customers for other men's cheap wares. Even their thought would seem to be mainly imitative. The orthodox is apt to tread the round of his own past eternally. The unorthodox is as apt to harness himself to the foreign present, with an equal blindness. In suicidal desperation, the would-be patriotic reiterate the war-cries of antagonistic sects, or moan for the advent of a new religion, as if, by introducing a fifth element of discord, the Indian peoples could reach unity. Nor does the education at present offered promise any solution of the problem. It is the minimum that is possible to the efficient clerk, and even that minimum is undergoing reduction rather than increase.

In spite of the absence of any theory of history that might elucidate the course of events in the East during the next two centuries, one truth reveals itself with perfect plainness. A nation becomes whatever she believes herself to be. She is made great, not by her relative superiority, but by her thought about herself. It becomes important therefore to ask—What conception of her own nature and power forms the inheritance of India?

As Roman Catholicism is but one element inhering in a great whole called Christianity, and as a man may well claim to be a good Christian without being a Catholic, so the religious system of Hinduism is only a fragment inhering in a vast social-industrial-economic scheme called the dharmma, and a man may well and rightly be the servant of the dharmma, without calling himself a Hindu. It is this dharmma, in its large and non-sectarian activity, that determines the well-being of every child of the Indian soil. The word itself is an ancient name for national righteousness or national good. It is true that the Brahmin who bows before one who is not the rightful king is held many times accursed by Manu. It is true that the Bhagavad Gîtâ is the only one of the world-gospels that turns on the duty of fighting for the true sovereign against usurpers. And yet it is also a fact that the person of the ruler is always a matter of singular indifference to the theocratic consciousness. It has been hitherto indeed a mere detail for military persons to fight out amongst themselves. The secret of so curious an attitude is reached when we discover that in the eyes of the Indian peasant, the sovereign himself is only the servant of the dharmma. "If he uphold it, he will stay: if not, he will have to go," they all say when questioned. Little do they dream, alas! that themselves and their children and their children's children may be swept into oblivion also by that same failure to uphold!

Thus, whoever was the master that an Indian statesman served, whether Hindu, Mussulman, or British sat upon the throne, it was the minister's duty, as the loyal and obedient child of an Asiatic race, to use all his influence in the best interests of his people and his country. It is this element in the national system that tends, with its great regard for agriculture, to rank the cow almost on a level with the human members of the commonwealth, making the Hindu sovereign forbid beef-eating within his frontiers. It was this that made a certain prince, in despair, hand over his salt-mines to the British Government, rather than obey its mandate to tax this commodity to his people, and thus derive personal benefit from their misfortune. It was this that made it incumbent upon many of the chiefs in the old days to provide, not only salt, but also water and fruit free to their subjects, a kind of "noblesse oblige" that has left the wayside orchard outside every village in Kashmir, till that favoured land is almost like the happy island of Avilion, "fair with orchard lawns, and bowery hollows crowned with summer sea." It was this power of the dharmma to safeguard the welfare of its people, through a law as binding upon the monarch as upon his subjects, that brought about the immense network of custom which regulated the relief of beggars, the use of water, the provisioning of pilgrimages, habits of sanitation, distribution of grazing-lands, the forest-rights of the peasant, and a thousand other matters of importance. The mere fact that the king's personal devotions were offered in a mosque could not interfere with his acceptance of the system, in any important measure. It was the language of rule, dominating all rulers alike, by every detail of birth and upbringing, and by the very impossibility of imagining any deviation. Hence it could never be more than a question of time till some new prince had assimilated the whole, and Mussulman co-operated actively with Hindu in the great task of enforcing and extending the essentials of the common weal. We may regret, but we cannot condone, the strange indolence by which the Indian people have permitted themselves to lose sight of these national and civic responsibilities of their ancient civilisation, and become absorbed in its personal and domestic rites. Nor can we for one moment admit that this substitution of the trees for the forest deserves the name of orthodoxy,—faithfulness to the dharmma.

It is, however, an essential weakness of theocratic rule that while it can tolerate any neighbour, it has no idea of dominating and unifying diverse elements round itself. The great mass of its subjects, too, see life indirectly through the nimbus of the supernatural. Instead of subordinating the priesthood in national affairs to the recognised leaders of the nation, exalting it only in its rightful capacity of influence upon the social and individual conscience, a theocracy is apt to require that its leaders move, encumbered by the counsels of the priests.

It was the Prophet's clear perception of these facts that gave its peculiar characteristics to Islam. He established a strong confraternity, and made subscription to a brief and concise formula its sole condition of membership. But Arab blood was comparatively unmixed, and the greater part of Mohammed's work was done for him, in the close bond of consanguinity that united his central group. At one bound, and without any means save that power of personality which is the first demand of the theocratic method, he performed the double task of creating an all-absorbing consciousness of nationality, and carrying his people through the required emancipation of thought. To this day the great Semitised belt that divides Eastern Aryans and Mongolians from Europe, reminds us, whenever we look at the map, of the reality of his achievement. And the history of the origins of European learning remains to attest the enthusiasm of freedom which he conferred on the Saracenic intellect.

Geographical conditions impose upon India the same necessity of unification at all costs, and yet combine with other facts to make her the meeting-ground of all races. Especially is this the case in modern times, when the ocean has become a road-way instead of a boundary. She is almost a museum of races, creeds, and social formations, some hoary with age, some crude with excessive youth. Thus her problem is vastly more difficult than that of Arabia before the seventh century. Yet she contains in herself every element of self-recovery.

If the fact had been open to doubt before, the British rule, with its railways, its cheap postage, and its common language of affairs, would sufficiently have demonstrated the territorial unity of the country. We can see to-day that India's is an organic, and no mere mechanical, unity. "The North," it has been said, "produces prophets, the South priests." And it is true that her intellectual and discriminating faculty, her power of recognition and formulation, lies in the South; that Mahratta, Mussulman and Sikh, form her executive; while to Bengal, the country that has fought no battle for her own boundaries, falls the office of the heart, which will yet suffuse all the rest with the realisation of the vast inclusiveness of meaning of the great word "India." Historically the Indian unity is obvious. And if socially it appear doubtful, the country itself could set aside the doubt in an instant by grasping that intuition of nationality which alone is needed to give the spiritual impulse toward consolidation.

But the bare fact of an actual social, historical, and geographical unity, waiting for precipitation as a national consciousness, is not the only possession of India at the present crisis. She has a great past to return upon, and a clearly defined economy for model. Her traditions are unstained. There is no element of national life—art, poetry, literature, philosophy, science—in which she has not at some time been exceptionally strong. She has organised at least two empires of commanding character. In architecture, three of the most imposing styles in the world have been hers—the Dravidian in the South, the Buddhist across middle India from Orissa to Bombay, and the Indo-Saracenic in the North.

There can be little doubt that her next period will confront India with the necessity of introducing some community of ritual as between priest and people; and this of itself must create fresh architectural needs, a new architecture of the communal consciousness which would be sufficient to make the required appeal to the national imagination, and at the same time give the needed scope to the passion of democracy.

For in looking to the growth of a sentiment oi nationality as the solution of Indian problems, we are of course turning away from kings and priests, and appealing to Woman and the People. A similar appeal, in the only form possible to the unmixed theocracy of that day, was made by Buddhism; and the whole history of India, from the Christian era onwards, is the story of the education of the popular consciousness, by the unifying and ameliorating influence of Hinduism, as it was then thrown open. To-day, if we adopt, moral and intellectual tests as the criteria of civilisation, we can hardly refuse to admit that in such issues the East has been more successful than the West. In strength of family ties; in sweetness and decorum of family life; in widespread understanding of the place of the personal development in the scheme of religion as a whole; in power of enjoyment of leisure, without gross physical accompaniments; in dignity, frugality, continuous industry without aggressive activity; in artistic appreciation of work done and doing: and above all in the ability to concentrate the whole faculty at will, even the poorest classes in India, whatever their religion, will compare favourably with many who are far above them in the West. Such are some of the results of the Buddhist period.

The Mogul Empire fell into decay and failed, simply because it did not understand how to base itself on a great popular conception of Indian unity. It could neither assimilate the whole of the religious impulse of India, nor yet detach itself completely from it. Hence, as a government, it succeeded neither in rooting itself permanently, nor in creating that circuit of national energy which alone could have given it endurance. Nevertheless, it contributed invaluable elements to the national life of the future, and it is difficult to see how that life could hope to organise itself without its memorable preliminary experiment.

The foreign character of the English period produced, as its first effect, a wide sense of bewilderment and unrest, which gave birth to a hundred projected panaceas. There were social reformers, who thought that by a programme more purely destructive than they then realised, their Motherland would be best served. And while we may deprecate the form taken by their zeal, we can but admit that no other testimony could have been given to the living energy of the race which would have been so convincing. If Indian civilisation had really been stationary, as is so sapiently supposed by the West, the embers could hardly have leaped into such flame, at the bare touch of new ideas. If, on the other hand, the country had accepted the superficial theory, and run agate in the endeavour to reform itself, we could not thereafter have conceived of India as possessing sufficient depth and stability to make hope possible. Meanwhile the reformers have not failed to bring forth fruit. They have produced groups of persons who represent what is valuable in Western thought and habits, without necessarily being denationalised, and they have demonstrated once for all the fact that India contains sufficient forces of restitution within herself to be completely independent of foreign advice and criticism.

Next came political agitators, who seemed to think that by entire deference to an alien idea their country would be saved. There can be no doubt that here also a valuable contribution had been made. The foreign idea can never save India—indeed, the use of the word "politics" in the present state of the country may strike some of us as a painful insincerity—but at the same time, the mastery and assimilation of the foreigners' *method* is an absolute necessity. The education of the people, also, to a knowledge of their common interests, and the throwing of a net of friendship and mutual intercourse all over the country, are great services.

Outside social and political movements, again, there are a hundred emancipations and revivals of religious centres, all of which are noteworthy symptoms of inherent vitality. And still a fourth school declares that the one question of India lies in the economic crisis, and that that once surmounted all will be well.

At this moment, however, a new suspicion is making itself heard, a suspicion that behind all these interpretations—the social reform, the political agitation, religious movements, and economic grievances—there stands a greater reality, dominating and co-ordinating the whole, the Indian national idea, of which each is a part. It begins to be thought that there is a religious idea that may be called Indian, but it is of no single sect; that there is a social idea, which is the property of no caste or group; that there is a historic evolution, in which all are united; that it is the thing within *all* these which alone is to be called "India." If this conception should prevail, it will be seen that social, political, economic, and religious workers have all alike helped to reveal it; but it can never be allowed that the whole problem is economic, grave as the last-mentioned feature of the situation undoubtedly is. It is not merely the status, but the very nature and character of the collective personality of a whole nation, occupying one of the largest areas in the world, that has to be recaptured. In the days when ancient Egypt made an eternal impression on human civilisation, the personal belongings of her great nobles were no more than those of an Indian cowherd to-day. It was the sentiment of fraternity, the instinct of synthesis, the mind of co-ordination, that were the secret of her power.

The distinctive spirituality of the modern world depends upon its ability to think of things as a whole, to treat immense masses of facts as units, to bring together many kinds of activity, and put them in true relation to one another. This is the reality of which map, census, and newspaper, even catalogue, museum and encyclopædia, are but outer symbols. In proportion as she grasps this inner content will India rise to the height of her own possibilities.

The sacraments of a growing nationality would lie in new developments of her old art, a new application of her old power of learnedness, new and dynamic religious interpretations, a new idealism in short, true child of the nation's own past, with which the young should throb and the old be reverent. The test of its success would be the combining of renewed local and individual vigour with a power of self-centralisation and self-expression hitherto unknown.

But before such a result could come about, we must suppose the children of every province and every sect on fire with the love of the Motherland.

Sikh, Mahratta, and Mussulman, we must imagine possessed each by the thought of *India*, not of his own group. Thus each name distinguished in the history of any part would be appropriated by the country as a whole. The Hindu would prostrate himself on the steps of the mosque, the Mohammedan offer salutation before the temple, the Aryan write the history of Islam with an enthusiasm impossible to those within its walls, the Semite stand forth as the exponent of India's heroic past, with the authority of one who sees for the first time with the eyes of manhood. For we cannot think that a mere toleration of one another's peculiarities can ever be enough to build up national sentiment in India. As the love of David and Jonathan, a love the stronger for distance of birth, such is that last and greatest passion which awakes in him who hears the sorrowful crying of the young and defenceless children of his own mother. Each difference between himself and them is a source of joy. Each need unknown to himself feeds his passion for self-sacrifice. Their very sins meet with no condemnation from him, their sworn champion and servant.

But has India to-day the hidden strength for such developments? What of the theocratic consciousness? What of warring religious convictions?

Whether or not she has adequate strength for her own renewal, only the sons of India are competent to judge. But it is certain that in the nationalising of a great nation, the two theocracies would reach, on the human side, their common flowering-point. Do not all kingdoms of God hold forth the hope of a day when the lame shall walk, and the blind see, the leper be cleansed, and the poor have the Gospel preached unto them? The theocratic consciousness is never jealous of the social good, but profoundly susceptible of it. It seeks it indeed as its true goal. What of the theocratic consciousness, what of religion, should a day ever come to pass in which men discovered that divine revelations were meant to unite humanity, not to sunder it? Surely the question is hardly serious. The old orthodoxy of the Arab would still be the austerity of the Mohammedan. The ancient piety of the Hindu would still and for ever be the church of the devoted life. Yet both would have found new purpose and common scope, in the re-making of the Motherland.

Nevertheless, the question remains. The road is clear, but has India strength to follow it?

Jackals prowl about the buried cities and deserted temples of the Asokan era. Only a memory dwells within the marble palaces of the Mogul. Is the mighty Mother not now exhausted? Having given to the world, is it not enough? Is she again to rouse and bestir herself for the good of her own household? Who can tell? Yet in all impotence and desolation of the present, amidst the ruin of his country and the decay of his pride, an indomitable hope wakes still in the heart of the Indian peasant. "That which is, shall pass: and that which has been, shall again be," he mutters "to the end of time." And we seem to catch in his words the sound of a greater prophecy, of which this is but the echo—

"Whenever the dharmma decays, and a-dharmma prevails, then I manifest myself. For the protection of the good, for the destruction of the evil, for the firm establishment of

THE NATIONAL RIGHTEOUSNESS

I am born again and again."